Eisenhower, Macmillan and Allied Unity, 1957–1961

Also by E. Bruce Geelhoed
CHARLES E. WILSON AND CONTROVERSY AT THE PENTAGON, 1953 to 1957

Also by Anthony O. Edmonds
THE WAR IN VIETNAM

Also by Anthony O. Edmonds and E. Bruce Geelhoed
BALL STATE UNIVERSITY: An Interpretive History

Eisenhower, Macmillan and Allied Unity, 1957–1961

E. Bruce Geelhoed

Director, Center for Middletown Studies and Professor of History
Ball State University

and

Anthony O. Edmonds

Professor of History
Ball State University

© E. Bruce Geelhoed and Anthony O. Edmonds 2003

All rights reserved. No reproduction, copy or transmission of this publication may be made without written permission.

No paragraph of this publication may be reproduced, copied or transmitted save with written permission or in accordance with the provisions of the Copyright, Designs and Patents Act 1988, or under the terms of any licence permitting limited copying issued by the Copyright Licensing Agency, 90 Tottenham Court Road, London W1T 4LP.

Any person who does any unauthorised act in relation to this publication may be liable to criminal prosecution and civil claims for damages.

The authors have asserted their rights to be identified as the authors of this work in accordance with the Copyright, Designs and Patents Act 1988.

First published 2003 by
PALGRAVE MACMILLAN
Houndmills, Basingstoke, Hampshire RG21 6XS and
175 Fifth Avenue, New York, N.Y. 10010
Companies and representatives throughout the world

PALGRAVE MACMILLAN is the global academic imprint of the Palgrave Macmillan division of St. Martin's Press, LLC and of Palgrave Macmillan Ltd. Macmillan® is a registered trademark in the United States, United Kingdom and other countries. Palgrave is a registered trademark in the European Union and other countries.

ISBN 0-333-64227-9

This book is printed on paper suitable for recycling and made from fully managed and sustained forest sources.

A catalogue record for this book is available from the British Library.

Library of Congress Cataloging-in-Publication Data
Geelhoed, E. Bruce, 1948–
    Eisenhower, Macmillan, and allied unity, 1957–1961 / E. Bruce Geelhoed, Anthony O. Edmonds.
    p. cm.
    Includes bibliographical references and index.
    ISBN 0-333-64227-9
    1. Eisenhower, Dwight D. (Dwight David), 1890–1969. 2. Macmillan, Harold, 1894– 3. United States – Foreign relations – Great Britain. 4. Great Britain – Foreign relations – United States. 5. United States – Foreign relations – 1953–1961. 6. Cold War – Diplomatic history. I. Edmonds, Anthony O. II. Title.

E183.8.G7 G275 2002
327.73041'09'045 – dc21
                                                                    2002028755

10 9 8 7 6 5 4 3 2 1
12 11 10 09 08 07 06 05 04 03

Printed and bound in Great Britain by
Antony Rowe Ltd, Chippenham and Eastbourne

Contents

Preface	vi
Acknowledgements	ix
Prologue	x
1 1957: Bermuda, Washington, Paris	1
2 1958: Arms Control, Washington, Lebanon	31
3 1959: Moscow, Washington, London, Paris	61
4 1960: Washington and Paris	97
Epilogue	132
Notes and References	158
Bibliography	186
Index	191

Preface

This is an old-fashioned book. It is not based on any overarching theoretical construct. It is not Marxist or Wallersteinian or modernist or postmodernist. Race, class, and gender do not figure much in what we say, except that almost all of our major actors are white males, as was overwhelmingly, if sadly, the case in Western international relations in the late 1950s and early 1960s. In some ways this work harks back to the old days of diplomatic history; our primary sources are diaries, memoirs, official government documents, and, especially, letters. We suppose that our use of the correspondence between Dwight D. Eisenhower and Harold Macmillan makes us the opposite of Stimsonian gentlemen, since we are reading other people's mail – with great profit.

If we have a central theme it is that personality and friendships do matter in international relations, especially in British–American relations. Put simply, the fact that Dwight D. Eisenhower and Harold Macmillan had known each other since the early days of World War II made a difference in the way that they and their advisors conducted foreign policy. Of course, there were tensions and disagreements and huffy complaints in private, but by and large Eisenhower and Macmillan got along famously. Especially crucial was their largely successful effort to reconstruct the Anglo-American "special relationship" after it had almost been shattered by the Suez crisis of 1956.

We focus on the period from 1957 to 1961, years that span Eisenhower's second presidential term and Macmillan's first four years as prime minister. A brief prologue deals with the origins of the friendship between the two leaders, their approaches to conducting foreign policy, and some historiography related to the British–American "special relationship." The four major chapters that follow each cover one year – 1957, 1958, 1959, and 1960, through the collapse of the Paris Summit Conference in May 1960. A brief epilogue discusses the last seven months of the "Ike–Mac" relationship, which ended with the inauguration of John F. Kennedy.

Scholars in the field will note that many international problems are not covered here. Cyprus and Far Eastern concerns, for example, receive virtually no mention. Because of space limitations, we decided to focus on major issues that both nations saw as crucial to their partnership. Those tended to center on Western Europe, the NATO alliance, and the

Middle East as they related to the Cold War conflict with the Soviet Union. We do a great deal with defense, disarmament, the Berlin question, and, above all, the concept of summitry. We conclude that the Eisenhower–Macmillan partnership was largely successful, with one major failure, of course: the collapse of the 1960 summit. And although Britain remained a junior partner of the United States during the late 1950s, it was a functioning and highly respected partner. Anglo-American relations, we argue, had come a long way since the dark days of Suez, and much of that progress was the result of the close relationship between Dwight D. Eisenhower and Harold Macmillan.

As authors, we wish to thank a number of helpful people who assisted in many parts of the project. The staff of the Eisenhower Library in Abilene, Kansas, was vital to our work. We wish to thank Thomas Branigar, archivist, and his colleagues for their assistance. Also, the staff of the Modern Political Papers section of the Bodleian Library, Oxford University, were enormously helpful – especially Helen Langley and Colin Drake. John Crouch and Talitha Greathead, Oxford students who are reading history at Harris Manchester College, gave up part of a weekend to help go through documents in the Macmillan Papers. Marc Geelhoed, graduate student at Indiana University, also researched materials relating to Harold Macmillan's visits to Indiana in the University Library at Indiana University.

The Honors College and Provost's Office at Ball State University helped to fund research terms in Great Britain, at various times, for both of us. Bruce Geelhoed spent a term at Westminster College in 1987 and Anthony Edmonds taught at Keele University in the autumn of 2001. A numbers of Edmonds's colleagues at Keele, especially John Dumbrell, made helpful suggestions. A special thank you goes to Professor Peter Boyle in the American Studies department at the University of Nottingham, who read the entire manuscript and made a number of helpful suggestions.

Bruce Geelhoed also wishes to thank the Naval Historical Foundation for a post-doctoral research fellowship award which enabled him to study the important aspects of naval history and defense policy in the 1950s as they related to this study. He especially wishes to thank Dean Allard, now retired, and the staff of the Operational Archives at the Naval Historical Center in Washington, DC for their assistance. He is also grateful to the University of Pennsylvania, especially Professor Martin Meyerson, president emeritus, for supporting research relating to the role of Thomas S. Gates in many of the events mentioned in this study.

Several of our students at Ball State University helped in the preparation of this study. Our thanks go out to Jennifer Anderson, Julie Gibboney, and, most notably, Jeni Sumawati, for their expert assistance.

Finally, we wish to thank our wives and families for enduring yet another lengthy book project. Deborah Geelhoed, loving wife of Bruce Geelhoed for 31 years, and Joanne Edmonds, loving wife of Anthony Edmonds for 38 years, patiently endured numerous stories about Eisenhower and Macmillan as this project unfolded. We continue to accumulate enormous debts to them for their patience, love, support, and cooperation.

E. BRUCE GEELHOED
ANTHONY O. EDMONDS
Muncie, Indiana

Acknowledgements

The authors and publisher gratefully acknowledge permission to use the following material:

From *Diplomacy* by Henry Kissinger. Copyright © 1994 by Henry A. Kissinger (New York: Simon & Schuster, 1994).

From *Freedom From Fear: American People in Depression and War* by David Kennedy, copyright © 1999 by David M. Kennedy. Used by permission of Oxford University Press.

Reprinted with permission of Simon & Schuster from *Eisenhower, vol. II. The President* by Stephen Ambrose. Copyright © 1984 by Ambrose-Tubbs, Inc.

Reproduced from *Harold Macmillan*, vols I and II by Alistair Horne (Copyright © Memsbury Press Ltd) by permission of Memsbury Press Ltd for the services of Alistair Horne.

From Harold Macmillan, *The Blast of War, 1939–1945* (1968); *Riding the Storm 1956–1959* (1971); *Pointing the Way, 1959–1961* (1972), by permission of Pan Macmillan, London, UK.

From the Conservative Party Archives, Bodleian Library, Oxford, UK for permission to quote from interview, Harold Macmillan by Robert McKenzie, 1972, in "Correspondence with the Party Leader (and ex-leader), Macmillan, 1963–1964."

From Winthrop W. Aldrich, "The Suez Crisis: a Footnote to History," *Foreign Affairs*, vol. 45, no. 3 (April 1967), 541–52. Reprinted with permission.

From Columbia University Oral History Research Office, Reminiscences of Winthrop Aldrich, 16 October 1972.

From John Foster Dulles Oral History Collection, Seeley G. Mudd Manuscript Library, Princeton University Library, Princeton University, Nathan F. Twining Oral History. Published with permission of Princeton University Library.

Prologue

On 10 January 1957, President Dwight D. Eisenhower sent a congratulatory letter to Harold Macmillan, the new prime minister of Great Britain. Eisenhower and Macmillan had known each other since 1943 when they met during the Allied campaign in North Africa. They had enjoyed a close friendship during the war and maintained a cordial, but less direct acquaintance since the war. In late 1956, however, the politically disastrous British military intervention against Egypt during the Suez crisis had resulted in the resignation of Anthony Eden as Britain's prime minister and created the circumstances for Macmillan's entry into 10 Downing Street. Eisenhower wasted no time in re-establishing an official relationship with Macmillan.

"Dear Harold," Eisenhower wrote,

> The purpose of this note is to welcome you to your new headaches. The only real fun you will have is to see just how far you can keep on going with everybody chopping at you with every conceivable kind of weapon. Knowing you so long and well I predict that your journey will be a great one. But you must remember the old adage, "Now abideth faith, hope, and charity – and greater than these is a sense of humor."[1]

Macmillan replied to Eisenhower's letter on 14 January, remarking that

> I too have vivid memories of the time when we worked together in North Africa, and of our association since then. You know how much importance I attach to the friendship between the two peoples of Britain and the United States, not least because of my own personal links with your country. I look forward to working with you once again to further this friendship.[2]

Between 1957 and 1961, Dwight D. Eisenhower and Harold Macmillan established a diplomatic partnership which cemented the Anglo-American "special relationship" as the centerpiece of the North Atlantic Treaty Organization (NATO), the alliance of Western nations created in 1949 to counter the threat of expansionism by the Soviet Union in Europe. During this period, the Cold War and the tensions which accompanied the breakup of the World War II alliance of the United States, Great Britain, and the Soviet Union dominated the international scene. Between 1947 and 1957, neither the Western democracies, led by the United States and Great Britain, nor the nations of the communist bloc, led by the Soviet Union and the People's Republic of China, had made any noticeable progress in resolving the great issues that divided them. The nuclear arms race had intensified; the future of Berlin was a flashpoint between East and West; and incipient guerilla uprisings, often sponsored by the communist powers, began to erupt throughout Southeast Asia and the Pacific.

In this environment of "permanent hostility short of armed conflict," to quote historian Robert J. Watson, the free world and the communist bloc viewed each other's intentions with great suspicion, despite occasional efforts to defuse some of the tension.[3] In July 1955, in Geneva, Switzerland, the United States, Great Britain, France, and the Soviet Union held the first major summit conference of the Cold War and, despite the atmosphere of the "spirit of Geneva" which transcended the conference, the meetings failed to produce any lasting agreements or even suggestions among the great powers as to how they might resolve their differences.

In some respects, British–American relations during the Eisenhower–Macmillan period functioned almost as an alliance within an alliance, where each country attempted to coordinate its foreign and defense policies within the broader framework of NATO strategy. Macmillan grasped the essential nature of this relationship when, at the Washington Conference in October 1957, he spoke of the United States and Great Britain, not as "a public and exclusive partnership," but rather "as an inner core working in unison gradually extending by example and influence their own harmony and confidence to all the free world."[4]

In his book, *Diplomacy*, Henry Kissinger discusses this ideal of Anglo-American cooperation as initially envisioned by the British prime minister Stanley Baldwin in 1935. As Baldwin expressed it:

> I have always believed that the greatest security against war in any part of the world whatever, in Europe, in the east, anywhere, would be the close collaboration of the British Empire with the United States of America. It may be a hundred years before that desirable end may be attained; it may never come to pass. But sometimes we may have our dreams. I look forward to the future, and I see that union of forces for peace and justice in the world, and I cannot but think, even if

men cannot freely advocate it openly yet, that some day and sometime those who follow us may see it.[5]

As Kissinger explained, Baldwin did not have to wait long to see his vision realized, first with the partnership between Franklin D. Roosevelt and Winston Churchill during World War II and then with the partnership between Eisenhower and Macmillan in the late 1950s.[6] And while it is tempting to view the Eisenhower–Macmillan relationship as the logical successor to the Roosevelt–Churchill partnership, some obvious differences in both policy and practice separate the two collaborations. Roosevelt and Churchill were largely unacquainted with each other before Adolf Hitler's ambitions for world conquest thrust them together in the period 1940–1945. By contrast, when Eisenhower and Macmillan began serving together as respective heads of state in 1957, they had known each other personally for 14 years. Furthermore, Roosevelt and Churchill met each other initially as heads of state; the Eisenhower–Macmillan partnership began when each man was serving as a subordinate to higher political authorities.[7]

More significantly, the aims of the two partnerships were different. For Roosevelt and Churchill, the overriding objective was to defeat the Axis powers, Germany, Italy, and Japan. Other aims, such as Churchill's desire to retain as much of the British Empire as possible and Roosevelt's ambition to dismantle as much of the European colonial system as possible, were secondary to the main pursuit. For Eisenhower and Macmillan, the overriding objective was to keep the peace by containing the threat of communist expansion in Europe and, occasionally, in other trouble-spots around the world, particularly in the Middle East. Although the Eisenhower–Macmillan partnership developed during a period of relative peace, rather than during wartime as that of Roosevelt and Churchill, the threat of nuclear war made the international setting more dangerous than at any comparable period in the post-Cold War era, with the possible exception of the Cuban missile crisis in 1962.

Certain aspects of the partnerships between Roosevelt and Churchill and Eisenhower and Macmillan were similar, however. Both Churchill and Macmillan assiduously courted and cultivated their relationships with Roosevelt and Eisenhower. Churchill needed Roosevelt's assistance to bring the United States into World War II as Britain's ally; he required American manpower and material if he expected to save Britain from military defeat.[8] Likewise, since Macmillan came to power in the post-Suez period when British–American relations had been strained severely, his first objective as prime minister was to restore the strong working relationship with Eisenhower as proof of his own competence as prime minister and as the best tool to maintain Britain's role in international affairs. Also, since he needed to call a general election by the spring of 1960 at the latest, Macmillan needed the invaluable political benefit which a close, visible association with Eisenhower could bring.

Admittedly, neither Roosevelt nor Eisenhower needed much convincing that a strong partnership between the United States and Great Britain served the interests of both countries. Roosevelt met with Churchill to adopt the Atlantic Charter before America entered World War II. Then, after the Suez crisis in 1956–57, Eisenhower sought out Macmillan, anxious to restore the "special" in the "special relationship." According to Andrew J. Goodpaster, Eisenhower's staff secretary and *de facto* advisor on political-military affairs, the president had a "visceral" attachment to the Anglo-American partnership and viewed it as central to international stability.[9] One could also add, parenthetically, that Eisenhower was willing to extend political assistance to the leadership of Britain's Conservative Party when the occasion seemed to call for it.

I

In personal backgrounds and life experiences, Dwight D. Eisenhower and Harold Macmillan were unlikely candidates for a close personal friendship. The contours of each man's life are well known to history but certain aspects of their experiences bear repeating. Dwight D. Eisenhower was born in Denison, Texas, on 14 October 1890 and grew up with his family in Abilene, Kansas, in the early 1900s. He was a middle son with two older brothers, Arthur and Edgar, and three younger brothers, Roy, Earl, and Milton. In Abilene, he acquired the boyhood nickname of Ike, a name which identified him to Americans and to the world for the rest of his life.[10] Ike's parents were David and Ida Stover Eisenhower. The couple had met as students at Lane University (now defunct) in Lecompton, Kansas. To support the family, David worked long hours in Abilene's Belle Springs Creamery and was a remote figure to the children. The task of running the household, including a good deal of the child raising, fell to Ida, a strict but loving mother. Ike's parents were devoutly religious. David learned the Bible in the original languages and read the Scriptures each night from a Greek translation. Ida also developed a prodigious knowledge of the Bible, once winning an award in college for memorizing 1,325 verses of Scripture.[11]

After graduating from high school, Eisenhower worked briefly to help support his family but then passed the entrance exam to the United

States Military Academy at West Point in 1911. A capable student, Ike distinguished himself more as an athlete during his first two years at West Point. He excelled as a football player and was considered one of the top players in the east until a knee injury, suffered in a riding accident, ended his athletic career after two seasons. The sudden end to his collegiate playing days hit him hard, and his academic standing suffered. Still, Ike graduated in 1915 and, shortly afterward, began the pursuit of a professional military career.[12]

Between 1915 and 1918, Eisenhower's assignments in the Army took him from Texas to Kansas to Pennsylvania. In 1916, while stationed at Fort Sam Houston in Texas, he met and fell in love with Mary Geneva "Mamie" Doud of Denver, Colorado. Mamie completely returned Ike's affections and the couple were married that year. Their first son, Doud Dwight, nicknamed "Icky," was born in 1917 but, tragically, died at the age of three, plunging his parents into a prolonged period of grief and sorrow. In 1922, Mamie gave birth to her second son, whom the parents named John Sheldon Doud Eisenhower.[13]

To his disappointment, Eisenhower remained stateside during America's participation in World War I, training troops for a prospective tank unit. In October 1918, he received orders to ship out for Europe and the Western Front, but the armistice which effectively ended the fighting was signed in November before he departed. Eisenhower believed that he had "missed the boat," from a career perspective, when he failed to obtain command and combat experience in the Great War.[14]

During the 1920s and 1930s, Eisenhower moved around the world and throughout the United States in his Army assignments. He served with General Fox Conner, a noted strategist and military theorist, in the Panama Canal Zone. He attended the Army's Command and General Staff School at Fort Leavenworth, Kansas, where he graduated first in his class. Briefly assigned to the American Battle Monuments Commission, he visited France to write a guidebook to the European battlefields where American troops had fought during World War I. He served with Army Chief of Staff General Douglas MacArthur in the 1920s in Washington and later when Roosevelt sent MacArthur to the Philippines to train a Filipino army in the 1930s.

During the interwar period, Eisenhower's assignments seemed routine and uneventful, hardly the jobs associated with a rapid rise in career status. Yet, Eisenhower's work always pleased his superior officers. Eisenhower was thorough, dedicated, dependable, and imaginative. "Eisenhower is the best officer in the Army," MacArthur said. "When the next war comes, he should go right to the top."[15]

MacArthur was correct. When the United States entered World War II, Army Chief of Staff General George C. Marshall summoned Eisenhower to Washington and placed him in the Pacific and Far Eastern department of the War Plans Division. Ike attacked his new duties with his customary diligence and imagination. In June 1942, Marshall was so impressed with Eisenhower that he selected him to command the combined British and American forces in the European Theater of Operations (ETO), choosing Ike for this coveted post ahead of 366 senior officers.[16] For Eisenhower, the rapid rise to command authority was exhilarating, especially after more than twenty years as a "lifer" in a peacetime Army. "I'm going to command the whole shebang!" he triumphantly told Mamie.[17]

The stage was thus set for the great triumph of the Allied armies under Eisenhower's leadership during World War II. As Supreme Allied Commander, Eisenhower oversaw the defeat of Axis forces in North Africa and Italy during 1943. In 1944, Eisenhower commanded Operation Overlord and directed the Allied offensives in the west which finally resulted in the German surrender on V-J Day, 8 May 1945. Victory in Europe catapulted Eisenhower to unprecedented fame and popularity. In 1942, he had left the United States as a relatively obscure soldier, but he returned to America as the man who beat Hitler.[18]

Eisenhower's skills as the Supreme Allied Commander extended well beyond the military realm, of course. The quality which most impressed Ike's superiors, including Roosevelt, Churchill, Marshall, the American and British military chiefs, and individuals like Harold Macmillan, was his ability to "fathom and manipulate the human equation," in the words of historian David Kennedy. "A careful student of war, Ike was a still more careful student of human psychology – especially of those elements that made up the mysterious compound of effective leadership."[19]

According to Alexander Macmillan, grandson of Harold Macmillan and the second Earl of Stockton, it was this capacity for human relations which endeared Eisenhower to the British. "What my grandfather always admired about Ike was his political skill, with a small 'p,'" Stockton said. "Ike always tried to understand the other fellow's point of view, negotiate with him, and then nudge him in the direction he wanted to go."[20] Added to that was Ike's demonstration of sincerity, fairness, and optimism. "I firmly determined that my mannerisms in speech in public would always reflect the cheerful certainty of victory – that any pessimism and discouragement I might ever feel would be reserved for my pillow," he once observed.[21]

In the immediate post-World War II period, Eisenhower returned to Washington as Army Chief of Staff. In June 1948, he took leave from the Army to accept the presidency of Columbia University, a decision which generated a host of rumors that Eisenhower intended to use his new position to launch a candidacy for the presidency of the United States.[22] In 1948, Eisenhower refused countless overtures to enter partisan politics, however. He remained at Columbia until 1949, when he once again entered active military service as chairman of the Joint Chiefs of Staff.

In December 1950, President Harry S. Truman named Eisenhower as the Supreme Allied Commander, Europe (SACEUR), and Ike became the first commander of NATO forces. He accepted an enormous assignment, rallying the nations of the Western alliance to furnish the money and manpower necessary to make NATO function properly. By this time, however, Eisenhower had parted company, philosophically, with the economic policies of the Truman Administration and the isolationist-inclined foreign policy of the Republican Party, exemplified by the views of Sen. Robert A. Taft from Ohio, the front-runner for the GOP presidential nomination in 1952. By late 1951, Eisenhower was poised to enter the presidential race and a full-blown Eisenhower for President campaign erupted in the spring of 1952.[23] Ike declared for the presidency in Abilene on 5 June 1952 and won the GOP presidential nomination after a bitter battle with the Taft forces at the Republican convention in Chicago in July. On 4 November, he convincingly defeated Governor Adlai E. Stevenson of Illinois, his Democratic opponent, receiving 55 per cent of the popular vote and 442 votes in the Electoral College.[24] His victory, along with the GOP's thin majority in the House and tie in the Senate, gave the Republicans control of both the White House and the Congress for the first time since 1928.

While Dwight D. Eisenhower had managed to rise from the modest origins of small-town America to the pinnacle of world leadership, Harold Macmillan's life experiences were considerably different in his climb to the summit of British politics. Born in London on 10 February 1894 (only four years after Eisenhower), Harold Macmillan was the third son of Maurice Macmillan and his wife, Helen Belles (Hill) Macmillan. The focus of the family's life centered on its prosperous and prestigious publishing firm, The House of Macmillan, publishers of the works of some of the world's most noted authors. Maurice Macmillan ran the company capably and effectively, devoting long hours to the success of the enterprise.

The dominant personality in the Macmillan household was Harold's mother, known as Nellie. Nellie Macmillan's life story was fascinating for any period, but especially so for the late nineteenth century. Born in 1856 in Indianapolis, Indiana, she was the only surviving daughter of five children born to Joshua and Julia Reid Belles.[25] When Nellie was six, her mother died. Two years later, Joshua Belles remarried; his second wife was an Indianapolis widow named Amanda Tull. The reconstituted Belles family then settled in Spencer, a small town south of Indianapolis, and Belles became the community's most prominent physician.

Nellie Belles received her education in both Spencer and at a finishing school in Indianapolis. In her late teens, she met and fell in love with John Bayliss (Jack) Hill, an aspiring painter and member of a prominent Indianapolis family. The couple were married in June 1874 but the marriage lasted only six months, for Jack Hill died suddenly in November at age 25.[26]

Not yet 20 and already a widow, Nellie Belles Hill remained in Indianapolis briefly, pursuing her interest in music. Later in the 1870s, Nellie left Indiana for Paris where she intended to study music and sculpture. "She was a fine singer," Harold Macmillan told an audience at Indiana University in September 1956. "Her singing is still remembered by some – in Church and chapel – in Spencer and Indianapolis. The last time she sang in her own country, I am told, was at the Indianapolis Women's Club in 1877."[27]

While in Paris, Nellie met Maurice Macmillan, and the couple were married in 1884. He was 30, she was 27, at the time of the marriage. The Macmillans took up residence at 52 Cadogan Place in London where Nellie became a devoted wife to her British husband and a demanding mother to her three sons, Daniel, Arthur, and Harold.

Some have argued that Nellie Macmillan was too forceful a mother to her children, bent on controlling every facet of their lives. Historian Richard Aldous notes that Nellie "was a stern and manipulative woman who dominated young Harold's life in an intrusive and persecuting way."[28] Harold Macmillan occasionally echoed the sentiments of his mother's critics by observing that Nellie "had high standards and demanded equally high performances from all about her. She had great ambitions, not for herself but for her children."[29]

Regarding Harold's future, Nellie harbored the dream that he would, someday, become one of Britain's great political leaders. "Don't kick that door," she admonished her grandchildren when they later came to visit at Birch Grove, the palatial Macmillan family mansion in Sussex.

"Someday this house is going to belong to a prime minister."[30] At some point, Harold became philosophical about his mother's relentless pressure and its positive and negative effects. While Macmillan often resented Nellie's intimidating personality, he also believed that his vigorous ambition for success came as a result of her influence.

Undeniably, Macmillan received an indispensable tutelage from Nellie about American life and politics as well as an appreciation for a close friendship between Great Britain and the United States. "My mother taught me that the future of the world depended on the alliance, the co-operation of our two great countries," he told an audience in Indianapolis in 1956. Also, in his address at Indiana University in 1956, he spoke about how his unique ancestry enabled him to understand the common bond which existed between the two great English-speaking countries. "The two countries to which I owe, from my double family tradition, an equal loyalty – Britain and the United States – have been partners and allies in two great struggles," Macmillan said, referring to the experience of World War I and World War II.

> In both these conflicts, two countries whose histories before held much of bitterness and misunderstanding were united in a deep and lasting loyalty. We had the same purposes and the same ideals. We made our great sacrifices partly in the defense of our own interests, as we have the right to do, threatened as they then were both from the Nazi domination of Europe and similar threats in the Far East. But in defending our own interests, we defended something much wider – the freedom of the whole world.[31]

Harold Macmillan received the systematic education customary for a member of one of Britain's privileged families, attending Eton and Balliol College, Oxford. Whatever other professional ambitions Macmillan entertained, he knew that a position always awaited him at the House of Macmillan. But World War I intervened, altering his life and permanently changing his outlook on politics.

After joining the Army, Macmillan was posted to the Scottish Grenadier Guards where he commanded a unit of soldiers drawn from Britain's working classes, "the best men in the world," he would say later.[32] Besides the influence of his mother, World War I was the signal event to that point in Macmillan's life. Few men could match Harold Macmillan's record of heroism and bravery during the Great War. In September 1915, during combat near the town of Loos in Belgium, Macmillan suffered a concussion and wound to his right wrist. Evacuated to London, he recuperated sufficiently to return to action on the Western Front. One year later, during a vicious encounter in the Battle of the Somme, Macmillan suffered wounds to his knee and pelvis. For twelve hours he lay motionless in a crater, in excruciating pain, feigning death as German soldiers passed by.[33] Feverish from infection, and never completely sure how he had been rescued from the battlefield, Macmillan was once again evacuated to London where he received medical attention from Sir William Bennett, the prominent British surgeon and friend of the family. Nellie Macmillan's prompt call for Bennett's services saved Harold's life. Even so, he walked with a slight limp for the rest of his life and his wrist never fully regained its strength.[34]

Yet, Macmillan had survived the fighting on the Western Front, despite five wounds, two brushes with death, and injuries which permanently afflicted him. "Alas, I am one of very few survivors of my contemporaries [from the University of Oxford]," Macmillan later recalled, and he made a promise to himself after the war "to make decent use of the life that had been spared."[35]

In 1919 Macmillan became the *aide-de-camp* to the Governor General of Canada, the Duke of Devonshire, where he met and fell in love with Dorothy Cavendish, the third daughter of the Governor General's family. Dorothy, too, was attracted to Harold and the couple married in 1920. Although the marriage lasted throughout their lifetimes and produced four children, Dorothy's long-standing, notorious extramarital relationship with Robert Boothby, like Macmillan a political aspirant in the Conservative Party, made the union a tense and difficult one.[36]

After a brief stint with the House of Macmillan, Macmillan won election to the British House of Commons in 1924 as the Conservative Party's representative for Stockton-on-Tees, an industrial town in northeast England. He served in Parliament until 1929 when he was defeated. He regained his seat in 1931.

During the 1930s, Macmillan became known as an interventionist in economic policy as the country experienced the devastation caused by the Great Depression. The grinding poverty faced by his constituents helped to convince Macmillan that the then National Government needed to develop new programs of assistance to help those who were becoming economically destitute. He also belonged to the anti-appeasement faction of the Conservative Party and became an admirer of Winston Churchill, who warned Britain about the dangers of German rearmament. Churchill became Macmillan's political hero, a leader who embodied Macmillan's notions of decisiveness, sense of destiny, and discernment. By most accounts, Churchill did not reciprocate Macmillan's admiration and respect, however.[37]

Nevertheless, in November 1942, Churchill appointed Macmillan as the Minister Resident to Eisenhower's Armed Forces Headquarters (AFHQ) in North Africa. Macmillan's responsibilities involved the representation of Churchill's views to Eisenhower and, in that capacity, he worked closely with Robert Murphy, Roosevelt's political representative to Ike. Both Macmillan and Murphy soon took on a greater degree of responsibility than their basic job descriptions indicated, as for the next two years, they trouble-shot their way through numerous imbroglios in North Africa and the Mediterranean, ranging from negotiations with the Free French to the defeat and surrender of Italy. As Murphy recalled:

> Macmillan and I became involved in one controversial matter after another... Macmillan was not a career diplomat, nor did he bring to Algiers any exceptional knowledge of French or African Affairs. What he did bring was exceptional common sense and knowledge of British politics. Churchill wrote Roosevelt that one reason he chose Macmillan was because, like Churchill himself, he had an American mother.[38]

After Operation Overlord, Murphy returned to the European theater to work on Eisenhower's staff. Macmillan remained in the Mediterranean where he became involved in the liberation of Greece and a host of problems relating to refugees and arrangements for postwar Europe.

It was in North Africa that Eisenhower and Macmillan met for the first time and began the friendship which lasted for the rest of their lives. In particular, two encounters emerged which were critical to each man's understanding and respect for the other. The first occurred on 1 January 1943 when Macmillan called on Eisenhower at his office in the St Georges Hotel in Algiers. At the time, Eisenhower was besieged with work and responsibility, even though the military situation in Algeria had improved considerably since the Allied landings of the previous November. Moreover, some uncertainty and confusion had developed as to whether Macmillan was to join Eisenhower's staff at AFHQ, and be responsible to him, or whether he was to be Churchill's autonomous representative to Ike and thereby remain accountable to the prime minister. In his memoirs, *The Blast of War*, Macmillan gave an account of what has now become his famous first conversation with Eisenhower.

Eisenhower: Pleased to meet you but what have you come for? I have been told nothing [of your appointment]. You are a minister but what sort of a minister are you?
Macmillan: Well, General. I am not a diplomatic minister. I am something worse.
Eisenhower: There is nothing worse.
Macmillan: Perhaps you will think a politician is even more troublesome.
Eisenhower: Well, I don't know about that. Perhaps so, but anyway, what are you going to do?
Macmillan: I will just do my best. I shall be told and will be able to tell you what are the feelings of the Prime Minister and his colleagues on anything that comes up.
Eisenhower: Oh, but I have got a fine man in Hal Mack who does that.
Macmillan: I am afraid that Mr. Mack will be wanted elsewhere, and you will have to rely on me. I can tell you that I have at least one advantage over you all. I know nothing whatsoever about the political problems here. I shall have to learn.
Eisenhower: Well, there's plenty to learn.[39]

The conversation was obviously proceeding to neither man's satisfaction so Macmillan tried a different tactic. He asked Ike if he knew that Macmillan's mother was an American. "What do you mean, your mother?," Eisenhower shot back. "Why should I know that?" "My mother was born in Indiana in a little town called Spencer," Macmillan said. "So I am a Hoosier."[40]

According to Macmillan, the knowledge that he had some roots in small-town America changed Eisenhower's attitude perceptibly. The supreme commander and his guest then began to converse in a more relaxed fashion about the problems which Ike was encountering in North Africa. Especially frustrating was the reaction in the British and American newspapers to his so-called "deal" with Admiral François Darlan, the collaborationist Vichy French military officer, whom Eisenhower had allowed to retain political control of the French troops in Algeria. Eisenhower believed that his "deal" with Darlan was a pragmatic method to save lives and keep the situation in the region under control. Besides, political considerations were a frustrating diversion from Ike's main objective, engaging the German forces in Tunisia. But other diplomatic, political, and journalistic circles on both sides of the Atlantic were uncharitable toward Eisenhower's use of Darlan. "I can't understand why these long-haired, starry-eyed guys keep gunning for me," Eisenhower complained. "I'm no reactionary . . . I'm idealistic as Hell."[41]

The first meeting between Eisenhower and Macmillan ended amicably, although its impact upon Macmillan was understandably more lasting than that upon Eisenhower. Three decades later, Macmillan told Robert McKenzie, an interviewer for the British Broadcasting Corporation (BBC), that his wartime association with Ike was

> a pure piece of luck. I made really a friendship with the President, with the General. He liked me; we got on, and I think I could help him over some things. At any rate, he felt so; he had complete confidence in me . . . although we didn't always agree. I could say anything to him and he'd answer it and we never quarreled.[42]

For his part, Eisenhower handled his initial contact with Macmillan routinely, never making any judgments, positive or negative, about his character. On 2 January 1943, Eisenhower wrote to the Combined Chiefs of Staff: "Mister Harold Macmillan has just reported . . . and explained his mission in this theater. I am convinced that he will be most helpful . . ."[43]

The second encounter occurred two weeks later when Macmillan, along with Murphy, received an order to fly from Algiers to Casablanca to attend the meeting between Roosevelt and Churchill. With a flair for the dramatic, Macmillan described the Casablanca Conference as a meeting of the Emperor of the East (Churchill) with the Emperor of the West (Roosevelt). Once in Casablanca, Macmillan was summoned to meet with Roosevelt at his villa. Entering the president's room, he found Roosevelt in conference with Churchill and Eisenhower. Greeting Macmillan warmly, Roosevelt said, "Harold, I am so glad to see you" and then launched into a reference as to when he had last seen Macmillan in the United States. After the meeting, Eisenhower turned to Macmillan and said, "I didn't know that you knew the president." "Well, yes, I've known him for some time," Macmillan explained. Eisenhower was mystified: how could someone who had known the president socially not have said so earlier? Even so, Ike appreciated the fact that Macmillan had not used his limited acquaintance with Roosevelt as a means of self-promotion. As Alexander Macmillan, a grandson of Harold, observed: "This [meeting] was something of a breakthrough. Ike now began to look at my grandfather as more than simply a somewhat effete Englishman."[44]

The Allied military campaign in North Africa lasted for almost six more months until the Germans were defeated late in May 1943. On 20 May 1943, Macmillan and Murphy held places of honor as the Allied armies paraded in victory at Tunis. Later, on the return flight to Algiers, Eisenhower and Macmillan observed a convoy of ships crossing the Mediterranean. Motioning to Eisenhower, Macmillan said, "There, General, go the fruits of your victory." Eisenhower replied, emotionally, "Yours, you mean, ours, Harold, that we have all won together."[45]

Several historians have commented upon the manner in which Macmillan's experiences with the Americans during World War II matured him and added to his self-confidence. As Robert Rhodes James has written: "[World War II] gave Harold Macmillan his opportunity [to bring out] his supreme negotiating skills with the Free French and the Americans. It also brought out an ambition that had not been noticed by his colleagues . . . His rise had begun."[46]

Just as importantly, Macmillan had formulated an approach to working with the Americans, an approach which consisted of equal parts admiration for their vitality; respect for their commitment to defeat the Axis enemy; and condescension toward their limited understanding of international relations. "We, my dear Crossman, are Greeks in this American empire," Macmillan told Richard Crossman, his principal wartime advisor. "You will find the Americans much as the Greeks found the Romans – great big, vulgar, bustling people, more vigorous than we are and also more idle, with more unspoiled virtues but also more corrupt. We must run A.F.H.Q. as the Greek slaves ran the operations of the Emperor Claudius."[47] More shrewdly, however, Macmillan also reckoned with the wisdom of a calculated deferral to the American prerogative, adding that the British should always "be a deputy or a number two" to their American counterparts. "This way you could often get them to do what *you* (authors' emphasis) wanted, while they persuaded themselves it was really all their idea," Macmillan contended. Such a process became the guiding philosophy for his future dealings with the Americans, including during his years as prime minister.[48]

Following World War II, Macmillan definitely had a future in British national politics, although his own career suffered a setback when he lost his seat in the Labour victory in 1945. Within three weeks of his defeat, however, he regained a seat in Parliament when he won a by-election for the constituency of Bromley, in Kent, the constituency which he served until leaving government in 1964.[49]

In 1951, the Conservatives returned to power with Churchill again becoming prime minister. Macmillan received the assignment to make good on the party's campaign promise to expand Britain's public housing sector. Appointed minister of housing in 1951, he served in this post for the next three years. In 1954, he became secretary of state for defence, a position which gave him some valuable experience in balancing the claims of military preparedness with the harsh realities of Britain's emerging economic difficulties.

In the 1955 general election, the Conservatives maintained power and even increased their strength in the House of Commons. Anthony Eden, who had succeeded Churchill as prime minister six months earlier, named Macmillan as his successor as foreign secretary, the Cabinet post which he long coveted. But relations between Eden, who intended to function as his own foreign secretary, and Macmillan were hardly cordial and, in 1956, Eden moved Macmillan to chancellor of the Exchequer, nominally the second highest post in the British government but one to which Macmillan never aspired.[50]

By this point in his life, Harold Macmillan, like Dwight D. Eisenhower, had discharged responsibilities of great authority. Capitalizing on the appointment which he obtained to Eisenhower's staff in 1942, "the great advantage that chance had given me," Macmillan had become a key figure in British–American relations during World War II.[51] He had earned the respect and admiration of a host of American and British military officers, diplomats, and administration officials. Then, he went on to hold Cabinet posts in two British governments and advised two prime ministers. He had acquired a working knowledge of leadership as it was exercised at the national and international levels.

So, despite the differences in their backgrounds and life experiences, Eisenhower and Macmillan shared some characteristics. Both came from a family dominated by the personality of the mother. Both grew up in a family of sons; the young men in the Eisenhower family and the Macmillan family all became successful professionals when they grew to adulthood. Both reflected conservative, and yet pragmatic, social and economic philosophies. Both were intensely patriotic, with a strong sense of duty, and spent their entire adult lives in service to their countries. Both were ambitious, from a personal perspective, and each man believed that he was the best qualified individual to serve as the leader of his country. Both men took pride in their knowledge of the other's country and its institutions.

Finally, both Eisenhower and Macmillan had experienced the horrors of war. Macmillan was a combatant in some of the worst fighting in the Great War and a diplomat in World War II. Eisenhower was the commander of the largest combined Allied force in history, a man who was forced to order thousands of troops into battle and, inevitably, send men to their deaths. And both men, as national leaders, were exceedingly reluctant to commit their countrymen to armed conflict. If negotiations were a reasonable alternative to military action, they were prepared to go to considerable lengths to exhaust that approach before contemplating a more drastic course.

II

When Eisenhower and Macmillan became the national leaders of the United States and Great Britain in January 1957, they quickly agreed upon a pattern of action which characterized their relations with each other and the conduct of their respective foreign policies. The pattern rested on three elements: the re-establishment and maintenance of the personal friendship which existed between the two men as the basis for frank, candid discussions of policy issues; a systematic series of regular bilateral discussions between themselves and the members of their national security offices to coordinate policy and thereby prevent misunderstandings; and, finally, a program of cooperation on military and defense policy. The process by which this three-part system was implemented between 1957 and 1961 was occasionally messy, and tempers often grew short in both London and Washington, but the system did preserve the Anglo-American relationship as the keystone of the western alliance.

First, both Eisenhower and Macmillan moved rapidly in early 1957 to renew the personal nature of their friendship. In March, at their conference in Bermuda (see chapter 1, below) Macmillan proposed, and Eisenhower accepted, the suggestion that they exchange a regular personal correspondence so as to give each man a glimpse into the thinking of the other.[52] Both leaders made a serious commitment to this correspondence: in the first five months of 1957, Macmillan sent 24 separate messages to Eisenhower and Eisenhower sent 19 separate messages to Macmillan.[53] This pattern of correspondence continued to the end of Eisenhower's presidency, although not always with the frequency of the early months.

Macmillan's initial proposal called for intimacy and confidentiality, the notion that the two men should exchange views without having their thoughts influenced by their respective bureaucracies. Regarding the matter of confidentiality, Macmillan agreed to one exception; Ike could show his letters to John Foster Dulles, the American secretary of state. As a consequence, after Eisenhower received a letter from

Macmillan, he asked Dulles, and later Christian Herter (who succeeded Dulles in 1959), to draft a response before he answered the prime minister officially. Nevertheless, the president did preserve the informality which Macmillan desired, addressing the prime minister as "Dear Harold," and closing the letters (usually) with the famous words, "With warm regard, As ever, Ike."

Likewise, Macmillan followed Churchill's example, who, as prime minister, had also carried on a correspondence with Eisenhower.[54] Often using the Churchillian salutation of "My dear friend," instead of the official "Dear Mr. President," Macmillan made it clear that he wanted to keep matters on a personal basis. The tone of the letters, with very few exceptions, was collegial.

The Eisenhower–Macmillan correspondence consists of a unique combination of material, ranging from discussion on serious matters of official policy to purely personal subjects such as wishes for good health and the exchange of birthday greetings. But, above all, it is a correspondence which reveals the thinking of two leaders whose countries had global interests. The correspondence also underscores the fact that both Eisenhower and Macmillan were master communicators. They loved to think, loved to write, loved to talk, and loved to confer. Eisenhower's writing style was businesslike and direct; Macmillan often resorted to historical analogies to justify his arguments for a particular course of action. In either case, the correspondence reveals a record of two leaders who were completely absorbed in the national security process.

The correspondence served a valuable purpose for both leaders. As Eisenhower expressed it in a letter to Macmillan on 6 January 1958: "It is indeed useful for us thus to 'think out loud' to each each other when, as is too much the case, we cannot sit down and talk together."[55] In similar fashion, Macmillan considered that the correspondence with Ike gave him entry to a privileged relationship with the president. "I have a strong feeling that private correspondence should remain private," Macmillan wrote to Eisenhower on 5 May 1959.

> In that spirit, I have, for example, never shown your letters to me even to my own colleagues, except from time to time to the Foreign Secretary.... The more I think about it, the more I feel that our relations, based as they are upon such a very long friendship, are of another character to those that exist even between statesmen of closely allied countries.[56]

Second, Eisenhower and Macmillan established a pattern of regular consultations which involved themselves and the officials responsible for national security policy in both the United States and Great Britain. These bilateral talks occurred at frequent intervals: at Bermuda in March 1957, after the Suez crisis; in Washington in October 1957, to reach agreement on the issue of nuclear cooperation; at Paris in December 1957 for a meeting of the NATO Council; in June 1958 in Washington, to discuss the Berlin situation and disarmament negotiations; at Washington in March 1959, to discuss Macmillan's recent trip to the Soviet Union; in London in August and September 1959, to discuss the upcoming Western Summit in Paris scheduled for December; at the Western Summit in Paris in December 1959 and in Washington in March 1960, to discuss plans for the upcoming four-power Summit in Paris; in Paris in May 1960, when the Four-Power Summit collapsed following the Soviet's downing of an American U-2 espionage aircraft; and finally in New York, in September 1960 after Nikita Khrushchev verbally abused the Western alliance in a speech at the United Nations. These meetings institutionalized the collaboration between the two countries and made for a more rational collaboration of policy-making between the United States and Great Britain.

Just as significantly, the pattern of consultation which Eisenhower and Macmillan established also reached into the lower echelons of their respective national security organizations. By the end of the Eisenhower presidency, many of these policy-makers in both the United States and Great Britain, like their leaders, were on a first-name basis with each other.

The process by which Eisenhower made national security policy has been extensively studied, of course.[57] We know that Ike placed a tremendous emphasis upon the deliberations and organization of the National Security Council as the key to formulating the American approach to international relations. But, within that context, Eisenhower worked with a wide array of people, ranging from Secretary of State John Foster Dulles, who dominated the national security process between 1953 and 1959, and other individuals such as Christian Herter, successor to Dulles as secretary of state; the three secretaries of defense: Charles E. Wilson, Neil H. McElroy, and Thomas S. Gates; Lewis Strauss and John McCone who chaired the Atomic Energy Commission (AEC) during his presidency; his treasury secretaries George M. Humphrey and Robert B. Anderson; his two ambassadors to Great Britain, Winthrop Aldrich and John Hay (Jock) Whitney; his staff secretary, General Andrew J.

Goodpaster; Henry Cabot Lodge, the United States representative to the United Nations; and a host of other officials at the sub-cabinet level.

The Eisenhower approach to formulating national security policy was once described succinctly by C. Douglas Dillon, ambassador to France, assistant secretary of state for economic affairs, and under secretary of state in the Administration. "President Eisenhower did believe that if he picked good people to run important areas of government, that they should have great freedom," Dillon recalled. "I think that is the best and really only efficient way to run our government. If the fellow that you have in a job isn't performing, then you can always replace him but you don't try to make all the decisions right from the beginning in the White House. That's the way the Eisenhower team worked."[58]

This decentralized approach to policy-making did not mean that Eisenhower abdicated the responsibility of decision-making, however. As John S.D. Eisenhower once observed, "I think that this [decentralized] aspect of Ike's style has been overdrawn somewhat. Ike ran national security policy pretty autocratically. He was used to commanding in this field, not simply accepting advice from others."[59]

By contrast, Harold Macmillan's approach was much more centralized than Eisenhower's, as befitting someone who had once served as his country's chief diplomat. During the Eisenhower presidency, Macmillan's foreign secretary was Selwyn Lloyd, who, like John Foster Dulles, was a professional lawyer. Macmillan did not give Lloyd the authority that Eisenhower granted to Dulles, but the foreign secretary nevertheless emerged as the prime minister's chief foreign policy advisor. Moreover, Lloyd and Dulles were comfortable with each other, despite their near-falling-out during the Suez crisis of 1956. Beyond Lloyd, however, Macmillan selected foreign policy advisors who functioned in more of a staff capacity to the prime minister. For example, Britain's defense ministers under Macmillan, Duncan Sandys and Harold Watkinson, were charged with managing their departments and generally were not active participants in the so-called "negotiating apparatus" between the United States and Great Britain. Both Sandys and Watkinson did form productive relationships with their opposite numbers in the United States, Neil McElroy and Thomas Gates, however, and the four men actively consolidated the program of defense cooperation between the two countries.

In the diplomatic realm, however, Macmillan came to rely on individuals such as Freddie Bishop and Philip de Zulueta, his foreign policy advisors; Sir Patrick Dean, who took the lead on arms control issues; Frederick Hoyer-Miller, the permanent secretary at the Foreign Office, and Norman Brook, the Cabinet secretary. Macmillan and Lloyd also dealt extensively with Sir Harold Caccia, the British ambassador to the United States, who was the courier for many of Macmillan's messages to Eisenhower. At the numerous consultations which occurred between Eisenhower and Macmillan in the period 1957–60, the advisors listed previously were generally extensively involved in the negotiations and discussions which transpired.

Finally, the Eisenhower–Macmillan diplomatic partnership owed much of its success to the program of defense cooperation which both leaders implemented. One suspects that this aspect of the Eisenhower–Macmillan relationship has been overlooked in favor of the frequent, visible public consultations which the two men conducted. As national leaders, however, both Eisenhower and Macmillan were realists on the issue of military forces and defense spending. As participants in World War II and strong anti-communists, both men understood the limitations which accompany any foreign policy which lacks the backing of a strong military establishment. Thomas S. Gates, Eisenhower's secretary of defense between 1959 and 1961, put it best when he observed in 1960: "National defense must always come first since only from military strength can foreign policy operate."[60]

But both men were also, in a sense, defense reformers who were instinctively cautious about permitting a rapid expansion in defense spending. Both Eisenhower and Macmillan wanted to achieve a balance where the proper functioning of the economy was not overburdened by defense spending. One of the major achievements of Eisenhower's first term was his ability to hold the line on military spending and, as some have argued, restrain the growth of the arms race.[61] For his part, Macmillan was also suspicious of more military spending, but for a different reason. In the post-World War II environment, the British simply lacked the economic capacity to support major international commitments. As minister of defense, he told Prime Minister Anthony Eden, "It is defense expenditure which has broken our back."[62]

During the late 1950s, cost-conscious approaches to defense spending led both the United States and Great Britain to focus on the modernization of nuclear forces, the establishment of a deterrent capability, and a reduction in conventional forces. Because the British economy was unable to support growth in its military sector, Macmillan, over time, turned to American technology as the most effective way to maintain British strength within NATO.

Fortunately, the American military establishment made unprecedented advances in its deterrent capability during Eisenhower's presidency, advances which made it possible for the Administration to institute a program of defense cooperation with its allies, particularly with the British. In retrospect, two decisions early in Eisenhower's presidency allowed the administration to undertake the modernization of its nuclear forces and deterrent capability. First, the Administration decided to resolve the Korean War diplomatically, a step which was achieved by July 1953. The end of that conflict significantly reduced the cost of military operations and allowed the Administration to focus on its primary objective of strengthening NATO forces in Europe. Second, the Administration decided in the spring of 1953 to reduce overall defense spending by more than $5 billion from the Truman budget estimates for the 1954 fiscal year. The responsibility for shepherding these reductions through Congress fell to Charles E. Wilson, Eisenhower's first secretary of defense. The former president of General Motors Corporation, Wilson had been savaged during his Senate confirmation hearings in January when he allegedly remarked, "What's good for General Motors is good for the country." Nevertheless, when the Administration and the Republican Congress drastically revised downward defense spending from the budget they had inherited from the Truman Administration, Wilson stood his ground and the Eisenhower reductions were approved, despite enormous criticism from the Democratic Party in Congress, the national press, and some prominent members of the military.[63] As a result of these two decisions, Eisenhower's defense budgets concentrated on modernization achieved through the vast advances in scientific research and development.

The result was remarkable, in terms of the growth of American military power during the 1950s. "The period from 1953–1961 was the most revolutionary in American history [relative to defense]," Robert B. Anderson, secretary of the navy, deputy secretary of defense, and secretary of the treasury in the Eisenhower presidency, once observed. "It was as striking a period as ever existed in American military history as far as capability was concerned. When we left office, we knew that we had the capability, for the first time in history, to destroy nations completely. The basic raw power existed."[64]

Thomas S. Gates put it more succinctly in a speech in 1960. "I came to the Pentagon in 1953," Gates said.

> In the short span of one man's service, let us look at what happened. In 1953, no ship afloat was powered by atomic energy. Today we have 13 nuclear submarines already in commission and 30 under construction . . . In 1953, the POLARIS system was merely a dream.

Before the end of the year, two of these submarines . . . will join our active forces. In 1953 an airplane which was expected for the first time to operate at speeds greater than the speed of sound was in the very early design stage. Today Mach 2 aircraft are part of our regular forces . . . These changes have occurred in less than seven years – the time that used to be regarded as par for the course in the development of a fighter aircraft.[65]

Thus, the growth in American military power during the late 1950s ensured that the Eisenhower–Macmillan diplomatic partnership was not a collaboration of equals. American power was reaching its apex, relative to the rest of the world, in the late 1950s. British military power, by contrast, faced a period of adjustment to the new realities of economic stringency and Macmillan needed to mold his foreign policy to a changing environment. "The dinosaur was [once] the largest beast but it was inefficient and therefore disappeared," Macmillan told a friend. "The bee is efficient, but it is too small to have much influence. Britain's most useful role is somewhere between the bee and the dinosaur."[66]

In conclusion, three diplomatic partnerships characterized British–American relations during the twentieth century: the Roosevelt–Churchill partnership of 1940–45; the Eisenhower–Macmillan partnership of 1957–61; and the partnership between Ronald Reagan and Margaret Thatcher during the 1980s. The British historian Robert M. Hathaway credits Roosevelt and Churchill for creating the alliance between Britain and the United States in the last century, Eisenhower and Macmillan for sustaining the alliance, and Reagan and Thatcher for renewing the alliance.[67] Of the three partnerships, however, only that of Eisenhower and Macmillan was implemented on the basis of a previous personal friendship. Because of the intimacy and candor made possible by their friendship, Eisenhower and Macmillan put their stamp on the foreign policy of the late 1950s and set a model of behavior which influenced future British–American relations after they left office. Indeed, one can argue that Eisenhower and Macmillan, with their stress on the personal aspects of their diplomacy and their concerns about integrating the defense policies of Britain and the United States, were central characters in the continuity of one diplomatic partnership and the preservers of future close relationships between the American and British political leaders who succeeded them.

1
1957: Bermuda, Washington, Paris

On the evening of 6 November 1956, Dwight D. Eisenhower watched the returns as American voters resoundingly re-elected him to his second term as the thirty-fourth president of the United States. His margin of victory over Adlai Stevenson, his Democratic opponent in both 1952 and 1956, was even greater than four years previously. In 1956, Eisenhower won 57 percent of the popular vote and 457 votes in the Electoral College, a triumph of landslide proportions.[1] Eisenhower's two victories in 1952 and 1956 made him the greatest vote-getter in the history of the Republican Party. Moreover, not since the days of George Washington (Eisenhower's hero, ironically) had an American leader occupied center stage, in war and peace, for as long a period of time as had Dwight D. Eisenhower.

For reasons of his own health and also as a shrewd political tactic, Eisenhower campaigned very little in the autumn of 1956. He made few political appearances on behalf of other GOP candidates with the result that his victory was especially personal. Eisenhower's landslide did not change the political balance-of-power in Washington, however. In 1956, the Democratic Party maintained the control of both houses of Congress, which it had acquired in the mid-term elections of 1954. Confronting an opposition Congress for the next four years was neither a heartening nor a daunting prospect for Eisenhower. In his first term, the president had proven that he could work cooperatively with the Democratic leaders of Congress, especially with the three Texans: Sam Rayburn, speaker of the House of Representatives; Lyndon B. Johnson, Senate majority leader; and George Mahon, chairman of the House Subcommittee on Defense Appropriations, who controlled the flow and content of important federal legislation. Eisenhower also realized that, if his first term's experience repeated itself, Congress would grant him virtually a free hand to manage America's national security policy, his major priority. "With Eisenhower as President and Johnson and Rayburn in the Congress, you always knew that on defense and foreign policy you'd win, though for political purposes they might give you hell," Tom Gates once stated.[2]

National security policy was clearly the main concern of the Eisenhower administration in November 1956. In fact, his re-election occurred at a tumultuous time in the history of the Cold War. When Americans went to the polls on 6 November, a full-scale crisis was underway in the Middle East as British, French, and Israeli forces were battling Egyptian forces in an attempt to restore international control of the Suez Canal after the Egyptian leader Gamal Abdul Nasser had nationalized the waterway in late July. The worst day of this six-month crisis may well have been 5 November, the day before the presidential election. On that day, British and French paratroopers landed in Egypt, after repeated American warnings to refrain from the use of force, and the Soviet Union, which supported the Egyptians, then threatened intervention in the region to combat "the spread of imperialism," a threat which raised alarms in both Washington and the European capitals. "Those boys [the Soviets] are both furious and scared. Just as with Hitler, that makes for a dangerous state of mind . . . If those fellows start something, we may have to hit 'em – and, if necessary, with everything in the bucket," Eisenhower said at the time.[3]

The Soviets had also taken advantage of the diversion of attention by the Western powers on the Middle East to crush a democratic revolt in Hungary, only two weeks after indicating a willingness to cooperate with the Hungarian reformers.[4] In the words of Ann Whitman, Eisenhower's secretary, "The day before [Election Day], the day for which we had worked so hard, was not at all a campaign day; it was a day of one crisis after another in the international field."[5]

I

The Suez crisis has become one of the most studied events of the Cold War and it has had an enduring impact upon the situation in the Middle East and relations between the great powers, as well as a profound effect on British–American relations.[6] From the beginning of the crisis in late July 1956, until the outbreak of hostilities between Israel, Great Britain, and France against Egypt on 29 October, the United States hoped to resolve the dispute by diplomacy. For a variety of reasons, Eisenhower opposed military action against Nasser. He did not want to arouse Arab animosity against the West and open the door to further Soviet influence in the region. He believed that action against Nasser by Western governments would be perceived in the non-aligned world as the reintroduction of colonialism into the Middle East. He also did not want to see a disruption in the shipment of Middle Eastern oil to Western Europe. Furthermore, he viewed armed intervention as contrary to the spirit and policies of the United Nations. As Alexander Macmillan once observed, "Ike got very nervous [about intervention in the Middle East.] Was this what the post-war world was going to look like? Fighting these damn little wars in some far-off place where you literally had to get out a map to find out where the crisis was."[7]

Another factor in the Administration's desire to resolve the Suez crisis diplomatically was the upcoming American presidential election on 6 November. Campaigning on a record of "Peace and Prosperity," the Administration wanted no involvement in any overseas conflict which could undermine its political standing. As the British writer M.R.D. Foot put it, "The [Suez] crisis could hardly have come at a less convenient time for Eisenhower, who was busy getting re-elected."[8] With time counting down until election day, one suspects that considerable frustration existed in Washington, based on the suspicion that the Israelis, British, and French were taking advantage of the American political calendar in order to advance their interests.

Regardless of these political calculations, the Israelis attacked Egypt across the Sinai on 29 October. The British and French promptly issued an ultimatum for a ceasefire, ostensibly to protect their interests in the Canal. Nasser rejected the ultimatum and on 31 October, British and French paratroopers landed in Egypt. Nasser responded by sinking ships in the Canal and, in effect, closing the waterway to commerce. Western Europe would have to look elsewhere for its oil shipments. That evening, Eisenhower addressed the country from the Oval Office, explaining American opposition to the action taken by the Israelis, British, and French. Sensing a potential emergency, Eisenhower also ordered the American Sixth Fleet in the Mediterranean to begin the evacuation of American citizens from the area.

On 1 November, the United States introduced a resolution in the United Nations calling for a ceasefire in the Middle East. By this point, Eisenhower was especially concerned about Soviet intervention into the region and sent a memo to Secretary of State John Foster Dulles, outlining his fears. "At all costs the Soviets must be prevented from seizing a mantle of world leadership through a false but convincing exhibition of concern for smaller nations," he told Dulles. "Since Africa and Asia almost unanimously hate one of the three nations, Britain, France, and Israel, the Soviets need only to propose severe and immediate punishment of these three to have the whole of two continents on their side ..."[9] On 3 November, British Prime Minister Anthony Eden rejected the proposal but the measure passed on 4 November, with the ceasefire scheduled to take effect on 6 November.[10]

At this juncture, an important factor intervened in the outcome of the Suez crisis, the health of two of its key players, John Foster Dulles and Anthony Eden. On 2 November, Dulles experienced a severe pain in his abdomen and went to the hospital for an examination. The medical news was bad: Dulles had suffered a recurrence of the intestinal cancer which had afflicted him two years earlier. He underwent immediate surgery and faced a lengthy hospitalization. Herbert Hoover, Jr., the under secretary of state, became the acting secretary in Dulles's absence and ultimately played a critical role in the resolution of the Suez crisis.[11] With Dulles hospitalized, however, Eisenhower became more directly involved in the day-to-day operation of American foreign policy.

In Eden's case, the prime minister continued to feel the effects of gall bladder surgery which he had undergone in 1953. Unfortunately, Eden never fully recovered his health after the surgery, and he was prone to debilitating episodes of high fevers and exhaustion. The stress of Suez aggravated his condition, and he often seemed on the verge of both a physical and an emotional collapse as the crisis wore on without any resolution.[12]

On 5 November, the crisis reached its pivotal point. Ignoring the UN Resolution, the British and French attacked Egypt at Port Said and Port Fuad. The same day, the Soviet leader Nikolai Bulganin issued a statement that the Soviet government was prepared to intervene on behalf of Egypt. He called on Eisenhower to authorize American cooperation with the Soviets in establishing a peacekeeping force in the region, a proposal instantly rejected by the Administration.[13] A larger concern, however, was whether the Soviets would send "volunteers" to Syria, further escalating the crisis.

By now, Eden was under tremendous pressure from virtually every side: from the Eisenhower Administration, from the United Nations, from the opposition Labour Party in his own country, from the British press, and even from his own Cabinet. He had calculated that the Eisenhower Administration would not oppose the invasion and had been proven wrong. Rumors of his physical and emotional exhaustion began to circulate in Britain as early as 3 November. The only course open to

Eden by this point was to accept the UN ceasefire. On 6 November, Harold Macmillan, Britain's chancellor of the exchequer, went to Eden with predictions of a dire economic emergency if Britain did not accept the ceasefire and begin the process of ricating itself from the military situation in the Middle East. Macmillan had already asked Secretary George M. Humphrey, the United States secretary of the treasury, for American economic assistance and was told flatly that none would be forthcoming without British acceptance of the ceasefire.[14]

Macmillan's role in the Suez crisis has been widely criticized. In August, he had been one of Britain's most vigorous hawks in calling for decisive action against Nasser. Then, on 22 September, he appealed to an American audience in Indianapolis for American support of the British position regarding Nasser's seizure of the Canal. Comparing Nasser to Mussolini and Hitler, he warned that Egypt and perhaps other Arab states unfriendly to the West were poised to take control of the world's oil supplies. "He must be stopped," Macmillan said of Nasser.

> If he gets away with his violations of treaties and contracts, Egypt will fall more and more under the Communist influence. There is much more to this than a disagreement over the Suez Canal. It is beginning to look as though the second half of this century will see a struggle between two systems – free and Communist.[15]

Following his speech in Indianapolis, Macmillan went to Washington for talks with George Humphrey on 23 September and with Eisenhower and Dulles on 25 September. These consultations should have enabled Macmillan and the Americans to reach a meeting of minds about the Suez crisis. In Macmillan's talks with Humphrey and Eisenhower, however, Suez was hardly mentioned and, in his talks with Dulles, he received a stern warning not to aggravate the international situation, at least until after the presidential election. Dulles reminded Macmillan that the Administration had tried to help the recently-elected government of Anthony Eden in 1955 by supporting a summit with the Russians at Geneva. It would be good to have British cooperation for the Americans in 1956.[16]

Once he returned to Britain, Macmillan badly misinterpreted his discussions with the Americans when he met with Eden. He gave the impression that the Americans would not oppose action by the British and French against Nasser. "Ike will lie doggo until after the election," Macmillan predicted.[17] By fostering the mistaken notion that the Americans would not oppose British and French action against Nasser,

Macmillan contributed to the momentum for military force which ultimately occurred between 29 and 31 October. Once the Americans refused to offer any economic assistance to Britain until it ended its military action, however, Macmillan told Eden and his colleagues that it was time to pull back, leaving Nasser in power with a greatly enhanced international reputation. As Harold Wilson, a leading member of the Labour Party, aptly put it, Macmillan was "first in, first out of Suez."[18]

Macmillan's critics in the British government wondered if Macmillan acted too quickly in deserting the objectives for Suez once American economic pressure came into play. Robert Rhodes James, the biographer of Anthony Eden, believed that Macmillan used the financial emergency as his method of bringing down Eden. James claims that

> it was not realized for some time [after Suez] that it had been Macmillan who had stopped it with figures of reserves pouring out of the country that were wildly exaggerated. Did Macmillan know that they were? Did he use his position as Chancellor of the Exchequer to destroy Eden? Eden certainly thought so, but his health was temporarily broken and his position beyond redemption.[19]

Once the French, the British, and the Israelis accepted the UN ceasefire, the Suez crisis entered its final stage. On 7 November Eden telephoned Eisenhower to request a meeting in Washington with himself and Guy Mollet, the premier of France. Eisenhower initially agreed but he reversed his decision after being advised that such a meeting would provoke an anti-American reaction in the Arab world.[20] Eisenhower's action served as a sharp rebuke to Eden who ascertained, correctly, that he was being isolated by the American administration. Winthrop Aldrich, the American Ambassador to Great Britain, described Eden's plight succinctly: "Eisenhower wouldn't have anything to do with Eden."[21]

By this point, the diplomatic efforts of both the United States and Great Britain were handicapped by the ill health of Dulles and Eden. In Washington, Harold Caccia, the new British ambassador to the United States, was not scheduled to assume his duties until 8 November. As a result, new players entered the diplomatic arena. In Great Britain, Macmillan and Richard Austen (Rab) Butler, the deputy prime minister, became directly involved, and, for the Americans, George Humphrey emerged as a strong force in Washington while Winthrop Aldrich became the crucial figure in London. Macmillan was first off the mark by attempting to rectify the situation through a direct appeal to

Humphrey for economic assistance and then by opening a channel of communication with Aldrich.[22]

In the crucial turn of events about to take place, the role of Winthrop Aldrich became especially important. A Harvard-educated lawyer, Aldrich was the son of the powerful former Senator Nelson Aldrich from Rhode Island and the brother-in-law of the influential philanthropist John D. Rockefeller, Jr. Through his relations with the Rockefellers, Aldrich had become an international banker, first with the family's financial interest in the Equitable Trust Company during the 1920s and later with Chase Manhattan Bank when it acquired Equitable in 1929. In 1933, he became the chief executive officer of the Chase Manhattan Bank and held that post until 1953 when he went to England as the American ambassador.[23]

On the surface, it was easy to dismiss Aldrich as simply another wealthy American businessman who used his political contacts to obtain a prestigious diplomatic post. But Aldrich possessed keen political instincts as well as solid diplomatic skills. During the 1930s he became well acquainted with Winston Churchill and, because of the Chase Bank's numerous business dealings in the Middle East, was knowledgeable about the region and even well acquainted with King Farouk of Egypt, who had been deposed in a military coup in 1952. Aldrich also belonged to a group of businessmen who traveled to Europe in 1952 to encourage Eisenhower to run for the presidency. After his victory, Eisenhower considered naming Aldrich as the secretary of the treasury but eventually decided against it because he did not want a "New York banker" in the post.[24] Instead, Ike appointed Aldrich ambassador to Great Britain, naming him to the post before nominating Dulles as secretary of state or even informing the British government ahead of time.[25]

While serving at the American Embassy in London, Aldrich grew frustrated with Dulles's habitual tendency to keep him uninformed on matters of policy relating to British–American relations. This was especially true with regard to Dulles's numerous conversations with the British during the Suez crisis.[26] With Dulles hospitalized, Eisenhower turned to Aldrich, who had by this time begun confidential conversations with other British leaders about the future of the government. For the record, Aldrich mentioned his separate channel with the British on two occasions, once when he gave an oral history interview to Columbia University in 1972 and second, in his article, "The Suez Crisis: a Footnote to History," written for *Foreign Affairs* in 1967.[27] In his article for *Foreign Affairs*, Aldrich mentioned that he "was enormously helped at the time by the willingness of several members of the British Cabinet to exchange views with me with great frankness, and to permit me to convey their views and ideas directly to Washington, without passing them through the Foreign Office."[28]

Aldrich did not refer specifically to the members of the British Cabinet with whom he was communicating directly. Based on other parts of Aldrich's discussion, however, we may assume that he was referring to Harold Macmillan and Lord Robert Salisbury, the Lord Privy Seal. And, of course, Aldrich also had established a channel to Churchill, whose influence was being felt off-stage. On 19 November, Macmillan spoke to Aldrich and informed him that he thought he could arrange for a majority of the Eden Cabinet to support a withdrawal of forces from Suez in return for some promise of American economic assistance to the British. Failing that, Macmillan warned that the British might have to break the ceasefire and renew hostilities against the Egyptians. Macmillan spoke of the need for some "fig leaves to cover our nakedness," the withdrawal of British forces from the contested region.[29]

Recognizing a dramatic change in the British political situation, Aldrich telephoned Washington and asked to speak directly with Eisenhower. Convinced that a change in the leadership of the British government was unfolding, he conveyed the substance of his conversation with Macmillan to Eisenhower. The Macmillan–Aldrich conversation on 19 November has become one of the most closely-examined discussions ever to occur between the British and Americans. In *Warriors at Suez*, Donald Neff interpreted Macmillan's action as a way of alerting the Administration that he had a plan to succeed Eden as prime minister, since Eden was too ill and demoralized to remain in office.[30] In *Dawn Over Suez*, Steven Freiberger contended that Eisenhower intended to depose Eden and create circumstances where the British Cabinet would turn to Macmillan.[31] Other writers, including Cole Kingseed and Alistair Horne, have been less critical of Macmillan.[32]

Two facts are indisputable, however. First, the Eisenhower Administration, chiefly Eisenhower but also George Humphrey and Herbert Hoover, Jr., had concluded that the Eden government was finished. This was obvious when Eisenhower cancelled his prospective face-to-face meeting with Eden on 7 November. On 20 November, Eisenhower met with Humphrey and Hoover to discuss the situation in Britain and plot a strategy to help the British government. But Eisenhower wanted Aldrich to express those assurances directly to both Butler and Macmillan. Even though he preferred Macmillan to Butler, while Humphrey, Hoover, and possibly Dulles preferred Butler to Macmillan,

Eisenhower was prepared to initiate some action, in effect, to offer some fig leaves, in order to "get the boys moving."[33]

Second, Eisenhower and Humphrey wanted to prevent the Conservatives from losing power in Britain and forcing the country into a hasty general election where the Labour Party might emerge victorious, as it had in 1945. If the Conservatives were voted out of office, Humphrey said, "then we have these socialists [the British Labour Party] to lick," and that prospect was not especially pleasing.[34] Eisenhower subsequently told Aldrich to inform the British that "as soon as things happen that we anticipate, we can furnish a lot of fig leaves."[35]

At this point in the crisis, Eden, taking his doctor's advice, left the country for a vacation in Jamaica on 20 November and stayed away until 14 December. He placed the government in the hands of Rab Butler, Macmillan, and Lord Robert Salisbury. As Aldrich had predicted, after Eden left the country, the jockeying for power began within the Conservative Party. On 22 November, the 1922 Committee, consisting of the backbenchers in the Conservative Party, met to hear from both Butler and Macmillan about the status of the Suez crisis and the situation in the country. During their presentations, Butler apparently failed to impress his colleagues while Macmillan gave an overly dramatic performance.[36]

In the certain leadership contest about to unfold, Butler appeared initially to have the edge over Macmillan by virtue of his longer experience of leadership within the Party. During December, however, Butler was forced to manage the problems associated with Britain's acceptance of the ceasefire and the eventual withdrawal of its troops. By contrast, Macmillan avoided most of the humiliations of Suez, and his allies in the Party began to focus on Butler's alleged association with the "appeasement" faction during the 1930s. In the words of Robert Rhodes James, Eden's biographer, this tactic used by Macmillan's partisans against Butler "was tough stuff, and unfair, but it was deadly effective."[37]

Eden returned to London on 14 December, eager to resume work as prime minister. The Tory Party treated him with indifference, however, including members of his Cabinet who knew that Eden lacked the support of his colleagues. Early in January, he became ill once again, when the fevers returned, and his physicians told him frankly that he could not expect to survive if he remained prime minister. Given the choice, as Rhodes James put it, between "his political lifetime and the real one," Eden chose the latter.[38] On 8 January, he and his wife Clarissa met with Queen Elizabeth II to announce his intention to resign as prime minister. On 9 January, he informed the Cabinet of his impending resignation.[39]

The task of choosing Eden's successor fell to Lord Salisbury and Lord David Kilmuir, the Lord Chancellor, with Salisbury responsible for informing the Queen about the preference of the Party. Salisbury met individually with each member of the Cabinet and asked for a declaration of preference between Rab Butler and Harold Macmillan. On 10 January, Queen Elizabeth summoned both Salisbury and Winston Churchill for their views. Butler realized that the game was lost. "I had no doubt what Salisbury's advice would be," Butler wrote. "I had served Churchill for ten years and for four as his Chancellor [of the Exchequer] but he told me 'I went for the older man.'"[40] At 2 p.m. on 10 January, the Queen summoned Macmillan and asked him to form a new government. He had now won the prize that Nellie Macmillan had sought for him; at age 64, he had climbed to the top of the greasy pole. Macmillan was now Britain's prime minister.

Historians have debated whether Eisenhower unethically meddled in Britain's internal affairs during the Suez Crisis.[41] At a basic level, Eisenhower had decided, perhaps as early as 7 November and certainly by 20 November, that the Eden government was in jeopardy. "Eisenhower did think Eden had to go," Andrew Goodpaster remembered. But Goodpaster also cautioned that meddling in anything as sensitive as a change in another country's political leadership was "beyond the pale" for Ike.[42] Support for Goodpaster's belief may be found in Eisenhower's response to Aldrich on 20 November, when the president instructed Aldrich to inform both Macmillan and Butler that the Administration stood ready to offer economic assistance if the British pulled back from their military positions. Ike even told Aldrich, "You see, we don't want to be in a position of interfering between those two."[43]

As for American economic support for the Tory government during its financial emergency, one must ask what other choice did the administration have? Following the British decision to withdraw their forces, the Administration authorized the release of emergency shipments of oil to Europe.[44] To refuse help to the British in December would have only made the economic situation worse. The Eisenhower Administration clearly had no interest in watching the failure of the government of its closest ally and then be forced to deal with a lengthy period of political instability once a new government took office.

Macmillan's rise to the premiership probably involved his own opportunism more than any pressure from the Eisenhower Administration upon the British political system. By mid-November, Macmillan could certainly see the difficulties which had overtaken Eden through the combination of American resistance, Labour Party opposition, press criticism, and, most importantly, his failing health. According to Winthrop Aldrich, Macmillan sought out the Americans on 19 November, not the other way around.[45] As a political opportunist, Macmillan played the strongest card in his hand, his close relationship with the Americans. Perhaps that was why Macmillan was the choice of the Cabinet: he seemed to have best chance of dealing realistically with the Americans. And, if in Washington, the bets were on Butler to succeed Eden, in London, it was something else. As Winthrop Aldrich wrote,

> For some reason Washington had come to the conclusion, that if Eden should retire, the new prime minister was going to be R.A.B. Butler (Eden's choice). I was convinced that the Queen would summon Harold Macmillan, since Salisbury, in whom I knew the Queen had great confidence and, who I felt sure would be consulted, had come to the conclusion that Macmillan was the person best fitted to deal with President Eisenhower because of the close association they had in Africa during the war. This proved to be the case.[46]

Nevertheless, the Suez crisis shook the confidence which the Americans and the British previously held in each other. As Philip de Zulueta observed, "My own view is that Ike got rather testy about [not being informed before the attack on Egypt] because his pride was affected. He was used to being the supreme commander and everyone doing what they were told."[47] For the British, the operative phrase was that they were "let down" by the Americans. Based on comments made by John Foster Dulles to the Eden government early in the crisis, the British had come to believe that the Americans would not oppose their use of force against Nasser. When Eisenhower assertively took the matter to the UN and then applied economic pressure against them, the British felt betrayed and humiliated. Such feelings died hard, especially within the Conservative Party. On 3 November 1995, almost forty years after Suez, it was Margaret Thatcher, then out of office and on a speaking tour of the United States, who said, "Eisenhower was a great leader but he was a bit cross with us."[48]

II

When Harold Macmillan became Britain's prime minister in January 1957, he faced a number of serious problems. The British economy had been dealt a setback by the Suez crisis; the Conservative Party's morale had declined sharply in the past six months; relations with the United States were badly in need of repair, and the Conservatives were trailing the Labour Party in the political opinion polls. Unlike Eisenhower, Macmillan needed to face the voters at least once more if he expected to remain in office and his policies inevitably were conditioned by the realities of domestic politics.

The situation was hardly hopeless for Macmillan, though, despite the pessimistic opinion that he had given to Queen Elizabeth II that his government might not last six weeks.[49] The Conservative Party recognized the need to unify around Macmillan if it expected to remain in power. The next general election was not legally mandated until April 1960, giving the Tories time to sort out their difficulties. Macmillan's personal friendship with Eisenhower also enabled him to search for some common ground between the two leaders without appearing to cave in to American pressure. As historian Nigel Ashton has argued, Macmillan viewed the revival of the Anglo-American relationship as a means of achieving British foreign policy objectives, rather than simply "as an end in itself."[50] Henry Kissinger has similarly pointed out that Macmillan "decided to embed British policy in American policy by skillfully handling relations with Washington. He readily conceded the center stage to Washington while seeking to shape the drama from behind the curtain."[51]

Moreover, Macmillan was an activist politician who was unwilling to let a difficult situation deteriorate around him. On 17 January, he spoke to the country on television, creating a sense of confidence and purpose in the new government.[52] On 22 January, Macmillan dispatched Duncan Sandys, his newly appointed minister of defense, to the United States for discussions on military policy. The visit by Sandys underscored the point that Eisenhower and Macmillan had chosen the issue of defense policy and military cooperation as the starting point for the re-establishment of harmonious relations between the two countries.

Sandys was in the United States from 23 January to 1 February. In addition to his talks with Secretary of Defense Charles E. Wilson and Secretary of the Air Force Donald Quarles, Sandys also spoke with John Foster Dulles. A son-in-law of Winston Churchill, Sandys was an acerbic man who expressed the full extent of British exasperation over Suez to Dulles. For once, Dulles even appeared somewhat chastened.[53]

In his discussions with the defense officials, Sandys dealt with the issue of the future deployment of American intermediate-range ballistic missiles (IRBMs) in Britain. He covered the range of British concerns about the stationing of them in Britain, especially about the matter of costs in view of Britain's impending scale-down of its defense spending. Wilson and Quarles believed that the time was right for an agreement between the US and Great Britain to base American IRBMs in England, but they failed to present a concrete proposal to Sandys. Sandys left the United States, therefore, without any definite agreement but with a commitment for the deployment of American IRBMs "in Britain at the earliest possible time."[54]

The effort to restore harmonious relations between the British and American governments received its strongest signal on 22 January, two days after Eisenhower's second inauguration, when Macmillan received word from the president of his willingness to meet personally with the prime minister. They agreed to hold a meeting in late March in Bermuda. The choice of Bermuda was intentional on Eisenhower's part. He had met with Churchill there early in his first term and the location symbolized continuity between the two nations. Eisenhower was prepared to meet Macmillan on British territory and negate the appearance of the prime minister having "to go to Canossa" to meet Ike.[55] As Alexander Macmillan recalled, "The real breakthrough [in repairing the special relationship] came when Ike agreed to meet my grandfather on British soil. He appreciated that gesture very much; it showed that the wartime relationship [between Eisenhower and Macmillan] was still strong. That was a very big gesture by the American president at that point in time."[56]

Macmillan and Eisenhower exchanged several messages in January and February leading up to the conference. On 23 January, Macmillan outlined his thoughts on the business of the conference. "I do not expect that either of us will want too many papers. What we want to do is to go over the canvas with a broad brush," Macmillan wrote. "But I certainly see this as an opportunity for joint decisions on broad issues of policy."[57] By 9 March, Macmillan had prepared a list of subjects which he expected to raise with Ike, including the future of the United Nations, relations with the Soviet bloc, the Middle East, Britain's economic relations with Europe, and trade with China.[58]

More ominously, on 5 March, however, Macmillan and Eisenhower conferred about the problems which defense spending was creating for the British economy. In a telephone conversation that day, Macmillan informed Eisenhower that the British would need to reduce their commitment of troops in Europe over the next two years. Then, Macmillan followed up with a message confirming the irreversibility of that action:

When we first spoke on the telephone this evening, I was not fully up to date on the position about our force reductions and I am therefore sending you this telegram because I do not wish you to be under any misapprehension, although I know that the Foreign Secretary [Selwyn Lloyd] has asked our Ambassador [Sir Harold Caccia] to explain our difficulties to Foster [Dulles] . . . We have made a great effort to meet General [Lauris] Norstad's [Supreme Allied Commander, Europe] views by agreeing that only a half of our proposed reductions shall take place during the financial year 1957/58 and that the second half will take place during the financial year 1958/59. Norstad seems satisfied . . .[59]

In the realm of substantive policy, defense demanded much of Macmillan's attention in the first few months of his premiership. He needed to present a White Paper on defense to the House of Commons by 15 April, and it was clear that the entire British military profile was under scrutiny. In effect, Macmillan was searching for the British equivalent to the American New Look strategy, with its emphasis on the nuclear deterrent and scientific modernization, and a de-emphasis of sizable armies and navies. In Macmillan's words, the British defense policy would focus on "big bangs and small forces."[60]

When Macmillan eventually released his defense White Paper, the emphases were clear: the end of National Service (obligatory military service); a reduction of the size of the British army, including the forces committed to Europe as part of NATO; a smaller navy; and renewed emphasis on a nuclear capability.[61] Now the challenge for Macmillan was maintaining Britain's historic role in international relations while, at the same time, reducing its military capability. And, in his upcoming meetings with Eisenhower, Macmillan was prepared to make the argument that a smaller British defense profile did not necessarily mean a withdrawal of British influence from the world.

On 18 March, Macmillan made a speech in Leicester where he touched on the importance of the upcoming meeting with the Americans. "Our object at Bermuda is to clear up any differences between Britain and the United States and to restore Anglo/American relations as the cornerstone to world peace," he said.[62] Macmillan intended to follow a course of patient diplomacy without needlessly provoking any disagreements with the United States. In late February, he had advised Viscount Bernard Law Montgomery, a critic of the Americans since World War II, to tone down a speech which the prime minister considered hostile toward the Americans. "I am not quite sure that it does good to say that if our action in Egypt had succeeded . . .

the United States would have applauded," Macmillan wrote to Monty. He urged a more subtle approach, arguing that "the best tactic with the United States is to be as conciliatory as we honestly can be in public, and as forthright in private."[63]

Macmillan also communicated with Anthony Eden before leaving to meet Eisenhower. "Sooner or later the Americans will come round," he wrote to Eden. "If they don't, Europe is finished, for I am certain the Russians are determined to get hold of the Middle East."[64]

The meeting in Bermuda was more important for Macmillan than for Eisenhower. The conference was vital to his strategy of drawing closer to the United States, and to Eisenhower personally, as well as to expand on the military cooperation between the two countries. On Wednesday 20 March the British contingent, consisting primarily of Macmillan, Selwyn Lloyd, the foreign secretary, and three advisers, Norman Brook, Freddie Bishop, and Patrick Dean, arrived in Bermuda in the early morning. Eisenhower and the American group which consisted of the President, Dulles, Donald Quarles, deputy secretary of defense, and Lewis Strauss, the chairman of the Atomic Energy Commission (AEC) came later in the day. At dinner that evening, Eisenhower, Dulles, Macmillan, and Lloyd generally restricted themselves to an exchange of pleasantries.[65] On 21 March, however, the British took the rhetorical offensive. Macmillan declared,

> Britain, my Government, will be staying in the game and pulling our weight. That is why I welcome free restoration of confidence and co-operation between our two countries. You need us: for ourselves, for our commonwealth, and as leaders of Europe. Powerful as you are, I don't believe you can do it alone. Chiefly because without a common front and true partnership between us I do not know whether the principles we believe in can win.[66]

At Bermuda, Macmillan introduced the concept of joint action between the United States and Great Britain, a theme to which he would turn repeatedly in the next four years. The United States and Britain, he argued, must "stay together." With the memory of Suez fresh in mind, the prime minister stated that disunity between the British and Americans would only lead to further opportunities for mischief by the Soviets.[67] "The next time," Macmillan speculated, "it might be Greece or Turkey, instead of some sand trap in the Middle East," Alexander Macmillan recalled when recounting his grandfather's opinions on the matter.[68]

Macmillan was obviously pleased with the first round of the discussions. His talks with Eisenhower were just like the "old days" in Algiers, and he even expressed sympathy for the difficult problems which the president faced. In America, Ike was "half-king, half prime minister, a rather lonely figure with few confidants."[69]

But other parts of Macmillan's remarks showed that he had not completely given up on his idea of deposing Nasser – and wanted American help to finish the job. In fact, he brought considerable pressure on both Eisenhower and Dulles to enlist in a joint effort for that purpose. "Mussolini started out as an Italian patriot and ended up as Hitler's stooge," Macmillan said. "Let's make it clear that we'll get him down sooner or later."[70]

It was the British position on Nasser that created the most difficulties for the Americans. As Eisenhower recalled the conversation: "We discussed all phases of the Middle East problem. Among the items that came in for special and searching investigation was the question of future relationships with the Middle East and a satisfactory arrangement for the use of the Suez Canal," Eisenhower recalled. But he added that "Foster and I found it difficult to talk constructively with our British colleagues because of the blinding bitterness they felt toward Nasser."[71] As a result, the two sides left Bermuda with Middle East issues largely unresolved.

There were other areas of agreement, however, which provided substantive evidence to prove that the conference was not an empty exercise. The United States agreed to join the military committee of the Baghdad Pact, a further indicator of the American intention to increase its involvement in the Middle East. The two powers also announced their intention to continue the testing of their nuclear devices in view of the absence of progress on the disarmament issue. Most importantly, the United States agreed to supply Britain with intermediate-range ballistic missiles and opened the path for the placement of American missile technology into the NATO theater. In Macmillan's words, this agreement "prove[d] to be an important addition to the deterrent power already based in the United Kingdom and the strength of NATO as a whole."[72]

Eisenhower and Macmillan held further meetings at the conference on 24 and 25 March. On 24 March at dinner, Eisenhower and Macmillan made their agreement to write to each other, "perhaps once a week or once a month, frankly and freely on any subject which we thought we should know each other's view. These communications, he would keep to himself, showing only to Foster Dulles."[73]

On 23 March, another important meeting had taken place involving Eisenhower, Donald Quarles, Lewis Strauss, Dulles, and Goodpaster to discuss the granting of IRBMs to Britain. Macmillan, perhaps reflecting the uncertainties involved in the British missile program, wanted access to American military technology; Eisenhower was willing to grant him that access, but not "until we have a successful missile." Quarles indicated that the missile program could meet that objective, with a "handful" of missiles committed to Britain within a year and full-scale deployment being put in place by 1959–60.[74] Eisenhower considered this agreement "of signal importance to the security of the free world." Once in place, the NATO alliance would have missiles "within striking distance of the U.S.S.R ..., a powerful deterrent to any atomic transgression by the communists."[75] The agreement called for the grant of 60 Thor IRBMs to the British, as these weapons became available. It would take another year for the two nations to finalize the arrangements for the deployment and expense associated with the missiles, but the fact that the Americans and British had entered into this program of strategic cooperation was a milestone in the history of NATO.[76]

With a sense of goodwill and mutual respect re-established between the United States and Great Britain, the Bermuda Conference adjourned. Both Eisenhower and Macmillan were gratified with the results. Eisenhower considered it "the most successful" of the meetings which he had attended since World War II.[77] For his part, Macmillan believed that the Bermuda Conference had succeeded in its main objective: restoring the Anglo-American relationship "to something almost approximately the old wartime intimacy of Algiers or at least, steps had been taken in that direction."[78]

Within hours of the end of the Bermuda Conference, however, an incident intervened that profoundly disturbed the two leaders. On Tuesday 26 March 1957, the *New York Times* carried a story written by Drew Middleton, its highly respected military correspondent, which summarized the entire conference. Obviously, someone from either the American delegation or the British delegation had leaked some highly confidential information to Middleton and the intrepid *Times* reporter had a major scoop. In fact, Middleton's story carried the somewhat explosive information that the United States and Britain intended to establish "joint intelligence and planning systems, to meet international problems."[79] In his story, Middleton also went on to explain that the Americans and British had signed on to "more than twenty-five agreements, directions and reports," none of which were mentioned in the communiqué issued after the conference.[80] "These documents," according to Middleton, "will serve as a guide to United States and British planners on various aspects of the Middle East, German, and Central European situations."[81]

No sooner had Middleton's article reached Eisenhower's desk than he immediately fired off a cable to Macmillan in Bermuda. "Dear Harold," Ike wrote,

> Will you please have someone get for you *immediately* [author's emphasis] Drew Middleton's article in Tuesday's New York Times (sic). The publication of this article disturbs me mightily, and of course I do not know what individual is responsible. Nevertheless, this leak creates doubt in my mind that we can talk frankly to each other in confidence on matters of import to us both. The publicizing and emphasizing of our intelligence ties makes it harder to maintain them, . . . what do you think?

And, just so Macmillan didn't miss the point, the president signed the telegram, "Dwight D. Eisenhower," not, "With warm regard, as ever, Ike."[82]

Eisenhower softened the blow a bit, however, when he sent Macmillan an "Eyes Only" letter, complete with a copy of Middleton's story. The part of the story that Eisenhower found most objectionable was Middleton's references to the "elimination of the words 'intelligence and planning' from the draft of the communiqué."[83] Complicating the problem was that Middleton's story appeared after Eisenhower and Dulles had briefed congressional leaders on the nature of the discussions in Bermuda, avoiding specifics as to intelligence operations which affected both countries. "We made the truthful assertion [to the congressional leaders] that no 'secret agreements' were arrived at," the president stated. "This morning some of them may be wondering!"[84] With that admonition Ike signed off, awaiting a reply from Macmillan which might clarify the situation.

On 27 March, Macmillan replied to Ike, in a businesslike tone which revealed his defense of his delegation. Macmillan replied that the Middleton article was given to him just prior to his departure but his initial enquiries "seem to show that any leak did not come from British sources."[85] On 29 March, he sent Eisenhower a letter which explained in more detail his understanding of the situation. The tone of the letter revealed that Macmillan, having spent a conference asserting the British position against the Americans, had no intention of buckling under to Eisenhower. "Dear Mr. President," he began, not "My Dear Friend." "I have now seen Middleton's article in the New York Times [sic] of March

26 . . . I have made very full enquiries about this." He went on to clear the British delegation, Selwyn Lloyd included, of any deliberate leaking of confidential information. He attributed the story to "intelligent guess-work" on Middleton's part, not leaks on the part of anyone connected with the conference. He concluded with the statement: "I dislike publicity as much as you do. I hate newspapers and am very bad at handling them and I remember your saying that you never read them." He further suggested that future meetings between the two should be kept more confidential and the number of advisors held to a minimum. "I do hope that the embarrassment of this article will not make us lose faith in the need for us to talk frankly and with confidence to each other." And, then with a devious p.s., he added, "Anyway, if we write to each other, nobody need read our letters."[86]

Eisenhower responded to Macmillan in a conciliatory fashion on 29 March. "As I should have told you before, I initiated . . . the same kind of inquiry here . . . and with some negative results," Ike wrote. "I believe with you that we should drop the matter and give our attention to the future, as you suggest in your last paragraph where you say 'the embarrassment of this article will not make us lose faith in the need for us to talk frankly and with confidence to each other.'"[87]

Eisenhower apparently had decided not to make the embarassment of the Middleton story a source of ongoing friction between himself and Macmillan. After doing some further digging, however, the Americans learned that the director of the Press Office for the British Foreign Office had given Middleton his story, for motives which were unclear. Eisenhower also learned from John Hay Whitney, the new American ambassador to Great Britain, that Macmillan was "just as mad" as Ike that the story had appeared so quickly after the conference.[88]

The flap over the Middleton story ended quickly after Eisenhower and Macmillan exchanged their correspondence on the subject. Even so, Macmillan must have breathed a sigh of relief that it had not damaged his carefully cultivated overture to Eisenhower. Writing to Selwyn Lloyd on 2 April, Macmillan expressed his overall view of the Bermuda Conference and its aftermath. In typical self-deprecating fashion, Macmillan said, "I feel like an inexpert fox hunter who as he jumps over one fence after another finds it is something of a miracle that he is still on his seat."[89]

III

Following the Bermuda Conference, Eisenhower and Macmillan used their correspondence to continue their conversations of the topics discussed in March. On 15 April, Macmillan sent the president a letter which ranged widely over a number of subjects, from defense policy to the Middle East to working relations between the two countries at the level of the foreign ministers. Macmillan expressed gratitude for the agreement on IRBMs reached at Bermuda, even though the "long-haired, starry-eyed boys" in Britain objected to the emerging strategic relationship between the two countries.[90] He told Eisenhower that Anthony Eden's surgery in Boston, just the day before, had gone well. "When I took [Eden's] job on I knew it would be pretty tricky with lots of hurdles ahead, rather like our Grand National Steeplechase," Macmillan wrote. "We have managed to scramble over the first hurdles well enough, but now we are approaching what I call the water jump, i.e. the Canal."[91] On matters relating to Nasser, Macmillan had obviously not changed his outlook appreciably. "I feel more and more convinced that Nasser and his regime are leading that country and the whole Middle East to disaster and there will be no peace until that system falls," he argued. "It was the same thing with Mussolini. These people start off with good intentions and mean to help their countries; but after the first few months or years they fall into all the temptations of dictatorship."[92]

On 28 April, Eisenhower responded to Macmillan's letter of 15 April, writing while on vacation at Augusta, Georgia. Like Macmillan, Ike ranged over a wide variety of subjects but left Macmillan with no doubt as to where the United States government stood on Middle East policy and, specifically, regarding Nasser.

> So far as the Canal is concerned, I agree with you that there is in sight no completely satisfactory solution. From the beginning that has seemed to me to be an ill-starred affair and I did my very best to keep it from developing as it did... If, in the Mid-East, one could completely separate the problems of the Canal from the age-old Israel–Arab dispute and deal with each of these individually, I am certain that we could reach a satisfactory arrangement in the lesser one, and make considerable progress toward improving the chronic one. To believe that such might happen soon is, of course, nothing but wishful thinking.[93]

Not wanting to put off Macmillan completely, he expressed his well wishes to Eden and commented, upon closing, "I am sending this from Georgia, where I am spending a few days. I should like to call it a vacation but I am frequently reminded that a man cannot take a vacation from his own thoughts."[94]

Despite Ike's kind words about Eden's health, Macmillan remained deeply frustrated by the president's stand on Nasser. In a letter to Eden, also dated 28 April, the prime minister complained, "You know all the American difficulties and the personalities. What is really irritating is that the American people, and I think Congress, are so sympathetic to us yet the Administration moves only slowly in our direction." Macmillan concluded that about the best he could hope for from Eisenhower was to "prevent the Americans from giving him [Nasser] money or any form of support."[95]

Nevertheless, through the summer and fall of 1957, British–American relations continued to move ahead, driven by the patient diplomacy of Eisenhower and Macmillan. In mid-October, Queen Elizabeth II made a successful visit to the United States to commemorate the 350th anniversary of the founding of Jamestown. The Queen was Eisenhower's guest at the White House and participated in a host of formal engagements designed to showcase the friendship which existed between the two nations. More importantly, perhaps, both countries announced shortly after the Queen's departure that Eisenhower and Macmillan were to meet in Washington for another set of consultations between 23 and 25 October. The purposes of this second round of discussions were to extend the program of military cooperation between the two countries and also to "institutionalize" their respective foreign policy procedures.

The Washington Conference began on 23 October 1957, against the backdrop of the Soviet launching of its Sputnik satellite earlier that month and, while the success of Sputnik was a considerable source of pride to the worldwide scientific community, it was a severe blow to the notion of American technological superiority. Eisenhower and his administration did not escape the criticism, either, and the suspicion that, for all their boasting, the Soviets had achieved a degree of technological superiority over the United States. The fact that competition in the realm of outer space might extend into the military realm was a source of further concern.

In a presidential news conference on 9 October, reporters wanted Ike to comment on the Soviet Union's space program. Asked if he believed that Sputnik had endangered American military security, Eisenhower responded by saying his views had not been altered "one iota." But press commentators ranging from Walter Lippman to Edward R. Murrow, as well as prominent Democrats in Congress, like Senator Stuart Symington of Missouri, a presidential aspirant and the harshest critic of the Administration's defense policy, expressed their dissatisfaction with the president's responses.[96]

The criticism which the Administration was receiving for its failure to be the first nation to put a satellite into earth orbit was especially frustrating, since Eisenhower and his advisors realized that the United States could have launched a satellite well in advance of the Soviets if not for one fateful decision in 1954. "We were coming up on something called the International Geophysical Year," Robert B. Anderson remembered.

> There was considerable pressure not to use our defense-related technology for purposes of outer space. We had rockets long before the Russians did that could have orbited the earth. But, under pressure from the scientific community and the educational community, the Administration did a silly thing. It tried to make a rocket that didn't duplicate anything we already had. It was like trying to make a Ford automobile without using Ford parts.[97]

Eisenhower intended to keep the military out of the space program and, for that reason, he decided not to use the Army's developments on the Redstone rocket in the program. If he had, the results would have been different. Moreover, the furor over alleged American technological deficiencies would not have materialized.[98] But, clearly, Eisenhower and the rest of the Administration had misjudged the extent of the public hysteria created by Russian satellites. "One of Dad's errors was underestimating the impact of Sputnik," John Eisenhower remembered. "He expected people to be more mature than they were [and] he didn't like to have to say the same thing more than once."[99]

The British perceptively noted the impact of the Soviet satellite upon public opinion in American as well as its effect upon the political environment. On 10 October 1957, one day after Eisenhower's press conference, Macmillan wrote a perceptive letter to the president, making particular mention of Sputnik. [What] are we going to do about these Russians?," Macmillan inquired. "I have been giving a great deal of thought to this in the last few days... This artificial satellite has brought it home to us what a formidable people they are and what a menace they present to the free world. Their resources and their knowledge and their system of government will enable them to keep up the pressure for a very long time – perhaps two or three generations. After that we must hope that the Communist ideology will be spent and that their people will revert to ordinary human behavior."[100] The program of British–American defense cooperation had been revitalized at Bermuda in March, but, in October, it was going to be pursued with a greater sense of urgency.

Macmillan had two scheduled meetings with the Americans on the first day of the Washington Conference. The main meeting was held at 3.00 at the British Embassy. Both nations brought large contingents. In the American group were Dulles, Christian Herter, the under secretary of state, John Hay Whitney, Livingston Merchant, United States ambassador to Canada, and Gerard Smith, assistant secretary of state. With Macmillan were Selwyn Lloyd, Ambassador Harold Caccia, Sir Norman Brook, Sir William Hayter, and Frederick Bishop, Macmillan's secretary for foreign affairs.[101] The discussion at the meeting generally focused on the Soviet threat and how the West needed to organize to meet it. Macmillan noted that "recent Soviet successes, including in the technical field, revealed how formidable was our adversary," a reference to the recent launching of the Sputnik satellite which had produced a near hysteria in the United States.[102]

On the minds of both Macmillan and Dulles was the capacity of the NATO alliance and Western nations in general to respond to a communist threat which was going to exist indefinitely. "How are fifty or sixty free and independent allies to be held as firm allies?," Macmillan asked.[103] Dulles also attempted to deal with the subject of allied unity, especially on the matter of relations between the United States and Great Britain. It was necessary to "institutionalize" the process of co-ordination so that unity did not rest on purely personal relationships.[104]

The other major subject under discussion, the transfer of nuclear technology, was considered at a meeting at the White House on 24 October at 10.30 a.m. Dulles expressed the view that "our future security will be accomplished increasingly by nuclear power delivered over long distances."[105] The free world has the capacity to defend itself and maintain sound economies "but not on the basis of everyone trying to do everything."[106] Continuing, Dulles stated that "Britain and the United States know and trust each other ... However, we cannot count on personal intimacy for longer than two years, since under our Constitution the president cannot serve another term and since Prime Minister Macmillan is subject to the political uncertainties of reelection."[107]

At this meeting, Eisenhower and Macmillan also expressed their views on the importance of Anglo-American unity. Ike noted that "the Free World needs a shot in the arm" and closer co-operation between the United States and Great Britain might provide a new burst of energy to the Western alliance.[108] For his part, Macmillan saw a long period of "leaning up against Communism" and the Western alliance, particularly Britain and the United States, needed to pool their resources for maximum benefit since "no country can carry all the load of maintaining the free world's interests alone," repeating the theme that he had mentioned at the Bermuda Conference.[109]

The most important meeting which occurred at the Washington Conference, however, occurred during a conversation at dinner on the night of 24 October. On that occasion, Eisenhower and Macmillan discussed the transfer of nuclear technology between Britain and the United States. They agreed to establish two working groups, one headed by Lewis Strauss and Sir Edward Plowden to consider nuclear weapons, and the other headed by Donald Quarles and Sir Richard Powell to deal with rockets and missiles. To Macmillan's great delight, Eisenhower was prepared to ask Congress for a revision of the 1946 Atomic Energy Act and to provide British scientists with access to American developments in the nuclear weapons field.[110]

The next morning, Eisenhower, Macmillan, and their respective advisers met at 9 a.m. to confirm publicly the nature of their agreements of the previous evening. In a "Memorandum of Understanding," the two countries spelled out the nature of the cooperation which they pledged for the short term.[111] In addition to the establishment of the working groups on nuclear weapons issues, Eisenhower and Macmillan established a procedure whereby diplomatic working groups, under the guidance of Dulles and Lloyd, would "consult from time to time [to agree] on particular areas of policy or specific problems ... which cannot be expeditiously and effectively dealt with through normal channels."[112] This document was followed by the more ambitious statement, entitled "The Declaration of Common Purpose," which identified the United States and Great Britain as the main guarantors of freedom in the Western world.[113]

The Washington Conference ended on 25 October. Eisenhower was pleased with the results, even though he knew that considerable work with Congress needed to be done before the Atomic Energy Act could be amended and nuclear sharing implemented. But Eisenhower had made a priority of extending the nuclear responsibility more effectively. "[The Joint Committee on Atomic Energy] was just anathema to Eisenhower," Andrew Goodpaster recalled. "He thought it was unconstitutional and that the United States had reneged on a wartime agreement to cooperate with the British."[114] On 3 July 1958, Congress passed the Agreement for Cooperation on Uses of Atomic Energy for Mutual

Defense Purposes, the fulfillment of Eisenhower's pledge to amend the McMahon Act.[115]

Eisenhower's sense of pleasure was probably less than Macmillan's exultation over the Washington Conference. As Alistair Horne recorded, the prime minister regarded the Washington Conference as a "Honeymoon," so productive were the talks and so completely had Britain re-emerged as a player on the international stage.[116] Writing to Ike on 25 October from the British Embassy in Washington, he used intensely personal language. "I cannot leave Washington without sending you a few hurried words to express my gratitude to you," he wrote. "What I want to say, but find it difficult to express, is the sense of inspiration which these last few days have given me and, I think, all our associates. We have got a pretty difficult job, but it is fine to feel that we are setting about it with such confidence in each other. We have got to spread that confidence through all our efforts all over the world, and I am very grateful for the theme which you developed that our two countries are working together not to rule or to impose our will, but to serve."[117]

IV

One unintended consequence of the Washington Conference was the opportunity which Eisenhower and Macmillan had to include Paul Henri Spaak, the secretary general of NATO, in their discussions. Eisenhower and Macmillan met with Spaak at 2 p.m. on 24 October and Macmillan proposed to make the upcoming North Atlantic Council meeting in mid-December a heads of government meeting instead of a meeting of the cabinet-level officials in the member nations.[118] Ever the cagey one, Macmillan initially had noted a lack of enthusiasm on Spaak's part for the suggestion but thought that Spaak might go along if he thought it would be presented as his idea. Almost prophetically, Spaak agreed with Macmillan, especially "if the President would accept, all the other heads of government would accept."[119] Eisenhower supported the idea and immediately booked a European trip on his schedule.

By November 1957, Eisenhower and Macmillan looked back upon a year of solid diplomatic progress. The tensions which existed between the two countries just one year earlier had largely disappeared. Macmillan was gratified with this significant turn of events. After returning to London, he wrote to Ambassador John Hay Whitney, noting that "he had not felt the same sense of elation since the days of the wartime alliance." He concluded with the plea that "we must try to get the world to accept that regular meetings between the Heads of Government are quite normal."[120]

For Eisenhower, restoring the "special relationship" with Great Britain did not change the fact that 1957 had been a demanding year, however. In addition to his diplomatic and national security concerns, he needed to look after some thorny problems at home. The load of the presidency had unquestionably taken its toll. On 17 November, he wrote to his boyhood friend Swede Hazlett "that he could not remember a day that has not brought its major or minor crisis," since 26 July 1956, when Nasser seized the Suez Canal.[121]

On 25 November, one week after his letter to Hazlett, Eisenhower suffered a stroke in the Oval Office. Feeling ill, he had called for Ann Whitman, his secretary, who found the president unable to talk clearly. Whitman summoned Andrew Goodpaster, who helped the president walk to his bedroom for some rest. Howard Snyder, Eisenhower's physician, Mamie, and his son John, then working as an assistant to Goodpaster, came to Eisenhower's room. For the next week, he experienced difficulty identifying and pronouncing words correctly, and the members of the Administration, chiefly Dulles and Vice President Richard M. Nixon, began to wonder if the president would have sufficient physical strength to finish out his term. Eisenhower rallied however, and, within a week, was tending to his official duties at the White House. Suddenly, the meeting of the NATO Council in mid-December took on an added importance. Despite personal appeals not to attend the meeting, Eisenhower made it a personal challenge to go to Paris and prove that he could discharge his responsibilities. If he wasn't well enough to attend, he entertained the possibility of resignation from office.[122]

When Macmillan learned of Eisenhower's stroke, he immediately wrote the president, expressing his concern. "Dear Friend, I have just heard the news of your illness," Macmillan wrote. "I am indeed distressed, and hope that you will make a very rapid and complete recovery. Pray take care of yourself, for you are very precious to us all. We will do our best to carry on the good work that we began in Washington. All good wishes, Harold Macmillan."[123]

Eisenhower responded to Macmillan on 30 November. "Dear Harold," Eisenhower wrote. "I cannot tell you how much I appreciate your message of the twenty-sixth. Fortunately, I am making better progress than the doctors originally anticipated and at the moment Mamie and I are enjoying a quiet Gettysburg weekend. It is gratifying to know that you and my able associates here are carrying on the programs that we discussed when you were here."[124]

A week later, Eisenhower began his preparations for the NATO meeting. Writing again to Macmillan on 4 December, he revealed his determination to press ahead with his responsibilities, paying some attention to the warnings of his physicians.

> My recovery from my sudden illness of ten days ago has apparently been steady and rapid. The earliest symptoms of my indisposition were sufficiently slight that the doctors did not class the difficulty as a "stroke." However, I did suffer a marked "word confusion," with, also, some loss of memory of words alone.
>
> In all other respects, I was not aware of any physical impairment, and within twenty-four hours I began to improve. While I still speak a bit more slowly and will occasionally mispronounce a word, I am sure that the doctors are most optimistic of my complete recovery.
>
> All this means, as of this moment, that I am planning to be at the NATO meeting in mid-month. It is possible that I will try to avoid any lengthy public addresses, but otherwise I see no reason to curtail my normal activity.
>
> Looking forward to seeing you in Paris, and with my warm regard,
>
> As ever, Ike.[125]

Conscious of the fact that he had had three serious illnesses in the space of less than three years, Ike needed some physical reassurance that he was up to the job, physically. Attending the NATO summit was a "drastic personal test," and Ike literally challenged himself to make this trip. "The test I now set for myself was that of going through with my plan of proceeding to Paris and participating in the NATO Conference . . . If I could carry out this program successfully and without noticeable damage to myself, then I would continue in my duties," Eisenhower wrote in his memoirs, *Waging Peace*. "If I feel the results to be less than satisfactory, I would resign."[126]

Eisenhower arrived in Paris on 14 December 1957 and received a tumultuous welcome from tens of thousands of Parisians who lined the motorcade route from the airport to the American Embassy in Paris where he was the guest of Ambassador Amory Houghton. To the dismay of his staff, Eisenhower stood in an open car in inclement weather.

The next day, Eisenhower met for an hour with Macmillan at 10 a.m. At 3.30 p.m., the conference officially opened and Eisenhower spoke to the assemblage, giving half of his prepared remarks and then handing his speech to Dulles to give the remainder of the speech.[127]

The main topic at the meeting was the issue of the forward deployment of American IRBMs to NATO. Since the British–American decision at Bermuda in 1957, there had been pressure from other European nations, particularly the French, to participate in the "nuclear-sharing" arrangements. On 7 November 1957, General Lauris Norstad, the NATO commander, had written to Eisenhower that the alliance needed the forward deployment of these missiles as "a matter of some urgency."[128] On 17 December, Dulles introduced the plan for deploying American IRBMs to NATO, with an accompanying offer, at Macmillan's suggestion, to hold another foreign ministers' meeting on the disarmament issue.

The plan which was adopted, later referred to as the Norstad Plan, was to unfold in three steps. First, American-made Thor or Jupiter missiles were to be made available to NATO in late 1958 or early 1959. The British and the French were to receive the first shipment of missiles. Second, NATO countries were to begin their own production of IRBMs, perhaps the Polaris missile, by 1960. Third, the plan called for an agency of NATO to develop its own third-generation missile. On 19 December, the North Atlantic Council approved the plan and issued its joint communiqué to that effect.[129] The agreement was a milestone in NATO history; as Macmillan said, "There is no division between NATO countries who approve the NATO rockets and those who disapprove, at least on ethical grounds."[130]

V

By the end of 1957, Macmillan could look back upon a remarkable year. The British political situation had stabilized at home; he had two successful conferences with Eisenhower in March and in October; he had obtained an agreement for the deployment of American IRBMs to Britain; and the North Atlantic Council had supported the introduction of nuclear weapons into the alliance. Under his leadership, Britain had managed to stay in the game and exercise its influence, usually by resorting to its close relationship with the United States.

In the area of defense cooperation, Macmillan and Eisenhower had taken two notable steps in 1957. The first involved the Administration's willingness to propose amendments to the Atomic Energy Act and allow the British to share American nuclear weapons research. As Alistair Horne concluded, the impact of this initiative on Eisenhower's part was substantial, enabling the British eventually "to produce smaller and more sophisticated missiles for her own deterrent, and be able to produce atomic-propulsion plants for her nuclear submarines."[131] The initiative also resulted in a "new and lasting relationship" between the defense planners in each country and was critical to joint action in many of the international crises which confronted the West in the next quarter-century.[132]

The second step involved the agreements reached at the North Atlantic Council meeting in December 1957, specifically the introduction of an IRBM capability under the direction of General Norstad and future NATO commanders. Admittedly, the post-Sputnik hysteria and the desire for closer military cooperation helped to drive this agreement, but it nevertheless represented an important departure in NATO military planning. McGeorge Bundy, former national security advisor in the Kennedy and Johnson Administrations, concluded that the Norstad proposal "marked the beginning of an effort to address the question of the kind of missile forces required for specifically European defense."[133] British–American military cooperation, announced first at Bermuda in March, paved the way for this movement into a strategic defense posture for the entire NATO alliance.

Macmillan felt perfectly comfortable in the conduct of foreign affairs. Moreover, as a national leader paired with Eisenhower, he laid the groundwork for foreign policy to be practiced the way he liked it, face-to-face, directly and personally with your allied opposite number, just like FDR and Churchill in World War II.[134] As Richard Aldous has observed, "Given Macmillan's admiration of Churchill, it is not surprising that as Prime Minister he should attempt to conduct foreign policy in a 'Churchillian' style... It was Churchill who provided the model for the way in which Macmillan conducted foreign policy negotiation using summitry and 'shuttle' diplomacy."[135]

Not that there were no payoffs for Eisenhower in the reconstituted relationship with the British under Macmillan's leadership. With Macmillan in office, Eisenhower was back in a familiar position, the acknowledged supreme commander, now in the diplomatic sense, of the world's most important alliance. He was familiar with the important personalities, both military and diplomatic, on each side and he was able to exercise the kind of policy coordination that he relished.

For example, in a telegram to Macmillan after the NATO Council meeting, Ike wrote enthusiastically, "Never have I experienced any greater degree of satisfaction in such conferences than in talks with you." He complimented the prime minister effusively: "Always your approach to any difficult task seems to be based on fact, logic, readiness to consider other viewpoints, and ... a never-failing friendliness."[136] While the rhetoric may seem a bit overblown, the genuine sentiment illustrates how far the two men had come since the dark days of Suez.

Having Macmillan in power in Great Britain put Eisenhower back into a comfortable position; American policy set the agenda for action and the British needed to adapt accordingly. It was almost like Algiers, where Eisenhower orchestrated, directed, and coordinated a joint American–British effort. Could two other leaders have restored British–American relations as quickly as Eisenhower and Macmillan did in 1957? Probably not, but that is not to say that other British or American leaders could not have accomplished the same result. In his meetings with Macmillan at Bermuda and Washington, Ike put the consultative process back into motion in order to restore the normal functioning of policy between America and Britain. The foundation had been laid for a more intimate coordination of policy between the Americans and the British, a process which would continue for the next three years.

2
1958: Arms Control, Washington, Lebanon

As Dwight D. Eisenhower and Harold Macmillan viewed British–American relations at the beginning of 1958, they witnessed a considerable change by contrast with 1957. The two leaders had spent much of 1957 mending fences and establishing a renewed basis for cooperation between the United States and Great Britain. In 1958, Eisenhower and Macmillan were forced to address the policy-making dimensions of their relationship. A particularly vexing problem for both the British and the Americans was the issue of arms control and disarmament and its impact upon relations with the Soviet Union.

In *Holding the Line: the Eisenhower Era, 1952–1961*, historian Charles C. Alexander analyzes the lack of progress which characterized the efforts of both the Western alliance and the communist bloc during the 1950s. On the American side, Eisenhower had made his proposal for "Open Skies" at the Geneva Summit Conference in July 1955. But the Soviet Union, characterized by the finger-waving of Premier Nikita Khruschchev, had rejected Ike's proposal and reverted to its own program of nuclear weapons development. For the Americans the objective in arms control negotiations became one of limiting the size of the Russian nuclear stockpile and its means of delivering these weapons. For the Soviets, who enjoyed a clear superiority in conventional forces in Europe relative to the Western powers, the goal became one of avoiding any agreement which would freeze the nuclear status quo in favor of the NATO countries.[1]

By 1957, therefore, both the NATO powers and the members of the communist bloc held a measure of deterrent capability relative to the other. In 1955, the Soviets were the first to explode a thermonuclear weapon from an aircraft, but the United States achieved the same feat in 1956.[2] NATO's deployment of the American superbomber, the B-52, during the 1950s gave it a sizable advantage over the Warsaw Pact in terms of aircraft available for strategic purposes. The Soviets chose to offset this advantage by accelerating their research and development in the field of ballistic missiles. The result of this feverish competition was a virtual military stalemate in Europe.

In March and April 1957, the Soviets made an attempt to break the log jam on disarmament. Valerin Zorin, the Soviet delegate to the United Nations Subcommittee on Disarmament, proposed a lengthy plan for aerial inspection of both the United States and the Soviet Union, a ban on nuclear tests, and a modest reduction in conventional forces. Many observers considered the Soviet proposal a major step in the right direction but the United States believed that the plan lacked sufficient guarantees on the matters of inspection and verification. Harold Stassen, the American delegate to the Disarmament Subcommittee, however, was convinced that the Soviet proposals presented a genuine opportunity for a breakthrough. Stassen complicated the picture, however, by consulting with Zorin without alerting the British and French negotiators.[3]

Upset by Stassen's behavior, Secretary of State John Foster Dulles inserted himself into the arms control picture. The West's response to Zorin occupied the next six months, and the Soviets reversed their position, calling unrealistically for "complete and total disarmament" and an end to military bases abroad. Both sides then reverted to their previous practices and began to expand their arsenals.[4]

In March 1958, both sides made some progress. The Soviets announced a unilateral suspension of nuclear tests and called upon Britain and the United States to do likewise. Under considerable pressure from world public opinion, Macmillan and Eisenhower responded to the Soviet offer by calling for a meeting of Western and Soviet-bloc nations in Geneva to produce a satisfactory inspection regimen. In August, 1958, after the Geneva negotiators issued their report, Eisenhower announced a one-year moratorium on nuclear tests, providing that the Soviets reciprocated. But once again, the Soviet Union derailed the proposal, citing differences over the number of non-Soviet inspectors who would be allowed into the country.[5]

In many respects, disarmament was tailor-made for Macmillan, who hoped to take this central issue and mold it to a solution of his choice. He believed that the eventual solution to disarmament required a rescue of negotiations from the bureaucratic realm and an elevation to the level of the heads of government. Thus, he began to advocate a summit meeting where, in a timely and constructive manner, national leaders would attempt to resolve the major issues which divided them. As he later explained in the last volume of his memoirs, *Pointing the Way*, "What I envision is a series of meetings, each one leading on to the next. Even if a summit meeting was not going to make any progress at all, I feel that it could nevertheless serve a useful purpose provided it led to a further conference."[6]

On the American side, however, Eisenhower, Dulles, the military chiefs, the civilian leadership of the Defense Department, and Lewis Strauss, the chairman of the Atomic Energy Commission (AEC), viewed summit conferences skeptically. The Geneva Summit in 1955 had turned out to be a disappointment and the Americans feared that an unsuccessful conference could damage the image of the United States in world opinion. While Macmillan believed that the process of summit meetings might lead to some easing of tensions between East and West, the Eisenhower Administration thought differently. Eisenhower and Dulles were interested in tangible results, such as verifiable agreements, which could lead to greater trust between the competing powers. Summit meetings which failed to produce those results could only deteriorate into propaganda victories for the communists. The Americans and the British were clearly divided on the matter of the utility of summitry as an approach to successful diplomacy.

In Macmillan's domestic political calculations, however, summitry was a potentially valuable weapon. He needed to call a general election within the next two years, and as British historian Robert Blake has written, the "next general election was in Macmillan's mind from the beginning."[7] Throughout 1957–58, the Conservatives remained behind the Labour Party by between 5 percent and 13 percent in the opinion polls, and the Macmillan government needed to reverse those numbers if it expected to win the next election.[8]

Macmillan's particular concern with his political fortunes involved the threat of nuclear war occasioned by Britain's entry into the group of nuclear powers and the agreements reached at the North Atlantic Council meeting in December 1957. He directed considerable political attention toward Aneurin Bevan, the Labour Party's shadow foreign secretary, who was preparing to use the popular fear over nuclear war as a winning issue against the Conservative government. On 15 May 1957, Britain had successfully detonated its first thermonuclear device and shortly thereafter, a chorus of opposition to Britain's development of the hydrogen bomb engulfed the House of Commons.[9]

Throughout the rest of 1957, Macmillan kept a wary eye on the antinuclear sentiment in the country and, specifically, on the attempts by the Labour Party to capitalize on it as an electoral issue. By September, he had decided to enlist Eisenhower's assistance in an effort to get "out front" on the disarmament issue. Focusing on Russian resistance to serious arms control negotiations, Macmillan wrote to Eisenhower on 18 September 1957:

> I have read what you said expressing your deep disappointment at the Russian attitude on disarmament. Everyone in this country feels the same; and for the first time for many months even the "long-haired, starry-eyed guys" seem to think that Russia is wrong. I have never known Left and near-Left opinion so critical of them or so understanding of us. In these circumstances, I am wondering whether we could not make a new gesture especially on the aspect which most worries ordinary folk – that is the nuclear. You and we are the two nuclear powers of the free world. You are very much the big brother, but we are now making quite a show of our own. Could we not together say that in spite of the Russian intransigence and immobility we were prepared to make a start?[10]

Nevertheless, the prevailing political attitude in Britain tended to support apprehension over a nuclear arms race. In February 1958, anti-nuclear activists formed the Campaign for Nuclear Disarmament (CND), an organization which advocated an end to the arms race by the destruction of nuclear arsenals, an end to nuclear tests, and the withdrawal of nuclear forces from Europe. From the standpoint of domestic politics, Macmillan could not ignore the anti-nuclear sentiment.[11]

In the United States, Eisenhower's domestic political problems differed considerably from those of Macmillan. From a policy perspective, Ike's goals were taking shape nicely after 1957. Plans for strengthening the NATO alliance had made considerable progress with the decisions to deploy IRBMs in Britain and to place nuclear forces at the disposal of General Lauris Norstad, the NATO commander.[12]

In fact, in 1958 the domestic demands upon Eisenhower in the realm of national security called for a greater, not lesser, commitment to national defense. The launching of Sputnik was followed by the revelation, within the government, of the secret Gaither Commission report during the winter of 1957–58. The product of a presidential advisory commission organized to study the civil defense environment, the report advocated increasing the defense budget considerably beyond its present $38 billion level. It also advocated a renewed commitment to new military technology, specifically missiles and satellites.

Obviously, the residual effects of the Sputnik hysteria were being felt in terms of discussions about the federal budget. "Sputnik almost revolutionized spending in this country on the grounds that money made all the difference, and it doesn't," Robert Anderson once said.[13] It took considerable persuasion on Eisenhower's part, including two televised addresses on 7 November and 13 November 1957, to reassure critics in Congress that the Administration was pursuing an effective military program.[14]

At the beginning of 1958, therefore, the British and the Americans obviously viewed the threat of nuclear war differently. General Norstad, responsible for meeting the Soviet threat in Europe, believed that the NATO alliance was strong enough to deter a Soviet military attack, but he feared that a possible miscalculation on either side could lead to a military conflict. "In my time, I think the position of NATO had become strong and our strategy was clear enough and our intentions were clear enough, our will well enough established, so I thought it was a relatively small chance [that hostilities might occur] and it would only happen if we made some mistake."[15]

For his part, Macmillan was also concerned about an outbreak of war, caused by accident or by a miscalculation on the part of national leaders. Therefore, he drew on his experiences from World War I and the notion that the war would not have broken out if "Sir Edward Grey hadn't gone fishing" and tended to the diplomatic situation instead.[16] Britain's proximity to the range of Soviet missiles and Soviet bombers concerned him mightily and conditioned his approach to the avoidance of a nuclear exchange.

Eisenhower was more concerned, however, about a surprise attack upon the United States by Soviet inter-continental ballistic missiles or long-range aircraft. It was in America's interest to attempt to slow down the arms race, but only after the United States and its NATO partners believed they had acquired the upper hand over the Soviet Union. "Actually, the only thing that we fear is an atomic attack delivered by air on our cities," Ike told a group of Congressional leaders as early as 1955. "It would be perfect rot to talk about shipping troops abroad when fifteen of our cities were in ruins."[17]

I

Macmillan set out his thoughts for the coming year in a lengthy letter which he sent to Eisenhower on 2 January 1958. Starting out casually, he proceeded to a serious discussion of issues which confronted not only the British and the Americans, but also the members of the NATO alliance. "As I promised, I have spent the past few days of this Christmas holiday in brooding over the problem of how to handle the Russians and, at the same time, what is equally important – how to rally the maximum support we can in the free world as well as in the uncommitted countries," he began.[18] Macmillan ranged broadly over a host of issues, ranging from nuclear weapons development, disarmament and arms control, and the buildup of conventional forces in Europe. He conspicuously returned to a theme of unity between himself and Eisenhower. "After all, we have kept the peace – or rather your great power has done so – for ten years . . . If you and I agree on a policy [relating to disarmament], I think we ought to be able to sell it to the rest of our allies," Macmillan said.[19] He argued that "we must work out an agreed policy for two countries on all of these issues. This is important not only from the point of view of any initiative with the Russians, it is important that we should carry all the NATO countries, especially Germany, with us in anything we propose."[20]

Macmillan also touched on the subject of nuclear tests, pointing out that the British position was that the tests should not be suspended, given the current status of negotiations. He warned against serious discussion of the recent Soviet proposal for the destruction of all nuclear weapons, viewing it as mere propaganda. "It may perhaps be the purpose of the Russians to achieve total nuclear disarmament leaving themselves with the immense superiority of numbers and the great advance they have made in conventional weapons," Macmillan contended. "They have built up a fleet of surface ships and submarines and large numbers of bombers which they are still trying to construct."[21]

After extolling the virtues of military strength and the need for firmness with the Soviets, Macmillan made a curious turn in the letter. Perhaps reflecting his sensitivity to the anti-nuclear sentiment in Britain and throughout Europe, he adopted a more conciliatory tone. "I think we ought to clear our minds about these fundamental problems, because we are now approaching a point when it may not be possible to rely any longer on throwing the blame on the Russians for the breakdown of negotiations," he wrote.[22] He then advanced the idea that meetings of the various foreign ministers might be more successful in breaking the deadlock on arms control negotiations than the disarmament panels, working under the United Nations. If that approach succeeded, Macmillan said, it might open the way for his most cherished objective, a summit meeting involving the various heads of governments. "If our two governments could reach clear and agreed views on all these subjects [through meetings of the foreign ministers] I myself would not shrink from what is called a summit meeting, at the right moment," Macmillan wrote. "The world seems to expect it. But we must insist on the necessary preparation, both on the diplomatic and foreign minister levels."[23]

On 4 January, Macmillan spoke directly to the British people in a national broadcast. His speech to the nation confirmed many of the points which he had raised in his letter to Eisenhower. He addressed the importance of nuclear weapons as a deterrent to war. "I look at it like this," he said:

> In a curious way, the knowledge of the immense devastation which would follow a world conflict does deter aggressors. The hydrogen bomb is a protection. For in a nuclear war, neither side can win a victory. The fact that our sure defense lies in our ability to destroy an aggressor as cruelly as he destroys others is to many a horrible idea. But we dare not let our revulsion from the idea of the H-Bomb deprive us of our best guarantee of safety from attack, and so the best guarantee of peace.[24]

In the broadcast Macmillan also praised the role of the Americans in the defense of Europe, in particular its newly announced program of military cooperation with Great Britain. The prime minister emphasized that the nuclear weapons in Britain could not be used without British approval and British safeguards. He spoke about the problems which had plagued disarmament negotiations to date and the necessity for the West to adopt a flexible position with the Soviet Union in nuclear weapons negotiations. In the process, however, he talked himself into a trap by referring to the negotiation of a "solemn pact of non-aggression" as it related to conventional war in Europe.[25] With the memory of World War II still fresh in mind, non-aggression pacts were hardly popular ways of proceeding with diplomacy.

The most important part of Macmillan's broadcast came toward its conclusion when he touched on two subjects. First, he spoke of making a fresh start in terms of negotiations between the free world and the communist bloc, "to clear away the rubble of old controversies and disagreements perhaps to get the path ready for a meeting of heads of government."[26] Out of sensitivity to the American point of view, Macmillan did not mention the word "summit" although the intent of his remarks was clear.

Second, Macmillan sought to dispel the views of those who felt British power had declined precipitously and that Britain had no role to play on the international stage. "We hear much loose talk today about the change of position of this country in the world," Macmillan admitted. "Some people even say that we are a spent force, but the world would be a lot different and less hopeful place if Britain did not exist."[27]

Eisenhower carefully read Macmillan's letter of 2 January, underlining several passages which provoked his interest. Ike's jottings can be seen throughout the letter, indicating points which he later covered in meetings with John Foster Dulles. When Macmillan referred in his letter to the placement of American IRBMs in Europe, Eisenhower jotted in the left margin, "Certainly I.R.B.M.s should be located west of the Rhine," so as not to provoke the Soviet Union needlessly. When Macmillan referred to his concern about finding fresh ways to engage the Soviets in the area of nuclear weapons, Eisenhower penciled in the margin, "propaganda problem," referring to the difficulty of having the West perceived as the one who wanted to build up their nuclear arsenals and endanger world peace.[28]

After reading Macmillan's letter, Eisenhower prepared a memorandum of 14 talking points that he wanted to discuss further with Foster Dulles. In point 11, he noted that on matters related to disarmament, "Harold suggests first a meeting by Ambassadors to discuss an agenda, then a Foreign Minister's meeting and finally if necessary, a summit meeting."[29] Later, in the memorandum, Ike expanded on what he perceived to be Macmillan's purpose. "He is obviously toying with a series of meetings, one of which might finally become a 'summit meeting,'" Ike wrote. "I think this subject will probably require more study on our part than almost any other. It is easy to get entangled in such a proposition but not so easy to get out of it."[30]

On 6 January, Eisenhower responded to Macmillan's letter. Ike referred to Macmillan's thoughts on the nuclear arms issue and also commented on the American reaction (mostly negative) to Macmillan's discussion of a non-aggression pact with the Soviet Union.[31] But the most important facet of Eisenhower's letter was his refusal to comment on Macmillan's suggestion for a summit. Clearly, Eisenhower had no desire to pursue such an initiative, at least at that moment.

Macmillan refused to give up on the idea so quickly, however. On 19 February, after a trip to the Commonwealth, he sent a reply to Eisenhower. "I believe that if we take a sober and dispassionate approach, public opinion not only in our own countries but also in the uncommitted areas will be consolidated in our favor," he wrote. "At the same time, there is an expectation all over the world that a summit meeting should take place. In our country and in the Commonwealth, this is strongly held, although all sensible people accept the view that there should be proper preparation."[32] Citing the considerable diplomatic pressure which could be applied to the Russians on that basis, Macmillan even boldly suggested a specific date for holding a summit meeting; "Let us say either late July or August subject, of course, to the preparatory work being done."[33] Reminding Eisenhower that he intended to be in the United States for two speaking engagements, one at the Citadel in South Carolina on 31 May and the other at DePauw University in Indiana on 8 June, Macmillan emphasized his willingness to confer with Eisenhower prior to a summit meeting. "If I were to accept [these speaking engagements], and if you thought it a good idea, I might meet quite informally with you and Foster in Washington between the two engagements," Macmillan suggested.[34]

Shortly after sending this letter to Eisenhower, Macmillan wrote to Emanuel Shinwell, a member of Parliament for the Labour Party, plaintively expressing his hopes for progress in this area. "I long for some break in the clouds and I would be content with some advance at a Summit conference no matter how small. If we could start somewhere, it would lead to better things later on."[35]

In his response to Macmillan's letter of 19 February, Eisenhower was cool to the idea of a summit but did not completely reject the suggestion, either. On 26 February, Ike wrote to Macmillan, explaining that he thought it would be a good idea for the prime minister to come to Washington after his commencement speech at DePauw University on 8 June.[36] On 19 February, Macmillan had delivered a speech in the House of Commons, dealing with the disarmament issue. Trying to strike a balance between guaranteeing the military strength of the alliance while offering the Soviet Union the opportunity to negotiate its differences, Macmillan tried to make some progress on the arms control issue. Eisenhower referred to Macmillan's speech in his response, noting that

> I hope that your presentation may cool off some of the burning, but completely unjustified, opinions that an unprepared "summit" meeting could do the free world any good. I think we should fully expect the opposite result. On the other hand, once the NATO nations are agreed among themselves as to what our positions on various matters should be, we could fix a date for preparatory work to be initiated with the Russians ... But I am quite certain that any

attempt to fix a date for the [summit] meeting merely on the Soviet promise to perform honestly in the preparatory would result in dismal failure.[37]

The jousting between Macmillan and Eisenhower via correspondence continued into March. On 3 March, Macmillan responded to Eisenhower's letter of 26 February, trying to accentuate the positive. He confirmed his intention to meet Ike in Washington on 9 June, the day after his speech at DePauw University. The Soviets had opened the door to a meeting of the foreign ministers and Macmillan was trying to keep it open. Macmillan was bothered by what he perceived to be the inflexibility in the American position. "The [American] arguments are certainly irrefutable," he said. "All the same, I am wondering whether it quite meets the mood in Europe."[38] The prime minister then proceeded to offer some suggestions as to how the two governments might remove some of the obstacles in the path of a summit conference, preferably by enabling the foreign ministers to agree on an agenda for the meeting.

The next day, however, Foster Dulles threw cold water on Macmillan's idea, responding to Macmillan's letter in a memorandum delivered to British Ambassador Harold Caccia. In his memo, Dulles raised a host of objections, ranging from the procedural, to the substantive, to the merely political. On the procedural side, Dulles wrote "the United States has preferred not to get into the composition of a possible Foreign Ministers' meeting at this time because it raises awkward questions as regards the allies and also the question of parity as it relates as regards relations with the Soviet Union."[39] On the substantive side, Dulles explained that the United States "will not accept a 'summit' meeting unless the advanced exploration by the Foreign Ministers indicates: a) that there is likely agreement on one or more significant matters; b) that there will be a serious discussion of the reunification of Germany." And finally, on the political side, even if all the preliminary matters had been settled, "the question of date and place [for a summit meeting] would have to be considered from the standpoint of the United States Congressional elections as we would not want to seem to be using this 'summit' meeting for political purposes."[40]

Eisenhower responded that same day, with a cable to Macmillan, repeating his conversation with Dulles and Caccia. Ike made the response his first order of business for the day, reading over Macmillan's letter at 7.45 a.m. "As you know, I am convinced that any summit meeting would be damaging to the free world unless some real agreements can be made with the Russians, one in which we can have some confidence. That is why I believe so much in adequate preparation."[41]

But later, Eisenhower tried to flatter Macmillan a bit on the summit issue when the president met with British Air Marshall William Elliott in Washington in mid-April. According to Elliott's report to Macmillan, Ike "went on to a very warm eulogy on yourself. You were not a person who allowed himself to be 'buffaloed.'" Although Eisenhower was "empathetic" about Macmillan's distress over American views on a summit, Ike nonetheless was "firm" that there would be no summit meeting "unless and until agreement was reached on an agendum."[42] Macmillan was essentially in a good news, bad news situation. The good news was that Eisenhower was talking about the possibility of a summit meeting with the Russians; the bad news was that he had raised some major objections to one ever taking place.

II

The stage was now set for the next round of direct, bilateral talks between Eisenhower and Macmillan, this time in Washington between 9 and 11 June 1958, the third such meeting between the two leaders since March 1957. Actually, this meeting had been in at least the discussion stage for close to a year. On 24 June 1957, Eisenhower cabled a note to Macmillan, indicating that he should expect to be invited to give the commencement speech at DePauw University the following June, based on the fact that his grandfather had once attended the medical college near the DePauw campus.[43] Macmillan subsequently accepted the invitation and the two leaders agreed to meet in Washington after Macmillan gave the commencement address at DePauw.

Then, on 2 April, Eisenhower and his brother Milton, the president of Johns Hopkins University in Baltimore, met at the White House and Milton inquired if Macmillan could also speak at his university's commencement and receive an honorary doctorate. Eisenhower agreed to explore the idea with Macmillan. Ike wrote to Macmillan on 3 April: "About forty miles away in the City of Baltimore, is one of our very fine universities, Johns Hopkins University. Its President is my youngest brother, Dr. Milton Eisenhower, a distinguished educator. He and his trustees are very anxious to invite you to come over to the university on Tuesday, June tenth, to receive an honorary degree from them and to make a commencement talk."[44] Macmillan accepted the offer and booked another speech on his itinerary.[45]

Harold Macmillan's visits to the United States provided poignant memories of his mother and her family. In September 1956, during the Suez crisis, he had visited Indiana to receive an honorary degree from Indiana University and to visit his mother's hometown of Spencer. On 22 September 1956, Macmillan thanked President Herman B Wells and the trustees of Indiana University for the honorary degree, adding that his "only regret [was] that my mother did not live to see me receive a degree from the University of Indiana (sic). It would have been a proud day for her."[46] Then, in October 1957, at the Washington Conference, Macmillan's thoughts once again returned to his mother when he met with Eisenhower and Dulles at the White House to work out the language for the Declaration of Common Purpose. "I thought how pleased my mother would have been to see me, as British Prime Minister in the American Cabinet Room, addressing a meeting presided over by the American President," he confided to his diary on 24 October.[47]

Nine months later, Macmillan was prepared to make a third visit to the United States in the space of about a year and a half. He left Britain on 7 June, accompanied by his wife Dorothy, Norman Brook, and two advisers, Freddie Bishop and Philip de Zulueta. The British met with Dulles and Harold Caccia to craft an agenda for their talks, and then Macmillan left for Greencastle, Indiana. As recorded in his diary, and then later published in his memoirs, Macmillan gave a detailed account of his day at DePauw University.

> [In Indianapolis] we were met by various dignitaries including the Governor and the Mayor, as well as by [Mr. Eugene C.] Pulliam, the owner of the *Indianapolis Star* and other newspapers. We drove from the airport to President [Russell J.] Humbert's house at Greencastle. All the route, about thirty to forty miles, was lined with people, who gave me a tremendous welcome. There were banners with "Welcome Mac," or "Welcome Home" across the streets in the villages. It was really most touching. There was rather a wind; otherwise a fine day and not too hot – about eighty degrees.[48]

Following his address, Macmillan attended a dinner given in his honor by Eugene C. Pulliam, who had also given a luncheon for Macmillan during his visit to Indiana in September 1956. In attendance were many newspaper publishers from the Midwest, including William D. Maxwell of the *Chicago Tribune*. Macmillan noted that "Kansas was well represented also."[49] Macmillan answered questions from the group, and later was gratified that the Midwest did not seem to be the hotbed of isolationist sentiment that his mother had earlier taught him about. As Alexander Macmillan later commented, "My grandfather was the one British politician who knew what it was like to stand in the middle of a cornfield in Indiana."[50]

Leaving Indiana, Macmillan returned to Washington for three days of talks with Eisenhower. The meetings covered a comprehensive set of topics: interdependence and the status of relations between the United States and Great Britain; the Middle East, including the problems in Lebanon; nuclear questions, including nuclear testing and disarmament; preparation for a summit meeting; and the economic and propaganda threats presented by the communist bloc.[51] Eisenhower and Dulles participated in all the meetings on 9 June, but Dulles met alone with the British delegation on 10-11 June.

At the outset, Eisenhower made it clear that he wanted no leaks of information about the substance of the conversations such as had occurred after the Bermuda Conference. "The President stated that he could see no reason why we should talk at all about the substance of these meetings in a communiqué and in extensive press briefings," said one account of one meeting. "The Prime Minister thought that we should just say that they had been talking about problems of common interest and that he just stopped by here in passing through from DePauw University. The Prime Minister and President agreed they would say to the press that we have discussed everything under the sun."[52]

The leaders participated in a lengthy meeting on the afternoon of 9 June which stretched from 3 p.m. to 6 p.m. In their discussions of British–American cooperation on nuclear weapons and arms control, both sides agreed that the sharing of nuclear information and weapons technology according to the amendment of the McMahon Act was going smoothly. Regarding nuclear testing and arms control, Dulles mentioned that on the next day, he intended to deliver a proposal to the Soviets for a meeting between the technical experts to discuss means of handling inspection in the event of a suspension of nuclear tests. The gist of the proposal was that the United States would agree to a moratorium of one or two years, contingent upon agreements in other areas of disarmament. Eisenhower emphasized that the means needed to be created for establishing inspection posts and not one with "just two or three inspectors." As many as twenty inspection stations might be necessary, although Lewis Strauss, the chairman of the Atomic Energy Commission, pushed for as many as forty to seventy stations worldwide. Dulles essentially captured the urgency of the issue when he noted that "the Soviet propaganda drive on suspension of nuclear tests" has convinced many people around the world that the Soviets are more peace-loving than the West.[53]

The two delegations also spent much of their time discussing the emerging instability in the Middle East. Predictably, Macmillan raised the subject of the West's response to Nasser and his efforts to undermine pro-Western governments in the region. Macmillan thought that the choice was one of "treating him woolly and supporting our friends on the one hand or attempting to buy him off on the other."[54] Macmillan then inquired if the United States intended to allow Nasser to obtain funds, possibly through the World Bank; he was obviously frustrated with the Egyptian leader's amazing endurance and ability to maintain power. What was needed was a strong Arab leader in the region who could oppose Nasser. Eisenhower interjected that Macmillan's suggestion was "desirable" but that all of the pro-Western leaders in the region, "[Camille] Chamoun [in Lebanon], [King Ibn] Saud [in Saudi Arabia], and Nuri [as Said] [in Iraq] all seemed to be weak" by comparison with Nasser.[55]

Dulles supported Ike. "The great difficulty with backing an Arab in opposition to Nasser is that Nasser is so popular with people in the Arab world," he said. "The Arab leaders want us to take the initiative in getting rid of Nasser but we cannot do so unless they are willing to stand up and oppose him."[56] The United States and Great Britain were reduced to a policy of supplying weapons to their friends in the Middle East with little likelihood that they would ever confront a fellow Arab state.

Following the points raised by Eisenhower, Macmillan, and Dulles, Sir Patrick Dean joined the discussion. "Nasser needs some victory every six months and . . . our task is to prevent him from winning these victories," Dean observed.[57] In response, Macmillan argued that "we must hold on to Lebanon [Nasser's next target for a "victory"], maintain the Arab Union and . . . see that he does not win a prestige victory."[58] Summing up, Macmillan stated that "it is hard for us to intervene usefully in this kind of struggle and find means of giving courage to anti-Nasser elements."[59]

The concerns of the Americans and the British about the problems created by Nasser extended to the status of the other countries in the region. In February 1958, the kingdoms of Iraq and Jordan formed the Arab Union, an organization which was to become a counterweight to Nasser's United Arab Republic of Egypt and Syria.[60] The United States and Britain had promised military assistance to the Arab Union and at their meeting on 9 June, the leaders reaffirmed their support for such action and even tried to accelerate the process. Eisenhower even went so far as to order an additional 4–6 combat aircraft for Iraq with British military personnel being in a position to maintain them.[61]

At the same meeting, Secretary Dulles expressed his serious concern about the necessity of maintaining a pro-Western government in Lebanon. "Under certain circumstances," Dulles said, the United States "would send armed forces into their country, primarily to protect American citizens, but also to maintain and support the present government."[62] Dulles added, however, that he felt the present situation was stable enough that Americans intervention was unnecessary.

The situation in Lebanon was considered serious enough to warrant its own specific discussion, however. The major source of political controversy involved whether Camille Chamoun, Lebanon's president, would run for a second term in office. With Lebanon almost equally divided between its Christian and Muslim factions, the pro-Christian Chamoun was under heavy pressure from Muslim elements both inside and outside of Lebanon to step down after finishing his first term. Eisenhower, Dulles, and Macmillan also firmly insisted that Chamoun should leave office when his term expired. "The Prime Minister expressed his belief that it would be very hard to keep Chamoun in power for a second term and the President agreed with him saying that if we should try, we would be asking for even more rebellion, since it was Chamoun who provided the spark in the current situation," read the notes of the meeting.[63]

Discussion then turned to a possible successor to Chamoun. The presumed favorite was Faud Chehab, commander of Lebanon's military, and an individual acceptable to both the Christian and Moslem factions in the country. William Rountree, the assistant secretary of state for the Middle East, agreed that "Chehab might be ... the best choice even though he has recently shown a lack of political interest."[64] It was left to Macmillan and Dulles to sum up. Macmillan advocated "watching the situation closely and [maintaining] our plan in a state of readiness."[65] Dulles was pessimistic; sending "forces into Lebanon is the lesser of two evils [but] even this course is still an evil," he argued. "It would be difficult to get them out once they are in, since the government that invites them may very well fall with great violence once they depart."[66]

The discussion also focused on Iraq where the situation was no better than in Lebanon. Macmillan argued that the Iraqis had their eyes on neighboring Kuwait as a third member of the Arab Union. The problem was that Nuri as-Said, the prime minister of Iraq, wanted the West to finance the economies of the states in the Arab Union. According to William Rountree, "Nuri wanted $37 million to cover the period from

July, 1958 to May 31, 1959 which is budget support at the rate of $50 million a year."[67] Macmillan felt that the West had to come up with the money: "If the Arab Union should collapse [as a counterweight to Nasser] it will be a terrible blow to our side."[68]

As for the inclusion of Kuwait in the Arab Union, Macmillan indicated that Nuri was attempting a "Nasser-style program of intimidation, and the ruler of Kuwait was resisting this pressure." Rountree gave a cogent analysis of the situation. In reply to a question from Eisenhower, he pointed out that "while Kuwait had few original inhabitants, there had been many recent immigrants from other Arab countries including Egypt and Syria who agitated strongly for joining with Egypt. Therefore, if the ruler showed an inclination to join Iraq in the Arab Union he will become most unpopular with [large segments of] his population. As well, he is certainly aware that the Iraqis are greatly interested in tapping his financial resources."[69]

Macmillan reacted strongly to the reports of Nuri's behavior and his "out and out" threats against Kuwait. Dulles also was dismayed by Nuri's behavior, which he compared to an attempt at "blackmail" to get more money out of the United States. Eisenhower's earlier fears were well-founded; the West did not have a friend in the Middle East who rivaled Nasser in terms of personal popularity.

On 10 June, Macmillan and Eisenhower took a brief respite from their talks to attend the commencement ceremonies at John Hopkins University at the request of Dr Milton Eisenhower. They traveled by helicopter from the White House to the Johns Hopkins campus in Baltimore and then rode by car to the ceremonies. Macmillan recalled, "My speech was shorter than the DePauw one – about fifteen minutes – but on the same general theme ... Economic interdependence is every bit as important as military [interdependence.]"[70] The speech may have been short but Macmillan took full advantage of the opportunity to take his idea for a summit conference out of the private confines of diplomacy and into the public setting of the commencement ceremony. "We must maintain these alliances – our sure shield – but I am not without hope that we may succeed little by little, if not all at once, in making progress towards the reduction of tensions in the world," he said. "Naturally I do not believe that at a Summit, or at any other meeting, five or six men can in four days bridge the immense chasm between these two concepts. It would be folly to suppose so. But, if conditions are favorable, and if the will is there, they might first make a little progress here, and then a little there, and so bring in out of a condition of stalemate into one of negotiation."[71] One can only wonder what was going through Eisenhower's mind as he sat in the audience, listening to Macmillan's words.

After returning to Washington, Macmillan addressed the Senate in the early afternoon, again making reference to his mother's observation that "being an American senator was the height of human endeavor."[72] Following that address, Macmillan and his team of British negotiators went to the State Department for another round of meetings with Dulles on the situations in Yemen and in Cyprus, two obvious areas of trouble for the British. There was also a meeting involving Macmillan and Treasury Secretary Robert B. Anderson which covered economic policy between the two countries as well as a session with Allen Dulles, director of the Central Intelligence Agency (CIA).[73]

That evening, Eisenhower and Dulles hosted a dinner for Macmillan attended by several men who formed an ad hoc committee to advise the secretary of state on disarmament issues. This committee consisted of General Alfred M. Gruenther, Eisenhower's successor as the NATO commander; General Walter Bedell Smith, Eisenhower's chief of staff during World War II, the first director of the Central Intelligence Agency and under secretary of state under Dulles; John McCloy, allied high commissioner in Germany after World War II and an international banker with the Chase Manhattan Bank; and Robert Lovett, former under secretary of state and secretary of defense in the Truman administration. Charles D. ("C.D.") Jackson, Eisenhower's special assistant for psychological warfare; and Neil McElroy, the current secretary of defense, also attended.

The conversation at dinner, primarily on Macmillan's initiative, turned to the issue of a prospective summit conference. As Dulles recorded in his notes of the conversation after dinner:

> Following the dinner, there was general conversation dealing primarily with a Summit Conference and disarmament, and more particularly, suspension of testing . . . The PM made rather an eloquent statement, pointing out the exposed position of the UK; that four or five nuclear bombs would wipe them out entirely; that they were willing to stand firm but did expect their government to do everything possible to mitigate the danger, and that they considered that a Summit meeting was at least an effort that ought to be made. The US speakers spoke with varying emphasis. If there was any general sentiment, it was that a Summit meeting should not merely provide the Soviets with a Roman holiday in terms of their finally winning a suspension of testing agreement, but that any Summit meeting

should be a place where the basic political problems of the world should at least be discussed. The Prime Minister suggested that the agenda might be of two parts – the first part dealing with a suspension of testing, etc., where agreement could be expected; the second part dealing with political discussions under some general heading such as European "political problems," where the political problems could be discussed without hesitation.[74]

One new item which crept into the talks between Eisenhower and Macmillan and their respective advisers at this conference was an appropriate response to the new government of Charles de Gaulle in France. Macmillan felt the discussion about France was appropriate but that de Gaulle already had a major foreign policy crisis on his hands with the Algerian situation. The French were also in some economic difficulty at the time. He also expected that de Gaulle would desire something similar to the close relationship which the United States and Britain had on the sharing of nuclear weapons information as well as on defense cooperation. Failing that type of agreement, he was likely to reject the placement of nuclear weapons in France.[75]

Eisenhower and Dulles saw the attractiveness of a tripartite (American/British/French) approach to the deployment of American IRBMs in Europe as well as a greater degree of information sharing with the French, but they doubted that the Congress would support such a measure. Passage of any legislation which eased nuclear restrictions, even a bilateral treaty with France, could not obtain Congressional approval, Dulles said.[76]

Nevertheless, Eisenhower argued that the Americans and British "cannot treat de Gaulle as if he were like God," and Dulles suggested a possible approach for the British and Americans in dealing with France. The United States and Britain would treat the French as members of a tripartite group on such matters as the summit and the reunification of Germany; on other issues, they would deal with France separately on a bilateral basis or through NATO, keeping each other informed in the process.[77]

The Washington consultations ended on the afternoon of 11 June with a meeting between Eisenhower, Macmillan, Dulles, and Harold Caccia. Prior to the meeting, Macmillan met individually with Dulles and also spoke to the National Press Club. The four men briefly reviewed the status of British participation in NATO, the progress of legislation leading to nuclear-sharing, and the expected date for the arrival of the

American IRBMS in Britain.[78] With good feeling all around, Macmillan left for Canada.

The talks between Eisenhower and Macmillan in June 1958 have not attracted the attention given that to other meetings between the two leaders. Despite the fact that no major agreements were announced, the June meetings were important, primarily because they afforded an opportunity for the two sides to discuss the troublesome situation in the Middle East, an area which soon required all of their attention.[79]

III

Since the Suez crisis had ended in early 1957, the United States and Great Britain had diverged slightly in their policies on the Middle East. The British and Macmillan, specifically, continued to view Gamal Abdul Nasser with the greatest suspicion, a menace to the supply of precious Middle East oil to the United Kingdom and Western Europe. The Americans tended to view Nasser "pragmatically" (a term hated by the British) and worrisome only to the extent that he might be considered to be an agent for the Soviet Union, willing to advance Russian interests in the region. American attention turned in the direction of building up oil-rich Saudi Arabia as a close ally and King Saud as a counter to Nasser.[80]

British and American policy received a severe jolt on the evening of 13 July, however, when Iraqi military leader General Abdul Karim Kassem staged a military revolt against the Iraqi government and the country's royal family. Kassem's forces stormed the royal palace in Baghdad, killing King Faisal II and Crown Prince Abdullah. Nuri as-Said, the prime minister, managed to escape on 13 June but was apprehended the next day by Kassem's forces and killed. Macmillan recorded that Nuri was "treated with the utmost barbarity, his body being dragged naked through the streets for the delectation of the lowest section of the mob."[81]

Kassem was obviously pro-Nasser, but the extent to which he was acting on Nasser's behalf was unclear. Nasser's propagandists in Cairo did, however, begin broadcasting a call for Nasser supporters throughout the Middle East to take action against the ruling families in the region. For the British, Nasser's words meant the destabilization of Jordan and King Hussein. For the United States, Nasser's threat meant the ruling monarchy of the House of Saud in Saudi Arabia. For the

United States, Great Britain, and Western Europe, it appeared to be another challenge by Nasser to pro-Western governments in the Middle East.[82]

Eisenhower spent 14 July responding to the crisis. Following the Suez crisis, Eisenhower had gained Congressional approval for a policy of American intervention in the Middle East to prevent any further communist influence in the region. Now this policy, known as the Eisenhower Doctrine, was about to be tested, although as historian Nigel Ashton has pointed out, the situation in Lebanon hardly presented a clear-cut contingency for the imposition of this new American approach to the Middle East.[83]

In practical terms, Eisenhower's primary concern involved support for the only acknowledged pro-Western government in the region. Following the coup in Iraq, Camille Chamoun issued an immediate request for American military intervention in Lebanon. Eisenhower first met with the National Security Council. Then he held a meeting with Foster Dulles, Allen Dulles, vice president Richard M. Nixon, Donald Quarles, Robert Cutler, the executive director of the NSC; General Nathan F. Twining, chairman of the Joint Chiefs of Staff; and Robert B. Anderson. Ike listened as both of the Dulles brothers gave their analysis of the situation and then he started giving orders. Foster Dulles was to instruct Henry Cabot Lodge, the United States ambassador to the United Nations, to request an emergency meeting of the UN for 15 July. Presidential assistant Wilton B. "Jerry" Persons was to contact the Congressional leadership for a meeting at the White House that afternoon. And Twining, once he had returned to the Pentagon, was to order the Sixth Fleet and a Marine contingent to Lebanon.[84]

On the afternoon of 14 July, Eisenhower consulted with the leaders of Congress, most of whom were skeptical about intervention in Lebanon. Presidential assistant William Bragg Ewald poignantly captured the moment:

> As Ike told the congressional leaders the Marines were going in, one lone observer, keen of eye and sensibility, heard the senators and congressmen draw in their breath with apprehension. And he happened to look at the President, and what he saw was this: one big hand (Eisenhower had outsized hands, with knuckles broken in football, made for wielding an ax or kneading dough for a pie crust), dangling on the arm of his chair – a hand relaxed, with no sweating palm, no agitation, no nervousness – a single arresting symbol of the man; of a capacity to make agonizing decisions which could entail death and

sorrow; of objectivity and command of detachment; of his ability to remove himself, to delegate details, to do his duty as he saw it; of that magnificent nervous system, the silent center on which a whole earthshaking event turned.[85]

After meeting with the congressional leaders, Eisenhower conferred once more with Allen Dulles, Foster Dulles, Twining, Quarles, Goodpaster, and press secretary James Hagerty, to settle on the details of the enterprise. The landings were to begin at 9 a.m. Washington time, 3 p.m. in Lebanon, and no one, including Chamoun, was to be informed in advance. Eisenhower then telephoned Macmillan at 5.43 p.m. Washington time.

Macmillan had also spent much of 14 July trying to make sense of the situation. He was genuinely saddened by the death of King Faisal, a young man who had been educated in Britain. Moreover, the British Embassy in Baghdad had been attacked by the mob which killed the royal family and one British officer was murdered. For the sake of safety, the British ambassador and his staff took refuge in a nearby hotel. Macmillan convened his cabinet and informed them of the precarious situation.[86] Then he spoke with Eisenhower. Segments of that conversation are summarized:

Eisenhower: You have all the news and intelligence on Iraq and how it exacerbates the Lebanon situation. President Chamoun has asked us both to go in. We have decided to implement the plan (for your very secret information). As I understand it, the contingent of yours is about 3,700 and it is apparently in the lift that gets in somewhere toward the rear of the procession.

Macmillan: Yes, that's right.

Eisenhower: It is just possible that in view of the Jordan situation that I understand has been put in your lap, you may want to hold those people a little bit in reserve as the situation develops in Lebanon.

Macmillan: Yes, but the thought is this: if we do this thing with the Lebanon it is only part of a much larger operation, because we shall be driven to take the thing as a whole, and want to feel that if we treat it as a whole it looks like a showdown.

Eisenhower: Of course, you must understand that so far as we are concerned, as of this moment, we can't talk about anything happening elsewhere. I agree with you that the situation must contemplate more than that.

Macmillan: Yes, I agree the situation is going to be hard. It will start off with all the pipelines, with the bigger things, but this will stand right up to them. If this thing is done, which I think is very noble, dear friend, it will set off a lot of things throughout the whole area. I'm all for that as long as we regard it as an operation that has got to be carried through.

Eisenhower: Now just a minute so that there is no misunderstanding. Are you of the belief that unless we have made up our minds in advance to carry this thing on to the Persian Gulf that we had better not go in the first place?

Macmillan: I don't think that, but I think that we have got to see it together, dear friend; there is no good in being in that place and sitting there a few months and the whole rest being in flames. As soon as we start we have to face it – we probably have got to do a lot of things.

Eisenhower: Well, now, I will tell you of course I would not want to go further. Today we tried in our discussions here, I and with the legislative leaders, the development of the situation, and that could take many forms. If we are planning the initiation of a big operation that could run all the way through Syria and Iraq, we are far beyond anything I have the power to do constitutionally. We have quite some trouble justifying to our [Congressional] leaders what we intend to do.[87]

The conversation revealed some apprehensions on the part of both leaders, even a fear that if certain actions occurred, the whole intervention could spin out of control. Eisenhower admitted: "I realize we are opening a Pandora's Box here, but if we don't open it, I think it is disastrous."[88]

Anyone reading the transcript of the conversation will recognize that Eisenhower intended to confine American action to Lebanon and then respond, if necessary, to the unforeseen. Macmillan, on the other hand, appeared to be willing to contemplate a general war in the Middle East, the unstated goal being the removal of Nasser. After the telephone conversation, however, Macmillan sent a cable to Eisenhower, clarifying some of his points and also changing some others. Macmillan voiced his concerns:

What I was trying to say on the telephone was that the action you contemplate must necessarily have great repercussions. It will set off a lot of trouble . . . I have talked this over with my colleagues and we are quite prepared to face these risks if it is part of a determination between us both to face the issues and be prepared to protect Jordan with the hope of restoring the situation in Iraq . . . But what I would like to feel is that it is our joint intention, not merely to be content with rescuing Lebanon (not very important in itself) but to face the larger issues together.[89]

In a separate telegram, Macmillan then addressed the problems in Jordan. "I have just read a telegram saying that the King of Jordan has specifically asked for an assurance from both your government and ours, that we will come to his assistance militarily if he thinks this is necessary to preserve the integrity and independence of Jordan," he wrote Eisenhower. "I very much hope that you will agree that we ought to give this assurance at once."[90] Macmillan then laid out a rationale for supporting King Hussein and for the necessity for joint action between the United States and Great Britain. He left no doubts as to where he believed that the enterprise would lead eventually. Macmillan concluded the cable with the comment that "There has been an attempt to subvert the Jordanian Army and the revolution in Iraq is clearly fostered and supported from Cairo."[91]

From Eisenhower's perspective, however, the initial intervention in Lebanon was not going to be a joint effort between the United States and Great Britain. The operation was going to be carried out by the Americans, lest there be charges that Americans and the British had colluded prior to the intervention, which they had, since Eisenhower carefully consulted with Macmillan before the intervention took place. Macmillan was probably disappointed that a lack of British participation from the outset would lessen the ability of the British to influence events down the line. "You are doing a Suez on me," Macmillan told Eisenhower when he learned on the telephone that the president had already ordered the Sixth Fleet to Lebanon.[92] Moreover, as Eisenhower reminded Macmillan on the telephone, the Americans had no desire to expand the intervention beyond the confines of Lebanon.

On 15 July, Eisenhower informed Congress and the American people that on that day US forces were to intervene in Lebanon. The landings began as planned, despite some initial confusion. Before the day was out, there were American and Lebanese forces patrolling the streets of

Beirut to keep the capital calm. Over the course of the next two weeks, the United States landed an impressive military force in Lebanon, including Marine forces traveling with the Sixth Fleet and Army units, which were sent from Germany, armed with Honest John rockets with nuclear capability.[93]

The mission also had its political and diplomatic dimensions. On 15 July, Ambassador Henry Cabot Lodge introduced a resolution in the United Nations calling for an international peacekeeping force to take over from the American forces once the situation became stabilized. Not surprisingly, the Soviet Union objected and called for the withdrawal of all "foreign troops" in the region.[94]

On 16 July, Eisenhower summoned Robert Murphy, deputy under secretary of state, for another mission to the Middle East. Murphy's basic role was to go to Lebanon and serve as the political representative for Admiral James Holloway, the commander in the Mediterranean who was overseeing the operation. But Murphy's instructions were "conveniently vague;" "he was to promote the best interests of the United States incident to the arrival of our forces in Lebanon."[95]

When Murphy arrived in Beirut, he found an almost incomprehensible situation. "By July 18, [there were] about seventy or seventy five warships near Beirut Harbor, providing quite a spectacle for the fashionable diners on the terrace of the Pigeon Rock restaurant," Murphy recalled, "Marine columns were marching past the luxurious St. George Hotel, where girls were sunning themselves on yachts in the hotel's private basin while Navy jets from the carriers *Saratoga* and *Essex* were shrieking over the city."[96]

Murphy's first responsibility was to meet with Chamoun, whom he found in a "tired and worried" state.[97] Eisenhower wanted Murphy to obtain a clear statement from Chamoun that he would not seek re-election. Murphy would then use America's good offices to assure the competing political factions in the country that the United States would help to make sure of a fair election. Between 17 and 30 July 1958, Murphy met with the leaders of Lebanon's Moslem and Christian factions, during a time of extreme tension with sniping and sporadic violence breaking out virtually every day. Murphy managed to reassure the Lebanese factions that the United States wanted a peaceful resolution to the factional strife in Lebanon. Chamoun finally agreed to lend his support to General Faud Chehab as his successor, hardly an overwhelming choice but the least objectionable of the prospective candidates. On 31 July, Chebab was elected president by a vote of 48 to 8 in the Lebanese Parliament.[98] Murphy left Lebanon to confer with Arab leaders in several other countries, including with King Hussein in Jordan, General Kassem in Iraq, and even with Nasser in Egypt.

The British also played a role in the Lebanon crisis, primarily with their support of Jordan and forestalling any possible Iraq-style coup against the government of King Hussein. On 16 July, the British foreign secretary Selwyn Lloyd left London for Washington where he was to confer with Eisenhower and Foster Dulles. By this time, King Hussein had requested British military support to protect his regime against a possible coup against his leadership and his family. At 11 p.m. that evening, Macmillan convened his Cabinet and his military chiefs to discuss a response to Hussein. The meeting lasted until 3 a.m., when finally a decision was reached in favor of assisting King Hussein. Correspondingly, the British ordered a contingent of 2,700 paratroopers to fly from Cyprus to seize the airport in Amman and protect the position of King Hussein. American participation in the effort, however, was limited to "logistical" support, rather than the dispatch of additional troops.[99]

The intervention in Jordan caused Macmillan a great deal of anxiety, but he nevertheless wanted to increase the stakes involved. Writing to Eisenhower on 17 July, he stated:

> Usually this is a situation in which we ought ideally to have had a proper joint long-term plan before embarking on any operations... Furthermore, I very much dislike from the military point-of-view the sort of operation to which we are now committed in Jordan, where our troops will have no port, no heavy arms, and no real mobility ... My great consolation is that we are together in these two operations in Lebanon and Jordan. We must at all costs not be divided now when we have been forced to play for such high stakes. I am sure that Selwyn [Lloyd] and Foster [Dulles] will be able to work out together a joint plan for the future. Now that we have started on this difficult road, I do not see how we can withdraw until we have somehow restored stability and strength, in at least some areas of the Middle East.[100]

Eisenhower responded to Macmillan's letter on 18 July, expressing some relief that the British and American "operations seem to be satisfactorily coordinated. I recognize that your decision as regards Jordan was a very close and difficult one. We have of course fully supported your decision."[101]

To maintain the position of their troops in Jordan, the British required extensive overflight privileges from Israel. Initially the Israelis granted the permission but then hesitated, under extreme diplomatic pressure applied by the Soviet Union. Between 19 and 21 July, with Russian threats floating around in the diplomatic atmosphere, Macmillan become convinced that the British position in Jordan was growing increasingly precarious. On 22 July, he wrote Eisenhower and requested additional military support, lest a "coup might take place under our noses."[102] Macmillan wanted American troops and a stronger assertion of American influence as it involved the supply and re-supply of the British contingent in Jordan. "I believe that this is a moment of crisis for Jordan and for our whole Middle East policy," Macmillan argued.

> What is needed is less military than political reinforcement – for this I believe the essential thing is that you should send some American troops to be alongside ours on the ground. Not only would this increase the military strength of the forces in Jordan, but it will have an extremely favorable political effect, since it will be visible proof of our support for Jordan's independence.[103]

Eisenhower refused Macmillan's suggestion, however. To be charitable to Ike, one might argue that he did not want to take the first step on a slippery slope leading to greater American military involvement in the Middle East. Responding to Macmillan on 23 July, Eisenhower indicated his sympathy for Britain's problems of supply, pledging the use of some American Globemaster aircraft to the British units in Jordan. but he refused to commit American ground forces. "The introduction of our ground forces raises much more difficult problems," Ike said. "Our public opinion and Congress would, I know, be extremely averse to seeing us take this further step. We believe, as you indicate, that your forces there already stabilize the situation and we hope that it will continue thus, until through the UN or otherwise you are able, logically, to lay down this burden."[104]

If one tended to lean toward Macmillan's view and become critical of the United States, an analysis was offered by Alistair Horne who said that the Americans decided "to leave Jordan exclusively to the British and only support them if they got in trouble."[105] Certainly Ike's conspicuous unwillingness to consider further action beyond Lebanon was a rebuff to Macmillan's position. And the fact that Eisenhower had chosen, on the face of it, to "go it alone" initially must have been a disappointment to Macmillan.

Unquestionably, American policy achieved its aims in Lebanon. Eisenhower wanted a show of strength to keep the region from tilting toward chaos and disorder and he had the military means to apply considerable force. At the time of the Lebanon intervention, John Foster Dulles was especially nervous about the introduction of American troops into the region, fearing that it would lead to a direct confrontation with the Soviet Union. General Nathan Twining, chairman of the Joint Chiefs of Staff, reassured him, however. "Mr. Dulles, I've heard your discussion with the President on this," Twining said:

> I've heard [Robert] Murphy and all of them talking. From what I gather, it's a politically sound thing to do. If it's not politically sound, that's up to you and the President. But we [meaning the Joint Chiefs of Staff] all think it is sound. If it is politically sound, you stop worrying right there. Because in the first place, we just know that the Russians aren't going to jump us. And the second thing, if they do jump us, if they do come in, they couldn't pick a better time, because we've got them over the whing whang [sic] and they know it.[106]

So Eisenhower supplied sufficient force in Lebanon to achieve the basic American objectives: to support a friendly government under internal threat; to convince Nasser that the United States possessed the capability to defend its interests in Middle East; to show the Administration's Congressional critics that the military had the means to respond conventionally, as well as strategically, to threats to the national interest; and to preserve the supply of oil from the Middle East to Western Europe.[107]

By the end of September, American and British troops had begun their departure from Lebanon and Jordan. By 25 October, American troops had completed their withdrawal from Lebanon and British troops had left Jordan by 2 November.[108]

After the Lebanon intervention, Eisenhower and Macmillan wrote separate letters designed to prevent any lasting differences. On 3 November, Eisenhower wrote to Macmillan, "Now that the missions of the British forces in Jordan and the American forces in Lebanon have come to a close, I think that your country and mine can take deep satisfaction in the successful undertaking of wide and historic significance," Eisenhower said. "Without firing a shot in anger ... our forces have achieved what they were sent to Lebanon and Jordan to do ... [preserve] the independence of these small nations against aggressive subversive forces directed from outside."[109] Writing back on 7 November, Macmillan also chose to strike a note of harmony, and especially the importance of acting together. "I have no doubt that there are further difficulties and troubles to be faced [in the Middle East], but so long as your country and mine continue to act together in spirit and deed, as we have over the last months, I am sure we can deal successfully with any eventuality," he wrote.[110]

Several months later, in conversations at Camp David in March 1959, both Eisenhower and Macmillan were still expressing their relief that the British and American intervention in the Middle East had not resulted in a major international crisis. Macmillan noted that the intervention in Lebanon and Jordan had been "a risky performance and that we had been lucky to get out as well as we did." Ike agreed, noting that "it had been the kind of intervention which had not left a nasty after-taste."[111] Years later, Philip de Zulueta commented that the British–American effort in Jordan and Lebanon had been one of the most successful joint operations ever attempted between the two countries and their combined action in 1958 helped to keep the peace in Lebanon for the next quarter-century.[112]

IV

Toward the end of 1958, Dwight D. Eisenhower reflected on the events of that year and then pronounced it as the "worst one in his life."[113] Certainly, a host of difficult problems crossed his desk in 1958 in foreign affairs. Moreover, an economic recession at home translated into major political gains for the Democratic Party in the 1958 congressional elections.

Already well into his final term, Eisenhower was bothered by the gradual decline of his domestic political influence. The morning after the Congressional elections, he attempted to be gracious, saying "There are a lot of [Democrats] that want to do what is good for the country."[114] But, every political leader wants to leave a legacy and, under Eisenhower's leadership, the Republican Party in Congress was considerably weaker at the end of his presidency than when he took office.

Sensing Eisenhower's disappointment, Macmillan wrote to him on 7 November, the day after the election. "I felt that I must write to you to say how much I am thinking about you," Macmillan said.

> You can rest assured that the affection which we all have for you is in no way dependent upon the political fortunes of the Republican

Party... The ups and downs of politics are very strange and sometimes very bitter... I remember well Churchill's feelings in 1945 when he was rejected by a people who had only survived through his leadership. I also remember my admiration for the way in which he accepted the facts and overcame them. If I may say so, I think that your position is not unlike his at the time. It was the Party that dragged Churchill down and not the opposite. Your record and your reputation will remain untarnished by temporary reverses.[115]

Eisenhower responded on 11 November. After thanking Macmillan for his note, Eisenhower unburdened himself about his frustration with the contemporary political scene. The first problem was the public's growing appetite for more government, "One thing bothers me," Ike wrote. "It is the seeming desire of the people of our country to depend more and more upon government – they do not seem to understand that more governmental assistance inevitably means more governmental control."[116]

Eisenhower's second frustration involved the disunity in the Republican Party. The party believed that it was hopelessly divided between its "liberal" and "conservative" wings. To Ike's dismay, the Democrats, while "representing the extremes of the political spectrum, can always unite for the election battle."[117] He concluded his letter by saying that "I'd like to take on the job of reorganizing and revitalizing the [Republican] Party" but he realized that the demands of the presidency made such as effort impossible.[118]

At the end of 1958, Macmillan had finished his second year as Britain's prime minister. In the realm of foreign policy, Macmillan had shown a clear activist tendency, especially on his initiative for a heads of government meeting to consider the problems of the Cold War. The fact that the Americans were lukewarm to the idea did not prevent him from continuing to advocate the view that a summit conference was in everyone's best interest. Macmillan foresaw an international environment where the summit conference "would become [an] annual event, looked forward to not with undue optimism, but accepted as the way the world was to be governed, replacing, in effect, the Security Council and the General Assembly [of the United Nations] which had completely failed to dominate any great issue, and leading to a gradual détente and agreement on more and more points."[119]

Macmillan's attention was also directed toward an upcoming election. Within 18 months, he would have to call a general election and the

Conservatives, in Great Britain, trailing in the polls, would need some bold efforts on Macmillan's part to improve their electoral prospects. As the events of 1959 quickly proved, the notion of summitry played a leading part in Macmillan's domestic electoral strategy.

3
1959: Moscow, Washington, London, Paris

In 1959, Dwight D. Eisenhower and Harold Macmillan were confronted with a new crisis, in addition to their concerns about disarmament, the Middle East, and even the situation in the Far East. On 10 November 1958, Nikita S. Khrushchev, the premier of the Soviet Union, told an audience in Moscow that the Western powers had violated their postwar agreements over the future of Germany. He called upon the United States, Great Britain, and France to end their occupation of West Berlin and said that the Soviet Union intended to negotiate a separate treaty with the German Democratic Republic (East Germany), thereby enabling the East Germans to control the access routes to Berlin. The Western powers, therefore, would be forced to negotiate a separate arrangement with East Germany, a country which they did not recognize diplomatically, in order to maintain their rights in Berlin. Khrushchev's speech was perceived as a tactic designed to force the West out of Berlin. Shortly after his 10 November speech, Khrushchev gave a six-month ultimatum for settling the Berlin issue, holding out the prospect of armed confrontation if a settlement was not reached.[1]

The Berlin crisis hung over the NATO alliance through the end of 1958 and into the winter and early spring of 1959. It certainly gave a new urgency to the problems of the Cold War. Khrushchev's insertion of the Berlin issue into great power relations forced the West to deal with him on personal terms for the first time. For Eisenhower and Macmillan, 1959 became the year of getting to know Nikita Khrushchev. Could Eisenhower and Macmillan realistically hope to do business with the Soviet leader? Beginning in February 1959, when Macmillan traveled to the Soviet Union to confer with Khrushchev and other members of the Soviet hierarchy and ending with Khrushchev's visit to the United States in September 1959, American and British foreign policy-makers tried to defuse the tension in the international situation by face-to-face meetings with the Soviet premier. Admittedly, Macmillan's visit to Moscow was carefully orchestrated to advance his domestic political fortunes by appearing as an international peacemaker. Regardless of the visit's obvious political overtones, however, Macmillan did succeed in making some slight penetration of the closed Soviet society.

Following Macmillan's visit to Moscow, he came to the United States for four days of talks with Eisenhower about the results of his trip to the Soviet Union and also to discuss other Cold War issues. The unstated purpose of the meeting was to start work on measures designed to change the climate of the Cold War from one of confrontation to one directed toward negotiations at the level of heads of government – Macmillan's prized concept of a summit conference.

In retrospect, it is clear that Khrushchev was also looking for some type of opening to the West. In July 1959, due to the crossings of some diplomatic signals on the part of the State Department, he obtained an invitation from Eisenhower to visit the United States in late September 1959, for a series of meetings with the president and a nationwide tour of the country.

In anticipation of Khrushchev's visit, Eisenhower made scheduled trips to the European capitals in late August and early September, consulting with Macmillan in London, Charles de Gaulle in Paris, and Konrad Adenauer in Germany. The purpose of these meetings was to reinforce Allied support for the prospective meetings with the Soviets and also to coordinate their respective policies. These talks were further steps toward the pursuit of détente with the Soviet Union, and with Khrushchev.

Eisenhower met with Khrushchev in late September 1959 but, even before that visit, the Americans made another attempt to understand Khrushchev when Vice President Richard M. Nixon visited the Soviet Union in late July. Nixon's trip resulted in the famous "kitchen debate" with Khrushchev at the American exhibit at the large trade fair in Moscow, an event which was a political triumph for the vice president but probably added little to the American understanding of Khrushchev or his motives.[2]

Khrushchev's trip to the United States was another matter. The Russian leader clearly enjoyed himself, although in public he mixed humor, bombast, and provocation. In his meetings with reporters, Khrushchev routinely denigrated American society as wasteful and inefficient. In his meetings with Eisenhower, he generally conceded nothing, but the mere fact that the two men were meeting led some to call this the "Spirit of Camp David." Khrushchev's visit held out at least some prospect for future success, especially at the summit conference which Macmillan advocated.

Once Khrushchev agreed to a summit meeting with Eisenhower, Macmillan, and de Gaulle, the Western leaders, including Chancellor Konrad Adenauer, met in Paris in December 1959 to make their final plans for the meeting. The various meetings, conferences, and consultations which transpired in 1959 were playing out in Macmillan's favor, and if international tensions eased somewhat, the happy circumstance would be in large measure the result of his tenacious diplomacy.

I

The backdrop for all of these meetings was the Berlin crisis of 1958–59. The chronology of the tension that Khrushchev initiated can be defined by a series of dates. On 10 November 1958, the Soviet premier made his celebrated speech in Moscow, demanding that the four-power status of Berlin be terminated and revealing his intention to hand over the control of the access to East Germany to the communist regime in Berlin. On 27 November 1958, he sent a diplomatic note to the United States, Great Britain, and France, demanding that West Berlin be turned into a neutral city with its access controlled by the East Germans. In effect, Khrushchev delivered an ultimatum: the West had six months to reach an agreement or the Soviet Union would sign a separate treaty with East Germany and give the East Germans control of the access routes to Berlin. On 10 January 1959, he presented the Western powers with a draft peace treaty that conformed to his view of the new structure of Berlin and East Germany.[3]

Khrushchev's threats tended to obscure the weakness of East Germany at that time. Since World War II, West Germany, under the leadership of Chancellor Konrad Adenauer, had developed into the economic and political powerhouse of Western Europe. Thousands of East Germans, especially in the professions, used Berlin as their point to flee the horrible economic conditions in the east.

Moreover, the Western powers refused to recognize East Germany diplomatically, a further humiliation in the eyes of the Soviet Union. In addition, in 1957, after the British–American agreements on defense and the acceptance of the Norstad Plan at the North Atlantic Council meeting, Khrushchev became anxious that the Allies intended to place nuclear weapons in West Germany, and even in West Berlin. The prospect of a rearmed West Germany, combined with the expansion of

NATO's offensive capability in Europe, was a source of serious concern to the Kremlin.[4]

Still, Khrushchev's motivations in fomenting the Berlin crisis remain unclear. Was he attempting to isolate West Germany – a country which was becoming stronger politically, economically, and militarily? Was he attempting to use the Berlin issue to force the Western powers to recognize East Germany and thereby strengthen the Soviet hold on Central Europe? Was he trying to split the NATO allies by playing to some possible differences on the status of Berlin? Was Khrushchev attempting to force the West into a summit meeting where the Soviet premier would be seen as the equal of Eisenhower and the other democratic leaders? Whatever his motivation, as long as Khrushchev kept the ultimatum in effect, the tensions remained.

Clearly Macmillan was deeply concerned about the Berlin problem. He seemed particularly worried that the United States might overreact to Khrushchev's moves. As early as 5 January 1959, he wrote in his diary that he "felt sure . . . that we must not overplay our hand" in regard to Berlin. However, he feared that "the Americans are so far not quite agreed."[5] Two days later, he confided in his diary the need to draft some sort of message to Foster Dulles "to undo some of the confusion which has taken place in Washington."[6] Ever the believer in personal diplomacy among friends, Macmillan concluded on 18 January that he needed to "talk with Dulles and the President," a "method," he noted, that had "worked very well for the past two years."[7]

In that environment, Macmillan also tried to obtain an invitation to visit the Soviet Union, ostensibly to ascertain Soviet intentions on arms control and the future of Germany. Working through diplomatic circles, and especially through Sir Patrick Reilly, the British ambassador to the Soviet Union, Macmillan managed to get his invitation, despite some tortuous negotiations, and scheduled a visit to the Soviet Union for the end of February and the beginning of March. Macmillan's plan to obtain the invitation was carried out in great secrecy; few British knew of his efforts and, once he received the invitation, he did not inform the Americans until late January. This was a solo effort on Macmillan's part, perhaps conditioned by Eisenhower's unwillingness to bring the British into full partnership during the Lebanon crisis.

Macmillan's desire for a visit to Moscow was also driven by domestic political concerns and the necessity to improve the Conservative Party's political fortunes before the next election. One year earlier, Macmillan had proposed to his Cabinet a visit to Russia, but his idea was rejected because the whole enterprise seemed too risky politically, at the time.

By 1959, however, with a general election looming, the Party's leaders needed to go along with Macmillan's move and risk the consequences.[8]

Not surprisingly, the Eisenhower Administration was unenthusiastic about the prospect of Macmillan's visit to the Soviet Union and believed that dangers lurked when the British and Americans did not coordinate their policies on the Soviet Union. The prime minister "can call there ... but he can't speak for us," Ike told British ambassador Harold Caccia. Macmillan's resort to independent action after the rhetoric of "staying together" made Eisenhower secretly hope that the British might return to London "with their tails between their legs."[9] Dulles was likewise convinced that Macmillan's motives were purely political. "Macmillan faces an election, probably in the fall, and wanted to be the hero who finds a way out of the Cold War dilemma," he told Ike.[10]

Nevertheless, Macmillan's impending visit to the Soviet Union forced the Administration to react quickly by sending Dulles to London for consultations with the British. His health failing, Dulles arrived in London on 4 February and immediately began discussions with Macmillan and Selwyn Lloyd. Prior to Dulles's arrival, Macmillan fretted about the secretary of state's views. Beginning with the issuance of Khrushchev's ultimatum on 27 November 1958 and continuing through the early weeks of 1959, the Americans had refused to alter their position on Berlin, although Dulles had floated the idea that East German officials might function as "agents" of the Soviet Union when it came to stamping the travel documents of those who entered West Berlin from East Germany. Of course, this proposal fell considerably short of formal diplomatic recognition of East Germany.

On 31 January, Macmillan again confided to his diary that "I feel rather depressed and frustrated. U.S.A. no 'give' at all on the great world issues, and no ideas."[11] As it transpired, his concern was misplaced. Dulles in fact said he did "not want major military moves into Berlin." Macmillan decided that "Ike [had] overrule[d] the Pentagon" and included in a dinner conversation with Dulles the observation that "above all we must not slip into the 1914 position – mobilization sliding into war."[12] As a bonus, Dulles said, "quite firmly," that "a summit conference, to which the president might come, ought not be excluded [from future talks]," thus coming closer to the prime minister's central diplomatic objective.[13] When Dulles left London, Macmillan was reassured about the American position on Berlin.

Macmillan departed London for Moscow on 21 February and, upon arrival, became the first British prime minister since Churchill to visit the Soviet Union. As Macmillan described it, his purpose in going to the Soviet Union was not "to negotiate" but, rather, "to ascertain Russia's real intentions and establish a better understanding. It was a reconnaissance rather than a negotiation."[14] That evening, he attended a dinner at the Kremlin where Khrushchev, apparently without notes, spoke about a possible "thaw" in the Cold War. Macmillan, likewise, hoped for a relaxation in tensions and mentioned his concern about a potential miscalculation which could lead to armed conflict.[15]

In the first three days of meetings, the British and the Soviets discussed a variety of topics, ranging from the German situation, to the prospects for a summit, to disarmament. Macmillan had promised to keep Eisenhower informed on his trip and on 23 February sent his first cable to Ike. The message was not altogether reassuring. "In spite of their great new power and wealth the Russians are still obsessed by a sense of insecurity," Macmillan wrote.

> I believe that these apprehensions are just as real as their misconceptions about western policy... On Germany and Berlin I detected no signs that there was any weakening in their purpose... I said that if the Soviet position was altogether inflexible as Khrushchev had indicated the situation was very serious indeed.[16]

Macmillan played a delicate game in discussing Berlin with the Russian premier. As he confided to his diary, "We want a negotiated settlement because we do *not* believe that (in spite of all the brave talk) the allies will face war over... the insistence that U.S.S.R. and not D.D.R. shall issue [the] necessary permits [for access to Berlin]" (emphasis Macmillan's). Nonetheless, he talked to Khrushchev "quite boldly about preparations for war."[17]

Eisenhower responded to Macmillan on 24 February, reinforcing the points which the prime minister had made in his cable of the previous day. "Thank you very much for the message giving your impressions after forty-eight hours in Moscow," Ike wrote:

> It seems that [Khrushchev] is intensifying his efforts to create division within the western group and thus weaken our resolution. In effect, he is saying, "We are destroying the western right in Germany and in Berlin, and if you make any attempt to defend those rights you are guilty of aggression and warlike acts."[18]

On 24 February, however, Macmillan's visit almost ended in disaster. While Macmillan and Selwyn Lloyd left early with Soviet deputy premiers Anastas Mikoyan and Frol Kozlov to visit a nuclear research station at Dubna, Khrushchev delivered a blistering attack on the West and its allies in the Middle East. As Richard Aldous has observed, Khrushchev also proposed an Anglo-Soviet Non-Aggression Pact, an offer that went nowhere. On 25 February, Macmillan again cabled Eisenhower. The "atmosphere has been very cool since [Khrushchev's] speech of yesterday," Macmillan wrote. "[All] indications are that he means to go ahead with his plans for turning over approaches to Berlin to [East Germany] and for making a peace treaty with them ... It is on this rather dark note that I am leaving for a four day journey around Russia."[19]

On 26 February, Khrushchev almost destroyed Macmillan's visit with a deliberate snub. Saying that he had a toothache, he told Macmillan and Selwyn Lloyd that he was unable to accompany them on their trip to Kiev. Noting the change in plans, the British press recognized the jeopardy in which Macmillan had been placed.[20] Macmillan called on Lloyd to rescue the situation. In Kiev, Lloyd made a clandestine visit to Vasili Kuznetsov, the Soviet Union's deputy foreign minister. Lloyd's olive branch came in the form of a British offer to recognize East Germany, as a "successor state [which] carried out the existing obligations in Berlin."[21] In his memoirs, *Riding the Storm*, Macmillan made no mention of the Lloyd intervention, saying only that he continued to carry out a "tough line" on Berlin.[22] Regardless, on 27 February, the British received a message from Khrushchev saying that he felt better; his dentist had cured his toothache by using a "British drill."[23]

On 28 February, when Macmillan and his group reached Leningrad, Mikoyan and Andrei Gromyko, the Soviet foreign minister, were present to meet them and gave them advance word of their desire to discuss the Berlin problem at a meeting of foreign ministers. The Soviets had dropped their six-month ultimatum on Berlin. With great satisfaction, Macmillan sent Eisenhower a cable on 2 March, although Lloyd's discussions with Kuznetsov were not mentioned. "The Russians have been showing us a fairer face since the scowl they directed at us last Wednesday," he wrote. "Khrushchev has recovered from his toothache – he even sent me a message in Leningrad to say so ... I think the attitude we tried to maintain of firmness allied with forbearance has paid a dividend. We shall go on maintaining it."[24] On 3 March, Macmillan returned to London and the British press generally applauded his efforts in Moscow.[25]

In the first bilateral meeting of any Western leader with Khrushchev, what had Macmillan accomplished? Certainly, he was able to interpret

Khrushchev's behavior to Ike and the other Western heads of state. In Macmillan's estimation, Khrushchev embodied many of the characteristics which the prime minister discerned in the Russian people: "clever, naïve, inexperienced, sensitive, suspicious of everybody else, and yet cynical themselves."[26] Macmillan believed that Khrushchev was "a mixture between Peter the Great and Lord Beaverbrook... [He] is the boss, and no meeting will ever do business [with him] except a summit meeting."[27]

The political payoffs and other tangible achievements of Macmillan's trip were more visible.[28] First; it was a natural media event. While Macmillan was abroad, he commanded the attention of the press and, although potentially dangerous politically, it also reinforced his image as a national leader. Moreover, with concerns about the tensions in Berlin and the threat of nuclear weapons, Macmillan was able to use his incumbency to identify the Conservative Party as the "Party of Peace" and, thereby, neutralize Labour criticism on that issue. In a sense, he was one of the first democratic leaders to steal the peace issue from his political rivals. To the extent that the imperatives of domestic politics drove Macmillan's visit to Moscow, they were deftly concealed. Even distant observers looked with some admiration on the political benefits of Macmillan's visit. Commenting years later on the trip and the political payoffs which Macmillan gained from it, Andrew Goodpaster summed up Macmillan's performance in two words: "pretty shrewd."[29]

Perhaps one should not be overly cynical about Macmillan's motivations and intentions about going to Moscow, and too clinical in addressing its significance to the diplomatic setting, however. Sir Patrick Reilly saw Macmillan's objectives in more personal terms. As he explained:

> [What] was remarkable was the truly dramatic effect that HM's obvious sincerity, and his hatred of war, his memories of 1914–1918, had in defusing what was undoubtedly a dangerous situation over Berlin... I think that was Macmillan's great contribution with the Russians, and undoubtedly had its effect over the negotiations with Berlin later on.[30]

Likewise, the American diplomatic historian Townsend Hoopes gives Macmillan considerable credit for defusing the tensions over Berlin during his meetings with Khrushchev. Despite taking a fair amount of rhetorical abuse from the Soviet premier, Macmillan had revealed Khrushchev's firm desire not to provoke a military confrontation with the West. As a result of Macmillan's insistence on future negotiations with the Soviets to resolve the Berlin dispute, first at the level of foreign ministers and eventually with a summit conference, Hoopes contends that "much of the intense anxiety was taken out of the 'deadline crisis.'"[31]

Regardless of the motivation behind the trip, the fact remained that Macmillan's visit to Moscow gave the Tories a boost in the opinion polls, pushing them ahead of the opposition Labour Party. On 3 and 10 April, Macmillan held two important political strategy sessions with the leaders of the Conservative Party. The Party's position in the polls was too risky to justify calling for a general election in the late spring or summer. They would have to go for the autumn, and use the intervening five months to reinforce their support with the voters. The election would be in October.[32]

II

Macmillan's trip to Russia in February was followed in March by visits to France, West Germany, and the United States. Not surprisingly, the French and the West Germans were hardly enthusiastic about Macmillan's recent attempt at personal diplomacy. President Charles de Gaulle was always suspicious of the close relationship which existed between the United States and Great Britain, a connection which, in his opinion, worked against the interest of France and its ability to influence events on the world stage. The emergence of the Eisenhower–Macmillan one bore too close a resemblance to the Churchill–Roosevelt relationship during World War II, and de Gaulle, of course, had his difficulties with both leaders. For Konrad Adenauer, Macmillan's diplomacy worked against his plan to cement the West German state more closely to the NATO alliance and away from the idea of an eventual peaceful reunification of Germany. Macmillan's talks with both leaders, first with de Gaulle on 10 March and then with Adenauer on 12 March, were difficult.[33]

Meeting with Ike was a different matter, obviously. On 2 March, Eisenhower cabled a message to Macmillan, complimenting him for the stand which the prime minister had taken on Berlin and inviting him to visit the United States. "At the very least, you demonstrated to the world that strength does not depend upon discourtesy, a great contrast to the provocative attitude and statements of Khrushchev. Thank you very much for the care you took to inform us on a day by day basis of your Russian experience," he wrote.[34] Also, noting that Macmillan intended to visit de Gaulle in Paris and Adenauer in Bonn, Ike advised

Macmillan that he was interested in the gist of these conversations. "I am quite sure that nothing is so important as to have any ideas and plans concerted among the four of us and, as far as possible, with the complete NATO group," he concluded.[35]

Macmillan responded with a letter to Eisenhower on 4 March. Accepting Eisenhower's invitation to visit Washington after he met with Adenauer and de Gaulle, Macmillan spoke of coming to Washington around 18 March. "Would this sort of plan fit in with your arrangements?," he inquired.

> I would propose to be accompanied by the foreign secretary. This afternoon, I made a statement about my visit to the Soviet Union in the House of Commons. The main point was the fact that the Russians now agree that they must negotiate over the Berlin and German questions and that there has been a retreat from their ultimatum attitude. This will give us a little more time to concert our ideas. As you say, it is of the utmost importance that the policies of the four powers, and of the whole NATO, should now be firmly aligned.[36]

Eisenhower returned a cable to Macmillan on 5 March, a message which contained an interesting offer. Eisenhower proposed to move the discussions involving the British and Americans away from Washington and to the presidential retreat at Camp David, Maryland. "About forty-five or fifty-five miles outside of Washington, I have a recreational spot called Camp David," Eisenhower wrote.

> It is an ideal retreat and while it has no recreational facilities (except for a movie room), it is very comfortable, with all the conveniences. If the idea appeals to you as well, I would suggest that you, Selwyn, your Ambassador, your secretary or other individual or individuals you would like, and we go up there about Friday noon, coming back at our leisure some time on Sunday... The helicopter trip is only thirty minutes.[37]

Eisenhower obviously wanted to move sensitive, high-level talks away from the glare of Washington and into the more private and confidential confines of the presidential retreat. It was the first time that an American president had chosen the Camp David site as the setting for high-level negotiations during an important moment in diplomatic history. It was also the first time in Eisenhower's presidency that he conducted high-level talks without John Foster Dulles, who was hospitalized once again.

Eisenhower's friendly invitation to Macmillan notwithstanding, the Administration continued to be wary of the effects of the prime minister's visit to Moscow and the direction of British foreign policy. On 14 March, Eisenhower conferred with Christian Herter, the under secretary of state, about the upcoming meeting with Macmillan and his concerns about the British positions on disarmament, Berlin, and the prospect of a summit meeting. Regarding the summit, Eisenhower expressed a willingness to consider such a meeting if the foreign ministers made some "progress" in their deliberations. But how was "progress" to be defined? According to the notes of the meeting, Eisenhower and Herter agreed that "the most we could expect from [the] Foreign Ministers was that they would define the areas of agreement and particularly the points of disagreement which the Heads of Government would have to negotiate."[38]

As for the prospect of reaching meaningful agreements with the Russians, Eisenhower was more pessimistic. The problems inherent in negotiating a "peace" treaty with a nation like the Soviet Union, "that is strong and growing and independent, are . . . practically insoluble."[39] As for Macmillan's motivations, Eisenhower believed that "there is something behind all this, even more than Macmillan's political ambitions and his forthcoming election." He "could not quite put a finger on what he feels lies behind Macmillan's maneuvers."[40]

With the two sides agreed upon yet another consultation between Eisenhower, Macmillan, and their advisors, the Administration prepared a lengthy agenda for the talks. Discussions on 20 March were to include Macmillan's visits to Moscow, Paris, and Bonn, his assessment of the Soviet attitudes on Berlin, disarmament, and a prospective summit meeting. The topics of Berlin, disarmament, and European security occupied a full day's worth of discussions on 21 March. On 22 March, another full day of talks were scheduled, ranging from the Middle East, to the Far East, to the world economy.[41]

These discussions occurred against the backdrop of the final illness of John Foster Dulles. Although the publicized cause of his latest hospitalization was the recurrence of a hernia problem, Dulles realized that his cancer had reached its terminal stages. On 19 March, Macmillan attended a dinner in his honor in Washington and one of the guests was Janet Dulles, wife of the secretary of state. "Janet Dulles wants [Foster] to resign," Macmillan described the conversation in his diary.

She told me that she wanted to take him away from Washington – to the South – for a bit. She clearly feels that he cannot live very long, and would like to make his remaining time as happy as possible. But I fear that to keep working is his idea of happiness, and that he clings to the job.[42]

In fact, the first order of business for the following day, 20 March, was for Ike and Macmillan to visit Dulles at Walter Reed Hospital. Macmillan recognized the poignancy of the moment; he was about to have one of his last conversations with an obviously dying Foster Dulles. "It was a strange scene," Macmillan remembered.

The President sat on a sofa, the Foreign Secretary and I sat in low arm-chairs in the sitting-room of this "hospital suite" ... while [Foster carried on about] Communism, Germany, Berlin, etc. He was strongly against almost everything. He was strongly against the idea of a Summit; he did not much like the Foreign Ministers meeting ... [But] Foster could not have been nicer or more genuinely glad to see us. He had particularly asked to see me and took my hand and held it clasped in his two hands for quite a few minutes when we said goodbye.[43]

Later, on the afternoon of 20 March, the discussions between the British and the Americans began at 3 p.m. at Camp David. The initial subject was Macmillan's trip to Russia and its significance. Macmillan opened by giving his summary of Khrushchev and his motivations. The Soviet leader was "a mixture of Napoleon and Lord Beaverbrook," the "undisputable boss" and "no business can be done with the Russians except with Khrushchev."[44] The Russians were very sensitive to the matter of espionage and believed that the West was undertaking a great deal of spying from a base in West Berlin, harboring "more than 200 western espionage organizations."[45]

The most comforting revelation from the discussion involved the conclusion by Macmillan and Lloyd that Khrushchev was, in effect, satisfied with the status quo in Germany. While stating that the Soviets would obviously resist a "roll back" of their satellite in East Germany, they were in no hurry to conclude a separate treaty with the East Germans. Lloyd reported that the Soviets did not expect Great Britain (or any other Western power, by implication) to recognize East Germany's borders diplomatically but instead to deal with it on its present basis. Macmillan recalled Khrushchev's remark, "where the tree has fallen, let it lie."[46]

According to Macmillan and Lloyd, the Russians were prepared to negotiate with the West on virtually any subject, but with strong conditions attached to any set of discussions. They were willing to discuss Berlin and the future of Germany, but not at the expense of disrupting the present situation. They were willing to discuss disarmament and arms control, but would never accept "inspection teams roaming around freely over their territory largely for purposes of espionage."[47] And they were willing to disregard the date of 27 May as the deadline for resolving the Berlin dispute.[48]

The next round of conversations dealt with Macmillan's perspective on his talks with Charles de Gaulle and Konrad Adenauer. He found that de Gaulle was very much determined to have the French become one of the world's nuclear powers but that he also was very firm on the need to remain in Berlin. Adenauer was another matter. Fearing that the British were going wobbly on Berlin, Adenauer had proposed to Macmillan that the allies offer Khrushchev a five-year "standstill" agreement on the status quo as the condition for accepting a summit conference with the Russians. Macmillan indicated that he had opposed such an idea, and attempted to clear up any misconception that the British had ever favored such a proposal.

Trying to add some levity to the discussion, Eisenhower ("jokingly," according to the minutes of the meeting) "stated that if we could get a commitment from the Russians to make no change in the *status quo* for five years then we could postpone going to the summit until the end of that period."[49] Turning serious, however, the president emphasized that he would not go to a meeting with "his hat in his hand."[50] The foreign ministers' meetings were crucial; the Soviets needed to demonstrate their serious intentions and willingness to negotiate in good faith as a precondition for a meeting of heads of government.

The two leaders then discussed the future of Berlin and its relationship to a possible summit meeting. Eisenhower began the discussion with the vigorous declaration that the United States "would absolutely refuse 'to throw the West Berliners to the wolves.'"[51] Macmillan responded by proposing two "acceptable" solutions for the Berlin issue; dealing with the East Germans as "agents" of the Soviet Union without formal recognition of East Germany or negotiating a treaty which would be registered with the United Nations that guaranteed Allied access rights to Berlin.

The discussion then turned to the topic of a summit meeting. Eisenhower's caution was obvious to everyone. According to the minutes of the meeting, "A prolonged summit conference, or a series of conferences, would be impossible for him by reason of the requirements of our Constitution."[52] Ike was concerned about the unsatisfactory situation which had been created when President Woodrow Wilson left the United States in 1918–19 for a lengthy period to participate in the conference at Versailles. "It might be possible for him to go for two or three days at the opening and leave Vice President Nixon as his personal representative, returning himself at the conclusion of the conference if the results warranted it," Eisenhower said.[53] Macmillan countered with a suggestion that the conference be held in the United States, "presumably as a means of avoiding the constitutional difficulties of a prolonged absence of the President from the country."[54] Macmillan then suggested Newport, Rhode Island as a possible site. "Perhaps the lavish beauty of the resort would appeal to the Russians' tastes. [We] are dealing here with ill-bred, uneducated, sensitive people who think they are gaining a better position by being reasonable and respectable."[55] Eisenhower turned down this suggestion but offered an alternative; perhaps the summit could be held at the Cow Palace in San Francisco which had been the site for the establishment of the United Nations.[56]

By 4.40 p.m., the conferees were ready for a recess, especially after they had aired their disagreements on the matter of a summit conference. Eisenhower offered to take Macmillan by car to his farm in nearby Gettysburg, Pennsylvania and the two leaders set off for a private conversation in the presidential limousine. According to Macmillan's version of the conversation, the summit issue was not mentioned. Instead, Eisenhower talked about Dulles's illness and the problems which it created for him in finding his successor. He realized that Christian Herter was the logical successor, but Herter's arthritic condition presented problems from a physical standpoint. Macmillan both liked and admired Herter, however, and thought he would perform capably. He entertained the hope that Herter would be more flexible than Dulles.[57]

On the ride, Macmillan also noted that in spite of Ike's "crudity and lack of elegance," the president did "have some very remarkable ideas" that transcended the specific agenda of the formal meetings. According to Eisenhower, "The thought that the U.S.A., U.K., Canada, Australia, etc. should make a Federation and combine in something like the European Common Market (to start with) ending in a political merger or Federal constitution" was ultimately "the only way to resist Communism and ... attract the neutral world."[58]

Discussions resumed between the British and Americans at 6.30 p.m. Andrew Goodpaster's and Livingston Merchant's notes of the evening meeting convey the tension between the two sides. According to both observers, Eisenhower and Macmillan disagreed vigorously on the preconditions for a summit meeting. Essentially, the issue came down to whether the summit depended on concrete results at a meeting of foreign ministers (the American position) or a Soviet agreement to participate in a foreign ministers' meeting followed by the setting of a date for a summit. When the drafts were discussed, and agreement was not forthcoming, Macmillan took the floor. According to Merchant's notes, "The Prime Minister became exceedingly emotional. He said that we were dealing with a matter which in his judgment affected the whole future of mankind. He said that: 'World War I – the war which nobody wanted – came because of the failure of the leaders at that time to meet at the Summit. [Sir Edward] Grey had gone fishing and the war came in which the UK lost two million young men.'"[59]

Macmillan's allusion to World War I did not persuade Eisenhower to alter his views. According to Merchant's notes, Ike expressed the view that there had been meetings before World War II and those meetings had not prevented a war. Macmillan shot back: "We were dealing with a madman – Hitler" at that time.[60] Macmillan then outlined a truly horrific scenario if he had to "take his people into war without trying the Summit first."[61] If a nuclear war was fought in Europe, Britain was largely defenseless against attack. "A substantial part of their people" would need to be disbursed to Canada and Australia. "Eight bombs," Macmillan kept repeating, "would mean 20 or 30 million Englishmen dead."[62]

Eisenhower then rejoined the rhetorical attack. In a nuclear war, Eisenhower told Macmillan, the United States would also suffer enormous casualties. The lower level of American casualties Ike "had seen estimated was 67 million. We don't escape war by surrendering on the installment plan."[63] He would not, according to Merchant's notes, "be dragooned to a Summit meeting."[64]

Equally determined, Macmillan countered by saying that he was "an old man" and the matter of a summit was "the most fateful decision he would ever have to take."[65] He said that he wanted to sleep on the issue and not discuss it any more that evening.

Andrew Goodpaster's notes of this important meeting roughly corresponded to Merchant's. He did, however, record Eisenhower as saying as many as 70 million people (rather than Merchant's more precise 67 million) would be the total of American casualties in a nuclear war.

"While others could talk about going to a Summit meeting under threat of attack by the Soviets, he for one would not attend and they could hold their Summit meeting without him," Goodpaster recorded.[66] With reference to meetings before World War II, Eisenhower stated that "Neville Chamberlain went to such a meeting and it is not the kind of meeting with which he intends to be associated."[67] The direct reference to Munich probably caused Macmillan to blanch, since he had been an outspoken opponent of Appeasement in the 1930s. The tone of Merchant's account leads one to suspect that a certain uneasiness and friction dominated the conversation while Goodpaster received the opposite impression, saying that [while] "the statements were made with great firmness and sharpness, there was no evidence of personal animosity – in fact just the opposite."[68]

The following day, 21 March at 9.30 a.m., the British and Americans reconvened at Camp David for another attempt to resolve their impasse over the summit. Macmillan began the discussion in a conciliatory mood but essentially repeated his position of the previous evening. Eisenhower was equally firm; he refused to participate in a summit meeting "come hell or high water" without first seeing measurable progress at a foreign minister's conference.[69] The two delegations then set about to reconcile their respective positions on the subject. Finally, agreeable language was approved by each side with the final result that the timing for the summit meeting would be dependent upon the success of the foreign ministers to clarify the issues involved. Livingston Merchant and Sir Anthony Rumbold were set to work to draft statements which could be sent to the French and West Germans, as well as the British and French NATO representatives.[70]

Having dispensed with the issue of a summit conference, the two sides turned next to a discussion of Berlin and how this issue was to be discussed either at the foreign ministers' level or by the heads of government. The situation hardly lent itself to a simple solution. Eisenhower argued that the West was in a relatively strong position in the city. Merchant's notes of the conversation record Eisenhower as mentioning that "we had sent some people over to take a look on the ground at exactly how the road, air, and rail communications to Berlin looked. So far the morale in the city was good and there were weaknesses in the Soviet position that might tend to make them want to negotiate."[71]

Eisenhower then introduced the concept of securing some "breathing space" for a "respectable agreement" with the Russians for the near future. The question of the relationship between East Germany and West Germany, as well as the possible reunification of the country be avoided in talks with the Russians. "What we must find was the best formula to maintain the *status quo* and give the Soviet Union the necessary face-saving," Ike argued.[72] Macmillan agreed with this sentiment, noting that

> everyone was in favor of re-unification in principle, but the curious situation was that nobody wanted it now, neither the Russians, Adenauer nor the French [though he did not say so, he left the clear implication that Britain too did not want it] Therefore, he concluded, a *de facto* approach seemed the only feasible one.[73]

On the afternoon of 21 March, the two delegations dealt with two thorny problems, "contingency planning" on Berlin in the event that the communists restricted Western access to the city, and disarmament. The discussion on contingency planning for Berlin was especially serious. Up to this point in the meetings, the participants had been restricted to Eisenhower, Macmillan, Christian Herter, Selwyn Lloyd, John Hay Whitney, the United States ambassador to Great Britain, Sir Harold Caccia, the British ambassador to the United States, and several other foreign policy experts. At this meeting, however, they were joined by General Nathan B. Twining, chairman of the Joint Chiefs of Staff; Donald Quarles, the deputy secretary of defense; Robert Murphy, deputy under secretary of state; John N. Irwin II, assistant secretary of defense for international security affairs (ASD/ISA), and Major John S.D. Eisenhower, who served as the assistant to Andrew Goodpaster. The meeting began with Goodpaster's rather ominous observation that "this meeting was concerned initially with contingency planning, in case the Communists obstruct access to West Berlin."[74]

Quarles then took charge of the discussion. He asked Irwin to comment upon a number of measures that the West had taken to alert its forces, including a re-examination of the inspection points. Irwin said that "these steps, although not observable to the public, will in all likelihood be picked up by the Soviets, and such in fact is the intent."[75] Twining then reviewed some additional military steps that had been taken, including moving submarine forces closer to the European theater, increasing the alert status for the Second fleet (Atlantic), Sixth Fleet (Mediterranean) and the First Fleet (Pacific) (alerted for the Persian Gulf). Air squadrons in Europe had also been placed on a higher state of alert.[76]

Eisenhower then turned to Macmillan and inquired if the British had made any additional preparations. The prime minister responded that the British would take any measures stipulated by General Norstad, the NATO commander, but Norstad had not made any requests at that point.[77]

Quarles then summarized the extent of plans and responses in the event that the communists closed off Western access. Four plans were in the process of development: to reopen access on the ground through local ground operations; to reopen access by air, presumably similar to the Berlin airlift of 1948; to take naval action against Soviet forces; and, ominously, "the initiation of measures of general warfare."[78] Lloyd then inquired of Quarles and Twining, "When we come to the breaking point, whatever it is, what would we do." In response, Twining stated if the Soviets use force to prevent the passage of traffic into Berlin, "this action would let us know that this is a major military operation." Did that necessarily mean war, however? On that point, Quarles was more reassuring. In such a situation, since the Soviets would "have the initiative and we are therefore on a tail chase, military actions on our side are not too desirable. Actions of a political character are better." Irwin emphasized that the use of a "substantial force" to deal with the Soviet tactics would only occur "after all political and other measures have been tried."[79] In the midst of this uncertain situation, Eisenhower "said it would be a good idea to ask the Soviets on May 11 what they planned to do."[80] Nevertheless, Eisenhower was clearly not prepared to sit idly by in the face of a threat from the Soviet Union. His major concern was having public opinion with the West in case any military action, "such as blockading the Dardanelles and the Baltic," was necessary.[81]

The final item on the schedule for discussion on 21 March involved disarmament. By this time, both the Western alliance and the communist bloc identified the inspection system for underground tests as the major sticking point. The Americans and the British continued to insist on procedures for an on-site inspection regimen; the Soviets continued to oppose it, not wanting to admit foreign inspectors onto their territory.[82]

Joining the meeting were Dr James Killian, head of the Presidential Science Advisory Committee (PSAC); and John McCone, who had replaced Lewis Strauss as the head of the Atomic Energy Commission. Killian and McCone summarized the technical aspects of the nuclear testing issue and the imprecise nature of being able to detect nuclear tests. Macmillan summarized the basic purpose of the inspections, from the Allied perspective. They were: to get rid of fallout; to limit the number of countries learning how to make nuclear weapons; and to make some forward movement in applying the principle of international control.[83]

Macmillan also related that the Russians had proven to be very obstinate on the question of inspections; once again their phobia was tied to espionage. Khrushchev had told Macmillan that the Soviet Union experienced 2,000 earthquakes annually and the proposal put forth by the Americans and the British "was designed for espionage purposes."[84] Macmillan attempted to reassure Khrushchev that nothing approaching 2,000 annual inspections was contemplated by the West but, if the Russians wished, an agreement might be reached putting a ceiling on the number of inspections that each side could make in a given year. With no serious consensus in sight, the two sides agreed to let the matter rest until the Geneva talks resumed in mid-April.

On 22 March, the two sides nevertheless engaged in a full day's worth of meetings. The morning meeting was given over to a general discussion of economic matters, the problems in the Far East involving the People's Republic of China and Nationalist China, and relations with de Gaulle. Eisenhower and Macmillan both expressed concern about the impact of continued large-scale defense spending on their national economies. Eisenhower bemoaned the fact that there were "built-in forces within our economy which tend to force prices up ... Defense plants have this tendency since their contracts are generally on a cost-plus basis."[85] Likewise Macmillan argued that the British defense industry was upsetting economic stability, mentioning that "the aircraft production industry ... is highly over-inflated, the reduction of which will inevitably cause major economic dislocation."[86]

The Washington talks ended with a final meeting between Eisenhower, Macmillan, Herter, Lloyd, Whitney, Caccia, and their advisors. There was no official communiqué, but Eisenhower and Macmillan signed the agreed minutes. According to Goodpaster's notes,

> The President thought this had been a most effective meeting and Macmillan agreed that the method used – of meeting at Camp David – had proven very fine. Despite reports about the cold, all had really been quite comfortable. The President noted that the meeting had been held without a communiqué and hoped that this would constitute a precedent. He said meeting with Mr. Macmillan has one advantage. Since he is not a Head of State, it is possible to avoid the ceremonial aspects of such a visit.[87]

In that fashion, the fourth bilateral discussion in two years between Eisenhower, Macmillan, and their advisors came to a close. The most important product to emerge was the design for a foreign ministers' meeting to be followed by a heads of government meeting at the summit. In a sense, the language of the agreement revealed a compromise between the views of both Eisenhower and Macmillan, and neither side was totally pleased with the outcome. The British believed that the Americans were dragging their feet on a possible meeting with the Soviets while the Americans believed that the British were in too much of a hurry to make concessions to the Russians.[88] Before the British left Washington, however, Eisenhower made one last request of Macmillan. "Would there be any problem in his visiting the British soil in the Bahamas?," Ike inquired. "There is a very pleasant golf course and place to stay at Eleuthera and he had been thinking of the possibility of a visit there." Macmillan answered, "[There] was no problem whatsoever."[89]

III

On 30 March, Khrushchev accepted the Western proposal for a meeting of the foreign ministers to discuss the outstanding issues of the Cold War: the arms race, disarmament, and the future of Berlin.[90] On 11 May in Geneva, Secretary of State Herter, Foreign Secretary Lloyd, Soviet Foreign Minister Andrei Gromyko, and French Foreign Minister Maurice Couve de Murville convened for their round of talks. Completely unproductive, the meetings of the foreign ministers recessed on 20 June, lasting only 41 days.[91] The problems encountered at Geneva led to some considerable concerns about the German situation and Khrushchev's continuing efforts to make threatening statements about Berlin.

Clearly, the priority which Eisenhower had placed on "progress" at the level of the foreign ministers was not generating the results hoped for by either Eisenhower or Macmillan. More seriously, the lack of progress endangered the prospects for a summit meeting. On 16 June, Macmillan attempted to play down the talks among the foreign ministers in a letter to Eisenhower. Coming quickly to his point, Macmillan proposed that Eisenhower should officially call for a summit meeting between the heads of government immediately after the conclusion of the meetings of the foreign ministers. If Eisenhower was unwilling to follow that suggestion, Macmillan indicated a desire to make the call for a summit himself. "The discussions [between the foreign ministers] so far give small grounds for optimism," Macmillan wrote.[92] "The Foreign Ministers cannot go on much longer at Geneva; and, if in the next few days deadlock on Berlin appears to be inevitable, I believe that the wisest course would be to suggest as a next step a meeting of the kind indicated above."[93]

Eisenhower was unpersuaded by Macmillan's latest overture on summitry. On 17 June, he sent a curt reply to the prime minister. "Dear Harold," Ike wrote, "I think that for the moment at least we are doing all that humans can do – and must hope for the best."[94] Macmillan still persisted, however. "We must maintain a public posture in which we can rally our people to resist a Russian attempt to impose their will [on Germany] by force," Macmillan wrote to Eisenhower on 23 June.

> All the same, it would not be easy to persuade the British people that it was their duty to go to war in defense of West Berlin. After all, in my lifetime we have been dealt two nearly mortal blows by the Germans. People in this country will think it paradoxical, to use a mild term, to have to prepare for an even more horrible war in order to defend the liberties of people who have tried to destroy us twice in this century.

Realizing the blunt, almost undiplomatic manner in which he was making these points, Macmillan concluded his letter as graciously as he could. "I wish of course that we could meet and talk. It is so difficult to put on paper all that one feels. I hope therefore that you will not mind my sending you these frank thoughts. Do tell me what you think."[95]

With the disarmament talks going nowhere and the foreign ministers' meeting in recess, Eisenhower decided to jump-start the negotiating climate. On 10 July, he told Herter, Douglas Dillon, who had become under secretary of state after the death of Foster Dulles, and Andrew Goodpaster that he wanted to talk personally with Khrushchev and was willing to use the opening of the Russian Exhibition in New York as a suitable occasion for a meeting. The offer called for Khrushchev to open the Russian Exhibition in New York, give a speech before the United Nations, and then remain in the United States for talks with Eisenhower. In return, Eisenhower would visit the Soviet Union in October after he had visited India as part of his international goodwill trip. The invitation to Khrushchev was to be conditioned on some progress at the foreign ministers' meetings, meaning that some concessions would be expected from the Soviets. Eisenhower turned to Robert Murphy to make the offer to Khrushchev.[96]

Murphy met with Soviet Deputy Premier Frol Kozlov in New York on 12 July and made the offer of the Khrushchev visit – without mentioning the precondition for progress at the foreign ministers' meeting.[97] In Andrew Goodpaster's words, "The Russians snapped it up just like that!"[98] On 22 July, Khrushchev announced his willingness to come to

Washington for a ten-day visit, a longer period than Eisenhower had anticipated. The fact that Khrushchev was coming without making any prior concessions irritated the president but, in his own words, he "would have to pay the penalty" and follow through on the invitation.[99]

In London, the news of Khrushchev's visit to Washington created considerable apprehension, just as the announcement of Macmillan's visit to the Soviet Union in February had generated alarm in Washington. Macmillan thought that Eisenhower's offer to Khrushchev was an example of "stupidity, naivete, and incompetence."[100] As Macmillan later told British journalist Robert McKenzie, he was "very upset because it gave the impression that the Americans were going to do a direct deal, one great vast country with the other, the great Eastern colossus with the great Western colossus, over our heads."[101] Many years afterward, Macmillan revised his views considerably. The Khrushchev visit was "not that at all. It was [that] dear Ike just asked him because he suddenly thought it would be a nice thing to invite him to have a look around."[102]

The possibility of being excluded from the diplomatic scene as Eisenhower and Khrushchev conferred in the United States led Macmillan to send a flurry of letters to the president. On 21 July, Macmillan wrote, offering "one or two comments from me which might be useful to [Vice President Richard Nixon]" in his forthcoming trip to the Soviet Union. In Macmillan's estimation, Khrushchev "has set great store by international relations. I suppose that he says to himself that Lenin built the Party and Stalin created the empire; what am I going to do?"[103] Then, on 30 July, Macmillan sent another letter to Ike, proposing that the Western heads of government agree to a meeting between themselves in August, followed by Khrushchev's visit to the United States in September, Eisenhower's visit to the Soviet Union in October, and then a formal summit meeting in November, with Quebec being the prospective site for the gathering.[104]

Lest Eisenhower forget the importance which Macmillan attached to the summit meeting, Macmillan wrote,

> I believe that you and I are pretty well at one on a plan for continued negotiations in the months ahead. There is, I think, only one real difference between us. You are reluctant to say now that there will be a Summit meeting, though I believe that you recognize that it is in fact inevitable. I, on the other hand, should like to get it settled and announced now that there will be such a meeting before the end of the year.[105]

On 5 August, Eisenhower announced that Khrushchev would be coming to the United States on 15 September for a ten-day visit. In preparation for his meetings with the Soviet leader, Eisenhower announced that he would visit Bonn, Paris, and London in advance for consultations with Adenauer, de Gaulle, and Macmillan.

Between 27 and 30 August, Eisenhower visited London for another round of talks with Macmillan, but this time there was an important difference. A British general election was in the offing, just as Dulles had predicted early in the year. Despite the differences between Eisenhower and Macmillan over Germany, disarmament, and arms control, the prime minister was obsessed with bringing Ike to Britain in the run-up to the general election. During the summer of 1959, he had dropped some not-so-subtle hints that Eisenhower should visit Britain. On 1 August, Eisenhower wrote to Macmillan that he intended to visit London at the end of the month, in preparation for meeting with Khrushchev.[106] A relieved Macmillan responded on 6 August and suggested that the two leaders hold some of their talks at Chequers, the country home of the prime minister, reminiscent of their meetings at Camp David in March.[107] Ike responded on 7 August, "Chequers will be fine," and then characteristically added a number of items for discussion.[108] Barely able to contain himself, Macmillan wrote back to Ike on 8 August. "I cannot tell you how much I am looking forward to your visit," he told the president.[109]

Eisenhower and his party arrived at London International Airport at Heathrow at 6.45 p.m. on 27 August. Given the time of arrival, Macmillan was expecting only a modest turnout of well-wishers along the route to London. He was wrong. As Macmillan recounted in his memoir, *Riding the Storm*:

> We drove together in an open car. The distance is seventeen miles. It took us nearly two hours. There was a wonderful turnout all along the route. It was a remarkable demonstration of confidence and goodwill. It was also impressive from another point of view. The car moved at a snail's pace. All of the roads and streets were crowded, and there was no security control of any kind. Most of the time, the President stood up and waved to the people, and some of the time, I stood up also and waved by his side.[110]

With respect to the purely political dimension of Eisenhower's visit, one must consider the fact that Macmillan took a certain amount of risk by inviting the president to Britain so soon before an imminent general election. British memories of the Suez crisis could have colored their enthusiasm for Eisenhower and might have made the situation embarrassing for the prime minister. Such a possibility was quickly dispelled, however.

Eisenhower never professed any worries about his reception in Britain. "I knew I had friends there and, in a sense, felt as if I were coming home," he wrote in his memoirs.[111] The Americans who were traveling with Eisenhower were likewise overwhelmed by the public response. On the ride from Heathrow to London, Andrew J. Goodpaster traveled in a car with Tim Bligh, an officer in the Royal Navy (who later became a good friend of Goodpaster's). Both men were awestruck by the reception given the president. "The crowds went on and on," Goodpaster remembered. "There was a tremendous outpouring of affection for Eisenhower. Some of this was personal for Eisenhower, who was always a hero in Britain. But it also symbolized that the British knew that the United States was with them."[112]

On 28 August, Eisenhower, his son John, and Macmillan flew to Scotland to spend the day with Queen Elizabeth II, Prince Philip, and their family at the royal castle in Balmoral. Although pregnant, the Queen hardly slackened from her duties as the hostess of the gathering. She insisted on doing the cooking and performing the kitchen duties. Ike washed the dishes.[113] It was a time of relaxation for Eisenhower who spent part of the time driving golf balls outside the castle grounds. The advisors remained behind in London to confer on the wide range of subjects which involved both nations.

Indeed, whenever Ike and Macmillan got together, extensive discussions were a fact of life. With a summit on the horizon, relations between the members of NATO, disarmament, and instability in the Middle East and Far East to consider, the two leaders had plenty to discuss. For example, the record of the visit showed that Eisenhower met on 29 August at the prime minister's country home, Chequers, to discuss, among other topics, "Laos" (a new subject), "contingency planning" (for Berlin), "President's Discussions in Bonn," and "Talks with de Gaulle." Early that same evening, Macmillan and Eisenhower had a lengthy, private discussion about Khrushchev's forthcoming visit to the United States as well as the disarmament issue.[114] The next day, Eisenhower and Macmillan met privately to discuss the test ban issue.[115] They were joined later that afternoon by their respective delegations for further discussions on the subject.[116]

The purely political part of the visit was a joint appearance by Eisenhower and Macmillan on British television on 31 August. The setting for the televised broadcast was the living quarters of 10 Downing Street, then undergoing renovation. It was to be a casual, extemporaneous conversation between two old friends who simply chatted about the nature of their friendship, the positive relations between their two countries, and the success of their talks over the past two days.

Actually, the idea for the broadcast had come during a conversation between Harold Evans, Macmillan's press secretary, and James C. Hagerty, Eisenhower's press secretary. Both men believed that a televised appearance by Eisenhower, in an informal setting, would be the best means of publicizing his appearance throughout Great Britain. Evans also believed that Macmillan's skills as a conversationalist and host would be put to great effect in a relaxed setting.[117]

But the televised broadcast was anything but extemporaneous and spontaneous. Macmillan left nothing to chance when it involved the political impact of a conversation with the most powerful vote-getter on the planet.

First, Macmillan used the Conservative Party's funds for paid political broadcasts (or PPBs) for his half-hour with Eisenhower. As Alexander Macmillan recalled, the prime minister "wanted to have absolute control over the broadcast." He chose not to use the "free time" offered by the British Broadcasting Corporation (BBC) for the event because he wanted no interference by BBC producers, directors, or reporters. The broadcast was completely controlled by Macmillan, including the selection of Norman Collins as the director of the program. As Alexander Macmillan recalled,

> Collins was an independent film producer who actually taught my grandfather how to operate on television. There was the famous occasion when my grandfather was going to make a speech to the country and he asked the general director of the BBC, "How many people will be watching?" The general director said, "16 million." [Macmillan] had never spoken to over 16,000 before and he said, "16 million, what an oration." So, when my grandfather entered the studio, Collins closed the door behind him, slammed his foot against the door so nobody could get in and literally shook my grandfather and said, "No, Harold, not 16 million, [but] two!" My grandfather threw his prepared speech into the waste basket, and did the speech as though he was talking to people in their living rooms... That was what he tried to achieve in his broadcast with Ike; the two of them sitting together in dinner jackets, very patrician. Ike knew what was

going on and I think he felt he was being manipulated quite a long way.[118]

Stylistic considerations aside, the broadcast was also far removed from the casual, intimate scene which the viewers saw on their television sets. The program was carefully scripted, and fortunately the historical record has been preserved of this highly organized broadcast. In Eisenhower's presidential papers is the actual script of the program, and Eisenhower's handwritten notes for the program. These documents provide a fascinating insight into the extraordinary length to which the two leaders went in capitalizing on this opportunity. The notes read as follows:

INTRODUCTION
Prime Minister– 1 minute leading to subject of
ANGLO-AMERICAN RELATIONS
Prime Minister– 2 minutes
President– 2 minutes
    1. Concur – since 1941 personally involved. Relations never better.
    2. Mention Canada
    3. Introduce NATO, organization to maintain peace.
PEACE AND WAR
Prime Minister– 2 minutes
President– 1 minute on character of war
    1. No winner – unless one side grows neglectful. Whole reason for these present meetings and visit with Soviet Premier is to explore to the bottom of every method for promoting peace.
    2. Introduce
UNDEVELOPED NATIONS
President– 2 minutes
    1. Serious problem – almost 2 billion people, lacking necessaries, must be helped.
    2. Civilization's responsibility – cooperation mandatory.
    3. Mention U.N.
Suggest to P.M. that Britain has a special problem in Britain and Commonwealth
Prime Minister– 3 minutes
President– 1 minute introducing <u>Importance of trade</u>
EXPANSION OF TRADE
Prime Minister– 2 minutes (wool??)
President– 3 minutes – Contacts

1. People-to-people
2. Ideas
3. Books
4. Science-health, etc.
   Histories-culture

<u>FINALE</u> (Dinner Guests waiting)
<u>Prime Minister</u>– 30 seconds
<u>President</u>– 30 seconds, opportunity to thank people for kindness to me and party ending on "God Bless Your Gracious Queen"[119]

Intentionally, the broadcast featuring Eisenhower and Macmillan touched on no controversial topics. But, at one point, Macmillan did press Eisenhower, ever so slightly, on the subject of the summit meeting. "I have always wanted a summit meeting and I believe your initiative will put us into position to get it under the best conditions," Macmillan said. Almost on cue, Eisenhower staked out his position. "I will not be a party of a [summit] meeting that is going to depress and discourage people," he stated. "Therefore we must have some promise of fruitful results."[120]

The other facet of the program which obviously stood out was the difference in the manner in which the two men addressed each other. Throughout the entire broadcast, Macmillan scrupulously referred to Eisenhower as "Mr. President." Also, throughout the entire broadcast, Eisenhower referred to Macmillan simply as Harold. "He called him Harold," Andrew Goodpaster remembered, "and that shocked more than a few of the British."[121]

Far from being offended by Eisenhower's dismissal of protocol in favor of his easy informality, Macmillan relished Ike's genuine friendliness. "It was a political plus," Alexander Macmillan remembered:

> The President was the head of state; he had to be called that. [For Eisenhower to call Macmillan by his first name] in Britain, particularly at that time, it implied a great intimacy. If Ike had called him Prime Minister, that would be too much the politician. But here he was, "buddy-buddy" with the most powerful man in the world. To be on first-name terms with the quarterback is pretty good, particularly when you're in the little league [yourself], to mix a metaphor.[122]

Following the broadcast, Macmillan's political opponents in the Labour Party sharply criticized him for "exploiting" Eisenhower's visit to Britain and for introducing the American president into the campaign. (To be fair, Secretary of State Herter met with several members of Britain's Labour Party while the Americans were in Britain.) In fact, once Macmillan called for the dissolution of Parliament on 8 September and the parties released their respective manifestoes, Hugh Gaitskell, the leader of the Labour Party, made one of Macmillan's statements on 31 August a point of contention. "In a television chat with President Eisenhower," the Labour Manifesto read, "Mr. Macmillan told us that the old division of Britain into the two nations, the haves and the have nots, has disappeared. Tory prosperity, he suggested, is shared by all. In fact, the contrast between the extremes of wealth and poverty is sharper today than eight years ago."[123] On 5 September, according to a cable sent to Washington by American ambassador John Hay Whitney the deputy leader of the Labour Party, James Griffith, accused the Conservatives of "blatant electioneering," a charge which was certainly true.[124] Even though an election had not been called, the Conservatives drastically increased their spending on political advertising, both in the newspapers and on posters throughout the country, prior to Eisenhower's visit.[125]

For the record, Macmillan refused to acknowledge any scheme to exploit Eisenhower's visit for partisan political purposes. In his memoirs, he simply acknowledged the criticism and then brushed it off. "Naturally, I was accused of arranging this visit for my own electoral purposes," Macmillan wrote. "But although the coincidence may have been happy, it was certainly not by my design."[126] At the time, Macmillan must have realized that he had pulled off a major political coup with Eisenhower, while his two Labour rivals, Hugh Gaitskell and Aneurin Bevan, were in Moscow, conferring with Khrushchev.[127]

If Macmillan, indeed, was guilty of exploiting Eisenhower for his own political purposes, Ike was hardly an unwitting victim. The visit also served his purposes, apart from politics. He had managed to reinforce British support for his meetings with Khrushchev and the preservation of his options as the leader of the NATO alliance when it came to negotiating with the Russians. As John Hay Whitney cabled to Secretary of State Herter after Ike's departure,

> Personal impact of President was enormous... President was acclaimed in manner exceeding that accorded any other foreign leader in peace-time years. Normally undemonstrative British people turned out in force to greet President everywhere along the way. He left them with image of vigorous, active, and healthy President,

sincerely dedicated to search for peace and willing to lead his country along untried but promising paths in the quest.[128]

Political considerations aside, the trip to Britain also met Ike's expectations. After his business in London, Eisenhower went to France for his consultations with de Gaulle before once again returning to Scotland, staying at Culzean Castle, the castle given to him by the Scottish people after World War II. He enjoyed two days of golf and bridge playing with several close friends who flew to Britain especially for the occasion. On 5 September, he sent a parting thank you letter to Macmillan. Eisenhower wrote:

> You express far better than can I the unique and friendly character of this latest of our conferences, a character that I am certain was engendered not so much by the warm welcome of the English people – heartwarming as it was, but by the close relationship between the two of us that seemingly grows stronger and stronger every time we meet.

Then Ike added, "I shall be pulling for you in the weeks ahead, as I am sure you know."[129] On 7 September, once Eisenhower had left the country, Macmillan asked Queen Elizabeth II for a dissolution of Parliament, and the general election was called for 8 October.[130]

Macmillan's careful preparations for the general election, including his historic visit to Russia in February and the timely visit of Eisenhower to Britain in late August and early September, strengthened his party's political position. Likewise, an expanding economy played into the Tory Party's hands and formed a political basis for Macmillan's remark in July, 1957 that, "most of our people have never had it so good," which ultimately led to the campaign slogan "Life's Better Under the Conservatives. Don't Let Labour Ruin It."[131] The Conservatives ran on the winning message of "Peace and Prosperity," strikingly similar to the Republican campaign slogan when Eisenhower was re-elected in 1956. When the votes were counted on 8 October, the results showed a surprisingly strong Conservative victory, with the Tories winning 365 seats in the House of Commons, Labour winning 258, and six seats for the Liberal Party. Macmillan had secured a resounding vote of confidence from the British electorate.[132]

Eisenhower responded immediately to the results of the British election, sending a cable on 9 October. "I have just heard the result of yesterday's elections," Ike wrote. "I want to tell you how much I look forward to the continuation of that spirit of close friendship and cooperation which has made our association so rewarding in the past."[133] Macmillan responded on 10 October, expressing the same sentiments. "Thank you very much for your kind message about our elections," Macmillan said. "Of course I am very pleased by this result. What gives me particular pleasure is the knowledge that I shall now be able to continue to work with you in all the negotiations and problems which face us. You know how much I believe that the alliance between our two countries is the foundation of peace."[134]

IV

Eisenhower's return to the United States from his European trip left him with two major diplomatic events left in 1959: Nikita S. Khrushchev's visit to the United States from 15 to 27 September, and the Western Summit in Paris between 18 and 20 December. The impending summit meeting between the leaders of the United States, the Soviet Union, Great Britain, and France lay at the heart of each of these meetings and Eisenhower clearly viewed them as an opportunity to ease some of the tensions of the Cold War.

Prior to the beginning of the Khrushchev visit, Eisenhower had the opportunity to read a profile of the Soviet leader which Macmillan had sent to him on 5 September. The impression of Khrushchev which appeared in Macmillan's profile was considerably at odds with the impression that most Americans had of Khrushchev as the threat-mongering, saber-rattling "Butcher of Budapest." Macmillan essentially made three points about Khrushchev's personality and temperament. First, "he is more like a human being than [Joseph] Stalin ever was."[135] Although a communist intellectually, Khrushchev struck Macmillan as a more pragmatic leader, willing to "allow personal prejudices and ideas to influence" him. Eisenhower did not have to rule out, completely, some flexibility on Khrushchev's part when it came to discussing the issues which divided them.

Second, according to Macmillan, "Khrushchev's basic philosophy is being influenced both by the increasing development of the Soviet Union and by the dangers of nuclear war."[136] In the prime minister's view, the threat posed by nuclear weapons presented the Soviet Union with a different international situation than the one which confronted Lenin and Stalin. Khrushchev understood that his war with capitalism was going to be fought according to a different set of circumstances than those confronted by his ideological predecessors.

Third, and quite significantly, Macmillan argued that, "as the memories of revolution and civil war die away, Khrushchev is anxious less to be regarded as the odd man out in international affairs and more as the responsible leader of a great bloc of countries."[137] According to that particular line of thinking, if Khrushchev regarded the Soviet Union as a country which was approaching a degree of military parity with the United States, so also did he view himself as emerging on a leadership status equal to Eisenhower's, the unquestioned leader of the Western alliance. The suggestion was quite clear; Khrushchev had sought a direct meeting with Eisenhower for a long time since it would confirm his status as a world leader or, in Macmillan's words, a "'respectable' member of the Heads of Government Club.'"[138]

Macmillan concluded his profile with a perspective on the type of expectations Eisenhower might entertain for his forthcoming meeting with Khrushchev.

> On the whole, this is not an unhopeful analysis. There seems at least to be a chance of bringing the Russians along at the same time Khrushchev's personal touchiness, which is almost a national characteristic of Soviet men, may even so lead to some tiresome scenes. If these occur they must be accepted with calm but it would be better to try to avoid them. During his visit to the United States, Khrushchev will probably be on his best behavior, he is coming as Head of State and he is bringing his family with him, both of which are good signs.[139]

On 10 September, Eisenhower sent Macmillan a lengthy letter which covered his analysis of his talks with President de Gaulle in Paris. Attached to the letter, prior to its being sent, was a note from Ann Whitman, Eisenhower's personal secretary.

> I reminded Andy [Goodpaster] that you had not acknowledged the letter from Mr. Macmillan about Khrushchev's character and suggestions for handling him – so he dictated this additional paragraph. Okay to add to letter? "Thanks very much for the character sketch of Mr. Khrushchev that you sent, and for your ideas as to the line I might take in discussions with him. I am grateful for all the help I can get."

Eisenhower initialed the note, "OK, DE," and the letter was sent to Macmillan.[140]

Nikita S. Khrushchev arrived in the United States on 15 September, the first head of state of the Soviet Union to visit the United States. His visit lasted until 27 September and was divided into three parts: two days of talks in Washington with Eisenhower and some formal dinners between 15 and 17 September; a nationwide tour between 18 and 26 September which featured an address by Khrushchev before the United Nations on 18 September in which he made an appeal for total disarmament (without inspection or verification, of course); and finally, two days of talks between Eisenhower and Khrushchev at Camp David.

The Camp David talks were notable for the frank discussions between Eisenhower and Khrushchev about the issues which divided the two countries. Although the talks occurred "in a generally dispassionate, objective, and calm tone," the results of the meetings showed that little in the form of substantive agreements took place. Regarding Berlin, Khrushchev essentially confirmed that the Soviets wanted to solve the problem through negotiation and denied any intention of taking unilateral action in Germany. Eisenhower staked out the American position: he would have to resign before he could accept any time limit for United States withdrawal from Berlin. According to the notes of the meeting, "the President made it clear that a summit meeting could not take place so long as the threat of duress in Berlin remained."[141]

Both Eisenhower and Khrushchev also spoke of pressure from their respective militaries to develop weapons and weapons systems which would provide an edge over their rival and how costly the entire enterprise had become.[142] Both men agreed to hold a summit meeting the following May, however, and Khrushchev finally dropped his ultimatum on the Berlin issue. In some respects, the Camp David meetings represented Khrushchev's desire to remove the West German dispute as an obstacle to further negotiations. Also, in what seemed to be at the time a relatively minor decision, Khrushchev and Eisenhower agreed to postpone Ike's visit to the Soviet Union until after the summit conference in Paris in May 1960.[143]

Otherwise, Eisenhower was disappointed with his apparent inability to establish anything resembling a rapport with Khrushchev. "I can't get anywhere with this guy," Eisenhower complained to Thomas S. Gates after one particularly unproductive meeting with Khrushchev at Camp David.[144] Khrushchev apparently felt differently, however, and spoke openly of a "Spirit of Camp David" after he returned to the Soviet Union and of how he and Eisenhower had established a meaningful, productive relationship.[145]

Eisenhower and Macmillan met for the final time in 1959 at the meeting of the Western Summit in Paris on 18–21 December 1959. The purpose of the meeting was to select the site for the upcoming summit meeting with Khrushchev as well as to agree on an agenda for the meeting itself. It escaped the notice of the statesmen involved – Eisenhower, Macmillan, de Gaulle, and Adenauer – that these items were, at one time, the prescribed business of the foreign ministers and that their lack of progress on them should have prompted an end to talk about a summit. By this point, however, Eisenhower had moved away from much of his earlier skepticism on the matter and was moving closer to Macmillan's position. After all, Khrushchev had dropped his ultimatum on Berlin and, in a gesture toward Macmillan, Ike "had no intention of bickering with one of my best friends."[146]

The four heads of state met for the first time at 9.30 a.m. on Saturday 19 December 1959. After de Gaulle made the welcoming statements, Macmillan took the initiative in outlining the business of the conference: the date of the summit meeting, the place for the meeting, the composition of the note inviting Khrushchev to attend the meeting, and finally the matter of an agenda. When the subject turned to a discussion of disarmament as an agenda item, Eisenhower made a statement which was certain to startle his Western colleagues. According to the notes of the meeting, Ike explained that he had changed his thinking about disarmament in recent months. At one time, when the United States had a monopoly of nuclear weapons, discussions about disarmament focused on the destruction of nuclear stockpiles. But now, Eisenhower argued, the emphasis should be on inspection and control of nuclear weapons testing, rather than the abolition of weapons. The summit meeting might provide an opportunity to take a step in that direction.[147]

The four leaders then turned to a discussion of the time and place for the meeting, a conversation that must have seemed almost comedic to the participants. First, as to place, Macmillan initially proposed Paris as a site. President de Gaulle then inquired as to the best time for the meeting. Adenauer suggested Geneva as a possible location, a logical suggestion in view of the fact that Switzerland was a neutral country, Geneva was the site of the 1955 summit, and "the facilities were available there."[148]

Macmillan then mentioned his idea of a series of summits, "rotating between the capitals; Paris, Washington, and London." And eventually even Moscow. To Macmillan's surprise, Eisenhower said "that this could be so."[149] Macmillan opposed the choice of Geneva as the site for a summit, since "negotiations there had never been successful and it would be good to break the curse on Geneva, where nothing ever seemed to go right."[150] De Gaulle agreed; the city was too crowded and Khrushchev could hardly be expected to like Geneva with its Calvinist history.[151] Paris was the final choice.

But, even before that rather roundabout discussion on choice of location, the four leaders had an even more comedic conversation. The notes of American Ambassador Amory Houghton's record of the conversation provided the account:

> Discussion timing conference then ensued. After some discussion de Gaulle indicated that he would like to come to the US prior to summit meeting. April 19–22 were indicated as probable dates for de Gaulle to visit US. President said he would attempt to have King of Nepal's visit moved up to April 22–24. Summit conference would then be held on April 27–May 1. Macmillan said he could even continue on May 2 but repeat not beyond as he had Commonwealth Prime Ministers meeting May 3–14. All parties agreed Soviets should know there would be fixed termination date for conference. De Gaulle said he would have liked to have summit conference in May, while Macmillan would have preferred mid-April. (Note: on the May 2 issue; Eisenhower explained that this "would be moving the King of Nepal and he had already been moved several times."[152]) Subject to checking there was general agreement on April 27–May 1 and it was also agreed that there would be a western summit April 26.[153]

This agreement overlooked the importance of 1 May, May Day in the Soviet Union, and the fact that Khrushchev would be spending the national holiday in Moscow. To accommodate Khrushchev, the date of the summit meeting was moved ahead to 16 May.[154] The Western summit, preceding the main conference, presumably became a casualty of the change in date.

The agenda for the summit meeting was left somewhat vague in discussions involving Eisenhower, Macmillan, de Gaulle, and Adenauer. Eisenhower initially proposed limiting the agenda to "disarmament and related questions." Both de Gaulle and Adenauer wanted to include the status of divided Germany but Eisenhower and Macmillan did not support this suggestion.[155] Regarding Germany, Eisenhower expressed a preference to study the "situation to see what could be done if the Soviets attempted to starve out Berlin while technically respecting our right of access to our garrisons there." Sensing some lack of resolve on the part of the others, Adenauer emotionally argued that Berlin was a "symbol and yielding there would [bring] fatal results for the West."[156] Seeing the difficulties inherent in the German discussion, the four leaders finally decided to limit their discussion at the summit to the issue of disarmament.

V

For both Eisenhower and Macmillan, 1959 had been a historic year. For his part, Eisenhower had become considerably more flexible in his approach to the Soviets following the death of John Foster Dulles in May. More inclined to work outside of the strictures which Dulles's behavior had prescribed, Eisenhower also sensed that time was running out on his presidency. In private conversations with him as early as his meeting in March 1959, Macmillan sensed that Ike was preparing to diverge from the views of his advisors on the issue of disarmament. With Dulles gone from the Administration, a visible change emerged in the flexibility of Eisenhower's position. His invitation to Khrushchev in the summer of 1959 appeared to confirm that change.

For Macmillan, 1959 had been a year of triumph. He had gambled on his initiative with Khrushchev, and it had paid off, both in diplomatic terms and in its domestic political benefit. If 1957–58 had been a period when Macmillan had successfully cemented his relationship with Eisenhower according to the philosophy of "collective action," 1959 was the year when he began to chart a more flexible, independent course and to envision the heady prospect of serving as a mediator between the United States and the Soviet Union.

Likewise, Macmillan's use of Eisenhower as a campaign prop was a political master stroke. Herbert Morrison, a longtime political foe of Macmillan's, gave the prime minister his due by acknowledging that the joint appearance on British television on 31 August "offered wonderful election propaganda on the eve of the announcement of the polling date."[157]

The death of John Foster Dulles also created an opportunity for Macmillan to play a greater role in Anglo-American diplomacy. As Richard Aldous and Sabine Lee have written: "Macmillan's illusions of British grandeur were at their most transparent in early 1959. With the chief playmaker of western strategy, John Foster Dulles, fatally ill, Macmillan set out to fill the vacuum in American foreign policy and take East–West relations into his capable hands."[158]

Without question, Macmillan had taken the lead in the advocacy of the summit meeting between heads of government. Macmillan's persistence, however, was not due to any overall strategy. He had, after all, pushed for a summit to be scheduled at different times, in different places, in 1959 before he, Eisenhower, de Gaulle, and Adenauer had finally settled on Paris in May 1960 as the appropriate setting. Perhaps Eisenhower also believed that a fundamental shift in the tensions of the Cold War was occurring. For both Eisenhower and Macmillan, the summit conference in Paris would provide the report card on the effectiveness of their diplomacy.

4
1960: Washington and Paris

As the year 1960 signaled the beginning of a new decade, so also did it open with a glimmer of hope for a positive change in the international situation. Largely due to the initiative of Dwight D. Eisenhower and Harold Macmillan, the Western alliance was poised to enter into meaningful negotiations with the Soviet Union for the first time in the Cold War. The success of these negotiations, of course, depended upon the willingness of Nikita Khrushchev and the Soviet leadership to entertain the prospect of acceptable solutions to the issues which divided East and West. In 1959, in talks with Macmillan in Moscow in February, at the "kitchen debate" in Moscow with Vice President Richard Nixon in July, and finally, with Eisenhower at Camp David in September, Khrushchev appeared willing to open a dialogue with the West.

Khrushchev's behavior, while welcomed in the West, had not resulted in any fundamental change in Soviet policy, however. The Soviet Union, the United States, and Great Britain remained divided over the issue of arms control and disarmament and they had not narrowed their differences appreciably on the Berlin problem, a crisis that had essentially been manufactured by Khrushchev. Yet, the major result of the numerous meetings between Macmillan, Eisenhower, and Khrushchev in 1959 was the understanding that a meeting of the heads of government was necessary to address these issues.

Macmillan was particularly enthusiastic about the prospects for success at a meeting of the heads of government and kept in touch with members of the British public about his hopes. For example, on 4 March 1960, he wrote to one British citizen, Jack Page, commenting on how hard he had worked "to reach a general agreement on the holding of a summit." Macmillan believed that "with goodwill we should make valuable progress which can be followed up at later meetings."[1]

The device to be used to resolve these issues was the Four-Power Summit in Paris, involving Eisenhower, Macmillan, Khrushchev, and French President Charles de Gaulle, scheduled for 16 May 1960. Presumably, the four leaders hoped for a historic breakthrough on nuclear testing and perhaps even the basis for resolving the dispute over Berlin. But the initial optimism for the conference ended abruptly when the Soviets shot down an American U-2 reconnaissance aircraft piloted by Francis Gary Powers on 1 May. Khrushchev reacted furiously to this trespass of Soviet air space and, failing to get a satisfactory apology from Eisenhower, used the flight as a pretext for torpedoing the summit conference.

The collapse of the Paris summit had profound consequences for the Cold War. The nuclear arms race accelerated; the atmosphere of suspicion between the Soviet bloc and the West intensified; and the prospect for serious negotiations virtually disappeared. The Soviet Union also began a conscious effort to sow discord throughout the world; in the Caribbean with Cuba, in Africa with the civil war in the Congo, and in Asia with the increasing amount of violence in Indochina.

The collapse of the summit and its tense aftermath was a major setback for Harold Macmillan. The repercussions of this failure did not affect his domestic political standing, but they did seriously damage Britain's capacity to act in the international arena. And, as the individual most responsible for promoting the summit, Macmillan was naturally the one who seemed most disheartened by its failure. Largely through Macmillan's patient diplomacy and the cultivation of his relationship with Eisenhower, Macmillan had managed to keep the British "in the game" as an effective voice in world politics. Now the collapse of the summit had called into question Britain's place in the diplomatic universe as well as Macmillan's skills as a statesman.[2]

I

The optimism which marked the end of 1959 continued into 1960, and President Eisenhower provided some momentum for the belief that progress at the summit was possible. On 11 February, he told a press conference of his willingness to accept a virtual moratorium on nuclear tests, be they atmospheric, oceanic, or underground, with appropriate safeguards for inspection. He was also willing to sign a treaty prohibiting tests in outer space.[3]

Eisenhower made this proposal to the Russians, despite the opposition of his own military advisors and the leadership of the Atomic

Energy Commission. On 19 March, the Soviets announced their support for Eisenhower's proposal but with one crucial exception. There would have to be no inspection of low-level underground nuclear tests. The countries would have to rely on the good faith of the other on that point. The skeptics within the Administration – chiefly at the Department of Defense and in the intelligence establishment – who questioned the value of arms control negotiations, opposed the Soviet offer. Even public opinion seemed to be against the president on this issue. Macmillan wanted Eisenhower to accept the Soviet proposal, however, at least as the basis for discussions. As on numerous previous occasions, Macmillan wanted to speak directly to Eisenhower about the latest Soviet offers and what they seemed to mean for prospects at the summit.

Eisenhower and Macmillan spoke twice on 21 March regarding the summit and disarmament. Macmillan hoped to extend any moratorium on nuclear testing beyond one year to make the agreement truly historic. According to their conversation at 10.30 a.m., Macmillan thought "we could get a moratorium for three years."[4] Eisenhower was not so sure; his term of office ended in ten months, and he questioned whether he could make any agreement which bound his successor. Macmillan then suggested an arms control treaty with the provision of a three-year moratorium. Eisenhower was pessimistic about that suggestion, also, since a treaty would have to be ratified by the Senate and sufficient time did not exist to conclude a treaty and have it ratified before he left office. In response, Macmillan pressed even harder: "it would be wonderful if it could be tied up by you," he declared.[5]

Macmillan and Eisenhower then talked about the possibility of a quick visit by the prime minister to the United States, perhaps within four or five days. Eisenhower suggested waiting for at least a week, but Macmillan was so anxious that "he would put everything off" in order to come to Washington to confer with Eisenhower, "perhaps at Camp David."[6] Eisenhower told Macmillan that he would talk with Secretary of State Herter and call him back.

At 2.30 p.m., Eisenhower called Macmillan. The Administration was still studying the Russian proposal and, until it had reached some conclusions, Macmillan should stay in Britain. Before ending the conversation, Eisenhower and Macmillan talked briefly about their recent trips abroad, Eisenhower's to South America and Macmillan's to Africa. Ike noted that "he was never as tired as he had been on completion of [the] South American trip." Macmillan said the same about his trip to Africa. Both agreed they had much to talk about, the president added, "like Gulliver."[7]

On 23 March 1960, Eisenhower called Macmillan once again. Eisenhower had cleared his schedule for another round of talks with Macmillan, beginning 28 March. The prime minister agreed immediately and both sides announced the meeting as a conference dealing with the issue of nuclear testing. Privately, Macmillan did "not feel very hopeful" about the compatibility of the British and American positions on disarmament, however. As he confided to his diary on 23 March, "Eisenhower seemed very friendly" but, "with an administration on the way out," opponents of a testing moratorium at "the Pentagon and [with] the Atomic groups" were "gaining strength."[8]

Nevertheless, Macmillan came to the United States between 27 and 31 March for a final round of discussions prior to the summit conference in Paris, then less than two months away. As in 1959, Eisenhower, Macmillan, and their advisers met at Camp David. On the afternoon of 28 March, they discussed the ongoing nuclear test negotiations and the tactics and strategy for the summit meeting. The British and the Americans discussed the length of the moratorium and eventually concluded that their differences on the issue were small. Macmillan remarked that, if one of Khrushchev's motives was to split the British from the Americans, he was not going to succeed.[9] Eisenhower speculated that perhaps Khrushchev's motives were to divide the British and the Americans from the French, who had said that they would not adhere to any arms control agreement dealing with nuclear weapons.[10]

The meeting also called for some speculation on Ike's part. He wondered whether the arms control and testing issues were somehow connected to the Soviet Union's concerns about the future of Germany. "The Soviets would [agree to almost] anything if in return they got assurances on the East German [situation]," Eisenhower surmised.[11] In his view, the Soviets "were really scared of a re-united armed Germany."[12]

Macmillan then steered the conversation back in the direction of a discussion about testing. The overall meeting had been helpful, Eisenhower summarized, adding that he was pleased "to find the British and [American] views close together. From what he had read and been told, he feared that the Prime Minister was coming over to try to sell him the full Russian line."[13]

On the morning of 29 March 1960, the two delegations met once again to discuss the technical aspects of the inspection systems for nuclear tests. Joining the group were John McCone, the chairman of the AEC, and George Kistiakowsky, the president's science advisor. In this meeting, Ike essentially swung over to Macmillan's views on the technical issues while moving slightly away from the views of the AEC and the military. Eisenhower confirmed that position and then defended it in a news conference on the following day.[14]

On the afternoon of 29 March, Eisenhower and Macmillan took another automobile ride from Camp David to Gettysburg. Eisenhower once again took Macmillan to his farm, and the two toured the various battlefield sights. By this point, Eisenhower appeared to have caught the summit contagion almost as severely as Macmillan. "Summitry had proved the occupational weakness of any incumbent of No. 10 [Downing Street]," Selwyn Lloyd once observed.[15] Now Eisenhower appeared to be as infatuated as Macmillan with the prospect of a diplomatic breakthrough at Paris. As Macmillan recorded their conversation, Ike

> talked a great deal and very freely about himself . . . his hopes of the Summit (he thinks we should be able to get some settlement on Berlin, if only we would guarantee to accept for the present the frontiers of Germany), his hopes for a Nuclear Test Agreement (he is really keen on this and – although he has not said much about it yet – would accept further concessions in the course of negotiations to get it) and many other matters.[16]

On 30 March, Macmillan had another extremely busy day. A luncheon with the Senate Foreign Relations Committee was followed by a brief speech to the Senate. Richard Nixon introduced Macmillan in the Senate chamber, and the prime minister's remarks were well received. Afterward, Macmillan shook hands individually with each senator. As in 1956, 1957, 1958, and 1959, Macmillan's thoughts turned to the memory of his mother. "How pleased my mother would have been," he confided to his diary. "She regarded a Senator of the United States as almost the highest degree of dignity and felicity to which mortals could aspire. (I told them that in the speech to the Senators and they enjoyed it. I added that although as a child I had always been rather skeptical about mother's view of the Senate, I now understood and approved.)"[17]

Following his address, Macmillan still had a number of appointments. He called on Janet Dulles, widow of Foster Dulles, met with the press, had dinner, and paid his farewell respects to Herter and Eisenhower. Departing for Britain at 11 p.m. on 30 March, Macmillan was satisfied that "all the omens were good" leading to the summit.[18] Once back in Britain, Macmillan wrote to Eisenhower. "I find it hard to express in the form of a letter how much I valued our talks over the last few days and how grateful I am to you for all your kindness and hospitality," Macmillan stated. "Looking back on it I am astonished at how much ground we covered."[19]

By this point, Eisenhower had accepted the notion that a summit meeting was the best route to negotiating some agreements which would ease the tensions of the Cold War. In press conferences in March and April, he repeated his desire to slow the arms race, end the proliferation of nuclear weapons, and divert these enormous military resources to peacetime uses, such as for school construction and the modernization of highways. As Stephen Ambrose has written:

> Eisenhower was prepared to go to Paris to seek a genuine accord. Never in the Cold War did one seem closer. A President of the United States was on the verge of trusting the Russians in the most critical and dangerous field, nuclear testing. He had de Gaulle and Macmillan with him, and Khrushchev seemed by every indication to be sincere in his own desire for disarmament.[20]

Ike almost certainly agreed with Macmillan; in April 1960, the omens for success in Paris were good.

II

In early April, the Eisenhower Administration began to prepare for the summit, amid the uneasy suspicion that the Soviets had reaccelerated their military program. A general belief existed within the Administration that Khrushchev had encountered some criticism from his military leadership once he returned from his meetings with Eisenhower in 1959. While the NATO countries were skeptical of any arms control agreement which lacked adequate safeguards for inspection and verification, the Soviet leadership did not want Khrushchev to accept any proposals that put a brake on the development of its overall military strength. In fact, the Soviets were aiming for an "orderly" expansion of their missile capability and a National Intelligence Estimate (NIE) prepared in January 1960 appeared to confirm that fact.[21] Eisenhower was sufficiently concerned about the implications of this buildup that, at a meeting of the NSC on 7 January 1960, he approved a further expansion in the American ICBM program.[22]

Eisenhower never accepted the notion that the Soviets held a great numerical superiority over the United States in overall missile capability, however. He knew the extent of the Soviets' military capability because of the success of a high-altitude surveillance aircraft, called the U-2, which had been conducting overflights of the Soviet Union since 1956 and brought back highly detailed photographs of its military installations. The project originated in 1955 when the CIA instituted a crash program to develop such an aircraft. The super-secret spy plane project, termed AQUATONE, was pressed with great determination, especially after the Russians had turned down Eisenhower's Open Skies proposal at the Geneva Summit in 1955.[23] The aircraft was eventually named the U-2, even though whimsical names such as "Dulles's Folly" (after CIA director Allen Dulles), were also suggested.[24] Dulles was not embarrassed at all; the U-2 flights provided photographs which revealed "every blade of grass in the Soviet Union."[25]

The U-2 made its first flight over the Soviet Union on 4 July 1956, taking off from a base in Wiesbaden, West Germany, heading first for Moscow and then Leningrad. The objective of the flight was to photograph the Soviet naval shipyard and a heavy bomber airfield, both near Leningrad.[26] By noon the next day, Richard Bissell, the deputy director of the CIA and the individual responsible for the operation of the U-2 program, had received a cable from West Germany saying that the flight had concluded successfully. As Bissell remembered: "[The] photographs were remarkable. We obtained perfectly beautiful high altitude photographs of Leningrad and Moscow in which one could literally count the number of automobiles in the streets."[27] On 5 July, Bissell reported on the success of the U-2 flights to Allen Dulles, who then went to the White House to inform Eisenhower. Eisenhower responded to the success of this intelligence breakthrough with one of his famous grins.[28]

In the early months of the U-2 program, the Eisenhower Administration enlisted the British in the surveillance program. The joint project began in 1956 during Anthony Eden's premiership when three U-2 aircraft were stationed at the Lakenheath air base in Britain. Test flights were undertaken from this base over Eastern Europe but not over the Soviet Union. Then, an unfortunate incident in Soviet espionage occurred when a Soviet cruiser was making a courtesy call at the British sea port at Portsmouth. British intelligence units sent a Royal Navy frogman underneath the ship to examine its signaling gear. Three days later, the frogman was found dead, his body floating in the harbor. Eden decided that it had become too risky for the Americans to carry out espionage from bases in Britain and the project ended.[29]

When Harold Macmillan became prime minister, he expressed an interest in resuming the program. The AQUATONE project became an agenda item at the Bermuda Conference in March 1957, and

Macmillan was willing to bring the British back into this enterprise. On 22 March, he sent a brief note to Eisenhower, while in Bermuda, outlining his intentions. "At our talk this morning," Macmillan wrote, "you asked me to send you some notes on one or two of the subjects we mentioned." "I now send you notes on the following subjects.

I. AQUATONE
II. Tripartite Alerts Procedure
III. Nuclear weapons for R.A.F bombers
IV. Nuclear bomb release gear for R.A.F bombers."[30]

Macmillan then included with the note a brief summary of the British position on each subject. For the AQUATONE item, Macmillan explained:

> At an earlier stage [during the Eden government] the United Kingdom government felt unable to agree that bases in the United Kingdom should be used for operational flights for AQUATONE. The United Kingdom government are now prepared to allow bases in the United Kingdom to be used for operations of this nature, if that would be of advantage to the United States government.[31]

Eisenhower responded to Macmillan's note the next day. Eisenhower stated, "[We] are pleased that you found your way clear to allow United Kingdom bases to be used for AQUATONE if it should at some time become necessary."[32]

Subsequent to this agreement at Bermuda, the United States began to train RAF pilots, and the British became involved in the operational details of the program. Before long, British pilots began flying U-2 flights from bases in the UK, Turkey, and Pakistan.[33] Like so much that happened between Eisenhower and Macmillan in 1957–58, the U-2 project had become a joint effort between the United States and Great Britain.

Between 1956 and 1960, the U-2 proved its value beyond simply the surveillance flights over the Soviet Union. The United States conducted U-2 flights extensively during the Suez crisis in 1956, the Lebanon crisis in 1958, and when the People's Republic of China threatened Nationalist China in 1958.[34] Most importantly, the flights provided valuable photographic information which showed what the Soviet military was doing, or equally importantly, what the Soviets were not doing, according to Andrew Goodpaster.[35] Eisenhower was able to design the

American military response to the Soviet Union with hard evidence of its capability. There was no need to overspend on defense, or to engage in "crash programs" designed to address a presumed American deficit in one area or another. As Richard Bissell later wrote:

> The U-2 was doing what it was designed to do. It was getting superb information on the Soviet Union, and it was doing so at what was recognized even then as a very modest cost. The aircrafts [cost] around $1 million each; the total personnel assigned to the project at its peak (both abroad and domestically) was about five to six hundred, excluding contractors.[36]

With the summit approaching, however, Eisenhower found himself under pressure to authorize additional overflights to make a final determination about the extent of Soviet missile development. By this point, he had grown increasingly apprehensive about the U-2 program, fearing that the loss of an aircraft or capture of a pilot could result in a major international incident. "If one of these things is shot down, this thing is going to be on my head. I'm going to catch hell. The world will be in a mess," Ike had remarked during the early years of the program.[37]

Despite his misgivings, however, Eisenhower still wanted the valuable information which the U-2 was providing about Soviet missile development. Since the inception of the flights, the Soviets had protested diplomatically but they lacked the military capability, at least until mid-1960, to shoot down a U-2. But both intelligence and defense officials were growing increasingly concerned that advances in the Soviet Union's surface-to-air (SAM) missile capability might soon make the U-2 overflights too dangerous.[38] It was necessary to get as much information as possible before the Soviets were able to shoot down a U-2. Accordingly, Richard Bissell went to Eisenhower on 7 April 1960, requesting permission for an overflight which had been recently postponed. On 9 April, the flight was made and completed its mission, although Soviet radar had detected the flight path and the Soviets had tried to intercept it with their SAMs. Moreover, a Soviet pilot who had attempted to track the U-2 had lost control of his aircraft and died in the resulting crash. The photography acquired from the flight revealed no new missile construction in the Soviet Union.[39]

Still, Bissell and the CIA wanted another flight to identify three prospective missile sites. Secretary of State Herter believed that additional U-2 flights over the Soviet Union, in the weeks leading up to the summit, were too provocative and should not be authorized. Curiously, however, Khrushchev had not protested the 9 April flight diplomatically, even though it was clear that Soviet radar had tracked the aircraft's path and that the Soviets had attempted to shoot it down. The lack of a protest indicated to the CIA that Khrushchev also was attempting to lay low before the summit and not engage in any provocative actions. Eisenhower remained concerned, but nevertheless authorized a two-week window for the flights, with a terminal date of 25 April.[40] Weather conditions were unsatisfactory through that entire period, however, and Eisenhower authorized a one-week extension for the flight, to 2 May 1960, the last date possible for any U-2 flight prior to the summit conference.[41]

At this point, and in view of the events which were to follow, some speculation is appropriate. Thoughts return to the conversation between Eisenhower, Macmillan, de Gaulle, and Adenauer at the Western Summit in Paris in December 1959, when the four leaders searched for a date for a meeting of the heads of government. Originally, they proposed a summit meeting in Paris for the third week or fourth week in April but, for a variety of reasons – Eisenhower's appointment with the King of Nepal; Macmillan's meetings with the Commonwealth ministers; de Gaulle's desire to visit Eisenhower in Washington before the meeting in Paris – the "early" summit date was discarded in favor of a "later" summit date which was set after 1 May, the date of the Soviet national holiday. More than likely, Khrushchev would have accepted any summit date, conveniently scheduled before or after 1 May. It is highly probable that, if the Western leaders had agreed on the earlier date, such as the 22–6 April proposal, the 9 April U-2 flight would have been the last flight before the summit conference. Under those circumstances, Eisenhower would not have authorized the 1 May flight by Francis Gary Powers.

Moreover, the U-2 flight on 9 April provoked considerable internal outrage within the councils of the Soviet government. "When will they poke their noses in again?," Khrushchev asked after the 9 April flight. The Soviet leader was perplexed: Why would the Americans risk an international incident so close to the summit? Had Eisenhower authorized the flight, or had it been the work of Allen Dulles and the CIA? There was no point in filing a diplomatic note of protest, Khrushchev said, since it would only be another acknowledgement of Russian weakness. Was the United States, as Khrushchev wondered, trying to expose Soviet weakness on the eve of the summit?[42] The answers to those questions were unknowable, but Khrushchev was certain that Eisenhower would not have authorized any U-2 flight between 9 April and the summit.

III

On 1 May 1960, Francis Gary Powers, the U-2 pilot selected for the 24th overflight of the Soviet Union, took off from his base in Peshawar, Pakistan, and entered Soviet airspace at 5.36 a.m.[43] Powers flew with a certain amount of apprehension; his flight had been postponed twice and the aircraft which he was flying was not the one originally assigned. Instead, he was flying U-2 number 360, which he considered a "dog." "Something was always going wrong with it," he later wrote.[44] After Powers had traveled well over 1,300 miles into the flight, the aircraft's autopilot malfunctioned. Flying over the Sverdlovsk region of the Soviet Union, one of the photographic objectives of the flight, Powers felt a dull "thump," followed by a violent convulsion, and then he lost control of the aircraft. Shrapnel from the explosion of a Soviet SAM had penetrated the outer skin of the U-2 and shredded its fuel system. Powers and his U-2 plunged to the earth, with fragments of the damaged plane falling everywhere.

Powers escaped from the doomed aircraft, opened his parachute, and plunged to the earth where he awaited certain capture by the Soviet authorities. As he fell toward the ground, Powers thought that the landscape below looked "like parts of Virginia. As if by wishing I could make it so."[45] Once on the ground, he was quickly apprehended, first by some Russian farmers, and then taken into custody by two police. In his possession, he had a poison needle which could be used to commit suicide. He did not use it.[46]

What had gone wrong? How had the Soviets managed to shoot down this particular U-2, having failed just three weeks earlier? Two versions of the fate of Powers's doomed flight bear some examination. One belongs to Richard Bissell, the other to Sergei Khrushchev, son of Nikita Khrushchev.

According to Bissell, "our luck just plain ran out."[47] While Powers was flying over the Sverdlovsk region, the Soviets fired three SAMs at his plane. One missile missed completely; a second struck and destroyed a Soviet MiG aircraft which was attempting to intercept Powers, and the third missile detonated close enough to Powers "to damage the outer layer of the aircraft."[48] Having lost control of the plane Powers eventually managed to struggle free but was unable to press the destruct mechanism for the plane. The Soviets, thereby, were able to capture him and the wreckage of his U-2.

In an interview with one of this book's co-authors several years before the publication of Bissell's account in 1995, C. Douglas Dillon essentially confirmed Bissell's conclusion. Dillon contended that the Soviets shot down the U-2 with a SAM, "from a battery which we knew the Russians were installing but which we didn't think was operational."[49] "We could see the Russian interceptors going up to 40,000 feet and fire their rounds at the plane and missing."[50]

Sergei Khrushchev's account of the Powers episode is considerably more detailed and differs significantly from that of Bissell. According to Sergei Khrushchev, the Soviets learned of the penetration of Soviet airspace by the "intruder," Francis Gary Powers, early on the morning of 1 May 1960. News of this latest flight left Nikita Khrushchev in a foul mood, since he had a full day's worth of activities planned for the Russian national holiday. Soviet missile forces were available, but their status was uncertain due to the national holiday. As the leaders of the Soviet air force watched the path of Powers's flight from their command center in Moscow, it appeared that the "intruder" knew exactly where to fly in order to evade the missile batteries on the ground below. Then, inexplicably, Powers changed the path of his aircraft and came back into the range of the Soviet SAMs. The Soviets gave the order to fire three missiles: only one was launched and it looked as though the "intruder" was about to escape.[51]

Then, at 8.53 a.m., a flash appeared in the sky, followed seconds later by a "faint sound of an explosion." On the ground, the Soviet air force officers initially thought that the intruder was performing an evasive maneuver to elude his attackers. Then a second battery fired three missiles at Powers, whose plane was not evading its attackers but was disintegrating and falling to the ground. The first missile had not hit the U-2 but had exploded behind it, creating the damage described by Bissell and Dillon. Then, in the second round of missiles fired at Powers, two missed but one hit the falling aircraft, only 18,000 feet above the ground. The damage to the aircraft caused by the force of the second missile enabled Powers to escape from the plane, open his parachute, and descend to the ground. One of the missiles did strike and destroy a MiG aircraft which had been dispatched to intercept Powers, however. The fact that the Russians had also lost a pilot in the attempt to shoot down Powers remained a closely-held secret in the Soviet Union for decades.[52]

On the ground, Powers was apprehended by several Russian citizens who drove over to him. They helped Powers to his feet and cut off the shroud lines to his parachute. They asked him how he felt. Powers responded unintelligibly. "Are you Bulgarian?," they asked. Powers nodded, to the negative. Then one Russian wrote "U.S.A." on one of the car's dirty windows, and Powers nodded affirmatively. His captors took him to the nearby state farm in Sverdlovsk where Powers was released to the KGB, destined to begin a two-year incarceration.[53]

When Powers failed to reach his destination at Bodo, Norway, feelings of concern spread in Washington. Was Powers alive or dead? If he was alive, where was he? Had the plane been destroyed or did the Soviets have any of its wreckage? Even if the Soviets had both Powers and the aircraft, would they say so? On that point, Foster Dulles once tried to reassure Eisenhower that even "[if] the Soviets ever capture one of these planes, I'm sure they will never admit it. To do so would make it necessary for them to admit also that for years we had been carrying on flights over their territory while they had been helpless to do anything about the matter."[54]

On 1 May 1960, Goodpaster contacted Eisenhower to inform him that the U-2 was missing and "possibly lost."[55] This was hardly good news but the Administration was not inclined to make any hasty statements at that point. The presumption, of course, was that Powers would not survive a crash of the U-2 and a "cover story" could be released to the press, saying that a "weather research plane" had been lost in a mission near Turkey.[56] On 3 May, that story was released under the provenance of the National Aeronautics and Space Administration.[57] Hardly a murmur of interest appeared either on 3 May or 4 May to challenge this rather unique story.

Little news about the ill-fated flight emerged during the next two days. But, at 4 a.m. on 5 May, Secretary of Defense Thomas S. Gates awoke to a telephone call informing him that the Joint Chiefs of Staff had put into operation a civil defense exercise at High Point, North Carolina, which required the evacuation from Washington of the president and several of his close advisors. After dressing hastily, Gates was driven by his wife, Anne, to a helicopter pad in northwest Washington, about ten minutes from his home, where he was to be flown to the evacuation site.

Arriving at the helicopter pad, Gates greeted his companion for the flight, Allen Dulles. Once airborne, Dulles reached inside his coat pocket and pulled out a single sheet of paper which contained a short message. "Here, Tom," Dulles said, staring straight ahead, "look at this."[58] Glancing over the message, Gates learned that Khrushchev had obtained the wreckage of the U-2 and he intended to reveal this shocking information in a speech before the Supreme Soviet in Moscow. The cover story would be shown to be a lie. A major international incident was unfolding.

On 5 May, Khrushchev made his speech to the Supreme Soviet where he confirmed the downing of the aircraft. More important, however, was what he left unsaid. No mention of Powers was made, nor was there any suggestion that the Soviets had recovered anything of value from the wreckage. Perhaps just as importantly, Khrushchev attempted to absolve Eisenhower of any responsibility for the flight, blaming "militarists in the Pentagon or the CIA."[59]

Meeting at the evacuation site, Eisenhower gathered his advisors to discuss the impact of Khrushchev's speech and a possible American response. In addition to Gates and Dulles, the group included Gordon Gray, Eisenhower's national security advisor; C. Douglas Dillon; and Andrew Goodpaster. The president and his advisors tackled several difficult subjects, including whether to admit publicly that the Administration had a definite program to obtain aerial surveillance of the Soviet Union.

Eisenhower left the meeting early in order to return to Washington to keep an appointment with General Nathan Twining. The normal diplomatic practice called for heads of state to disclaim any responsibility for intelligence activities and this approach appeared to be safest at that particular moment.

On 6 May, however, Khrushchev turned up the temperature, ever so slightly, by showing a photograph of the wreckage of the plane, except that it was not the wreckage of Powers's aircraft. As Sergei Khrushchev recorded, Nikita Khrushchev was biding his time, waiting for the proper moment to embarrass the Americans. "Let them [the Americans] worry about it," he said. "Let's see what the State Department dreams up. When they've become completely enmeshed in lies, we'll show them the living pilot. But in the meantime – not a word!"[60]

At the meeting on 5 May, however, Gates was troubled by the recommendation that the president should not accept responsibility for the flights. Gates had developed a tremendous respect and appreciation for the U-2 program and the surveillance photography which it provided. He viewed the U-2 missions as an effective counterweight to the elaborate espionage system which the Soviets had developed within the borders of the United States. Like Eisenhower, Gates realized that the U-2 program was risky and yet he considered it necessary, even if a summit meeting was upcoming.

Furthermore, Gates was not convinced that Powers was dead, and the possibility that he might be alive conditioned his approach to the matter of Eisenhower's response to the Soviet charges. Gates would not dismiss the possibility that Powers was alive until he learned conclusively to the contrary.⁶¹ For that reason, he pressed the argument that both the president and the Administration should admit the overflights and not involve the prestige of the presidency in an "international lie."⁶² A strong case could be made for the flights from the context of American national security, the extensive Soviet espionage network in the United States, and the closed nature of Soviet society. As damaging as the admission of the revelation of aerial surveillance might be, it would be far more destructive to American prestige and the president's credibility if Eisenhower was trapped in his own falsehood. In Gates's view, Eisenhower should take the responsibility for the flights, announce their suspension, explain his position, and then deal with whatever consequences might result. The position advocated by Gates did not prevail, however, and on 6 May, Lincoln White, the spokesman for the State Department, repeated the cover story which the Administration had clung to since the first days of the crisis.⁶³

Khrushchev appeared content to play a waiting game but then events conspired to force his hand. On 6 May, Rolf Sulman, the Swedish ambassador to the Soviet Union was speaking with Yakov Malik, the Soviet deputy foreign minister, at a reception in Moscow. Malik responded to a query from Sulman about the "fate" of the U-2 pilot. Malik answered, "I don't know exactly. He's being interrogated," thereby confirming that Powers was alive and in Soviet custody.⁶⁴ In possession of this explosive information, Sulman excused himself from the reception and contacted Llewellyn "Tommy" Thompson, the American ambassador to the Soviet Union. Thompson then notified the State Department about Powers's survival. His cable reached the department too late for the Administration to alter its cover story.⁶⁵

On 7 May, Khrushchev spoke once again to the Supreme Soviet. In this speech, he showed photographs of the "real" wreckage of the aircraft and of Powers, who was "quite alive and kicking." Eisenhower found the news "unbelievable;" Gates later recalled that he was also "astonished beyond imagination" by Powers's survival.⁶⁶

By this point, officials in the State Department and the CIA were trying to protect Eisenhower, ultimately settling on the line that Eisenhower had not specifically authorized the flights.⁶⁷ Since Khrushchev was trying to lay the blame for the flights on unnamed "Pentagon militarists," Gates was furious at the State Department's unwillingness to specify who had authorized the flights. But Secretary of State Herter held firm to the position that Eisenhower needed to be protected.⁶⁸

In London, Harold Macmillan was undergoing his own private anguish, beginning on 7 May when he learned of Khrushchev's speech acknowledging the capture of Powers. Macmillan was at Chequers, making preparations for the forthcoming meeting of the Commonwealth prime ministers. Admittedly, he had known about the loss of the airplane as early as 5 May but he had been hopeful that the incident would not develop into anything more serious, certainly not serious enough, to jeopardize the summit conference in Paris. Nevertheless, he did express his fears, just the same: "The Americans have created a great folly . . . One of their machines have been shot down by a rocket it is said, a few hundred miles from Moscow . . . The Russians have got the machine, the cameras, a lot of the photographs, and the pilot," he confided to his diary on 7 May.[69]

Macmillan's first concern at this point was to attempt to salvage the summit. He also wanted to keep from having to disclose any British involvement in the U-2 flights.[70] Communicating through Robert Murphy, Macmillan suggested that the Americans try to change the subject simply by refusing to discuss intelligence matters. But, since the American response to the loss of the U-2 had undergone so many changes, Macmillan was pessimistic that the Americans could work their way of what was an exceptionally embarrassing situation.[71]

Khrushchev was also behaving mysteriously. In public, he lashed out at the Americans for conducting the flights and threatened retaliation against Pakistan, Norway, and Turkey – countries which were providing bases for the U-2 flights. Privately, however, he was conciliatory. On 10 May, following a diplomatic reception in Moscow, he asked to speak with Ambassador Thompson, virtually pleading with him to get some softening of the American position on the overflights. "This U-2 thing has put me in a terrible spot," the Soviet premier told Thompson. "You have to get me off it."[72]

Khrushchev also sought Macmillan's help, writing to him on 8 May. While complaining about overflights, Khrushchev still kept open the prospect of the summit conference. Macmillan wrote a conciliatory reply to Khrushchev's letter, concluding in a helpful tone, "I look forward very much to renewing on 16 May the friendly acquaintance and intimate discussions which commenced during my visit to your country last spring."[73]

Macmillan hoped that the Eisenhower Administration would let the matter rest until the four leaders met in Paris on 16 May, but, as Sergei Khrushchev has pointed out, "both sides misjudged the situation."[74] Khrushchev's persistent refusal to blame Eisenhower for the U-2 flights, and his attempt to absolve Ike from responsibility for the surveillance program, showed that he wanted to maintain the relationship which had been established at Camp David the previous September. But Eisenhower, once the Soviets had conclusive proof of the American U-2 surveillance program, and more importantly had demonstrated their ability to shoot down a spy plane, could not indefinitely refuse to accept responsibility for the flights. He needed to refute Khrushchev's charges that "militarists in the Pentagon and the CIA" controlled national security policy without presidential oversight. Ike refused to admit that he was not in control of his administration. He also refused to find a convenient scapegoat for the failure of the flight. The path which Khrushchev had outlined for Eisenhower, perhaps out of a desire to preserve a strained relationship, was simply unacceptable to the president.

Therefore, at 10.29 a.m. on 11 May, Eisenhower held a press conference to clarify the Administration's position on the U-2 crisis. "No one wants another Pearl Harbor," Eisenhower said, reading from prepared notes. The fear of a surprise nuclear attack upon the United States by the Soviet Union was a prime concern and it justified, in the president's mind, a host of preventive measures, including espionage. The failure of the Russians to consider Eisenhower's Open Skies proposal at Geneva in 1955 revealed the "fetish of secrecy" which characterized the Soviet political system.[75] By contrast, despite the Soviet Union's "theatrical behavior" and attempt to propagandize the U-2 incident, there was nothing provocative about the U-2 flights, since the plane was "unarmed and non-military." Regardless, the flights would be stopped and Eisenhower fully expected to meet with Khrushchev in Paris as well as keep his visit to the Soviet Union in June. Eisenhower accepted responsibility for the overflights; "To deny my own part in the entire affair would have been a declaration that portions of the government of the United States were operating irresponsibly, in complete disregard of proper presidential control."[76]

Eisenhower's acceptance of responsibility for the U-2 flights was exactly what Harold Macmillan did not want to hear. Macmillan believed that Khrushchev might have accepted "silence or some formal disclaimer from Eisenhower," but Ike's admission of responsibility led to a hardening of the Soviet position, in Macmillan's estimation.[77]

According to Sergei Khrushchev, the Russians left Moscow for the summit with their minds open to the possibility of negotiations with Eisenhower, Macmillan, and de Gaulle, but while on the flight to Paris, Khrushchev suddenly reversed course and decided to torpedo the summit, primarily by making a set of essentially non-negotiable demands upon Eisenhower. Sergei Khrushchev quoted his father:

I thought we had to set conditions, an ultimatum to the United States of America: they must apologize for insulting our country by sending over a spy plane. We must demand that the president of the United States retract his statement that they have the right to send intelligence flights over our territory . . . By the time we arrived in Paris we had complete approval of our new position and when we landed in Paris their content was quite different.[78]

IV

In mid-May, the four leaders met in Paris primarily to discuss disarmament, but also to consider the future of Germany and East–West relations. Eisenhower and Macmillan both arrived on 15 May and were apprehensive when they reached Paris. Khrushchev left Moscow on 14 May and arrived in Paris in a defiant mood.

Some of the preparatory work for the summit began on 14 May when Secretary of State Herter met with reporters prior to Eisenhower's arrival. Of course, the reporters wanted to discuss only the effect of the U-2 on the conference. Herter was asked if the United States intended to continue overflights of the Soviet Union. He was evasive; the United States, in his view, had a "responsibility for doing whatever we could to, not only on our own behalf, but also for the whole free world, cover the threat of surprise attack and that . . . we intended to maintain that responsibility."[79] He also indicated that he thought that Khrushchev's pre-summit "theatrical behavior" was "a diversionary tactic" designed to focus attention away from the substance of the summit meeting. "Well, here I get into the field of speculation entirely, and some of our experts have been going over this incident and the reaction to it very carefully," Herter stated. "There have been some indications that Mr. Khrushchev has been having a pretty hard time, particularly with his military people. The cutting down of the navy . . . has certainly caused a great deal of heart-burning in military circles and, I think, some very active opposition." Herter was then asked if Khrushchev "is under some pressure from the military to take a harder line." Herter responded, "I think he may be. I think that there are undoubtedly within the Presidium and in the important circles in Russia, people who do not sympathize with the softer line he has been taking . . . The Chinese criticisms have been in that same field."[80]

The speculation about Khrushchev's intentions ended early on 15 May when he met with de Gaulle and Macmillan, submitting a list of demands that Eisenhower must accept before the Soviets would participate in the conference. In his meeting with Macmillan, the Soviet premier outlined the demands: Eisenhower must condemn the flights, express regret, discontinue the flights, and punish those responsible.[81] Khrushchev had hoped to use Macmillan as his intermediary to Eisenhower but, in this case, the problem was not with the messenger but rather with the message.

Later that day, Eisenhower responded in a statement to Khrushchev's charges. "I came to Paris ready to discuss overflights and other forms of espionage and to seek agreements with the Soviet Union which would lessen, and hopefully, in due course eliminate the necessity for such activities," the statement read. "Mr. Khrushchev was certainly perfectly aware of this, but it now seems clear that, for reasons which I do not understand, he had already decided to use this incident in order to disrupt the meetings of the Chiefs of State and Heads of Government in Paris."[82]

Between 6 and 7.40 p.m. Eisenhower, Macmillan, and de Gaulle and their advisors met at the Elysée Palace in preparation for the formal opening of the conference on the next day. Both de Gaulle and Macmillan explained the substance of their individual meetings with Khrushchev. Macmillan interpreted Khrushchev's behavior as indicative of someone with domestic difficulties. Regardless of Khrushchev's attitude regarding espionage, Eisenhower said that "he was not going to be the only one at the conference to promise not to undertake something [that] everybody else was doing."[83]

Both Macmillan and de Gaulle expressed the view that Khrushchev was attempting to use the U-2 incident as a lever for discussions on the future of Germany. De Gaulle even thought that he could visualize an agreement: the United States would promise not to overfly the Soviet Union while Khrushchev would agree not to negotiate a separate treaty with East Germany. The discussion then moved off in the direction of disarmament and Berlin.[84]

Khrushchev's erratic behavior on 15 May troubled the American delegation, which consisted of Herter, Tom Gates, and John Irwin, assistant secretary of defense for international security affairs. With thoughts of surprise attack in mind, the fact that Khrushchev appeared nowhere in public without being in the presence of General Rodion Malinovsky, the Soviet defense minister (known as the "Rocket Marshal"), seemed ominous to some. Indeed, Macmillan was convinced that Khrushchev was "on a very short leash" because of Malinovsky's presence and that his behavior was bound to be unpleasant and even destructive.[85]

Therefore, on the night of 15 May, Gates contacted James H. Douglas, the deputy secretary of defense, in Washington. Douglas then contacted General Nathan Twining who, in turn, was authorized to raise the alert status of American forces around the world. This military alert was intended primarily for communications purposes and did not mean any upgrading of American military preparedness. But in still another bad stroke of luck for the Americans, the alert ceased to remain secret and news of it soon reached Paris. The reality of an American military alert contributed to a further increase in tensions at the summit meeting.[86]

On 16 May, Eisenhower, Macmillan, and their advisors had breakfast at the American Embassy. Macmillan, who had not slept well the night before, thought that Eisenhower "looked depressed and uncertain" and "the Americans were in considerable disarray."[87] John Eisenhower, however, thought that a meeting of this type brought out the best in his father who was "drawing upon the ideas of all, regardless of station, observing no difference of the rank of the adviser . . . When he left the [Embassy] for the first meeting of the Summit . . . he walked with amazing bounce."[88]

The opening meeting of the summit began at 11 a.m. The American delegation reflected the tension and before the leaders convened, Herter sent a cable to Douglas Dillon in Washington. "Mounting evidence suggests Soviets intend wreck conference at opening session on U-2 issue. Please inform Vice President," the cable read.[89]

Shortly after the representatives from the respective countries were seated, Khrushchev demanded the right to speak. As presiding officer, de Gaulle consented, and the Soviet premier, as described by Macmillan, "with a gesture reminiscent of Mr. Micawber . . . pulled a large wad of typewritten papers out of his pocket and began to speak. Khrushchev tried to pulverize Ike (as Micawber did Heep) by a mixture of vitriolic and offensive, and legal argument. It must have lasted three quarters of an hour."[90]

Certainly Khrushchev minced no words, making generous use of such adjectives as "provocative," and "treacherous" to describe the actions of the United States government. He also returned to his earlier statement that "militarists" in the Pentagon were largely responsible for the violations of Soviet air space. "I wish to address the people of the United States of America," Khrushchev said:

> I was in the USA and met there with various sections of the American people and I am sure that all the strata of the American people do not want war. An exception constitutes but a small frantic

group in [the] Pentagon and in [its] militarist quarters which benefit from the armaments race, gaining huge profits, which disregard the interest of the American people and in general the interest of the peoples of all the countries . . .[91]

Khrushchev waited almost until the end of his diatribe before withdrawing the offer for Eisenhower to visit the Soviet Union, scheduled for 10 June. "The President of the USA was to make a return visit to our country. Our agreement was that he would come to us on June 10. And we were being prepared to accord a good welcome to the high guest," Khrushchev declared. "Unfortunately, as a result of provocative and aggressive actions against the USSR there has now been created such conditions when we have been deprived of a possibility to receive the President with proper cordiality."[92]

For those attending the meeting, Khrushchev's histrionics were interpreted as mere theatrical gestures intended primarily for a domestic constituency. Tom Gates, present during Khrushchev's outburst, described the scene as "true theater, great theater. Eisenhower managed to hold himself together and keep his legendary temper in check. But both his face and the back of his neck grew redder the more Khrushchev carried on."[93] Likewise, Macmillan was aghast at Khrushchev's behavior. "Oh, it was terrible," he told interviewer Robert McKenzie in 1972. "It was insulting. Ike looked very uncomfortable."[94]

In their remarks following Khrushchev's tirade, both Macmillan and de Gaulle searched for a method of continuing with the conference. Macmillan asked:

> Could we not make note of these statements [those of Khrushchev and Eisenhower] and put them aside and put them for study in their written form and in the meantime get on with the Conference after a short recess rather than to make a hasty decision now without opportunity to study these statements?[95]

Following the prime minister's comments, de Gaulle likewise indicated a willingness to postpone the conference for a day until tempers cooled somewhat.

Khrushchev continued to create rhetorical road blocks, however. In his statements, Eisenhower referred to his previous Open Skies proposal and his intention to submit another Open Skies proposal to the UN for its consideration. Khrushchev was having none of it. Having rejected Open Skies once before in Geneva in 1955, he was not about to embrace the concept in Paris in 1960. Referring to Open Skies, Khrushchev said, "I heard it in Geneva in 1955. At that time we declared categorically that we were opposed to it, and I can repeat it now. We will permit no one, but no one, to violate our sovereignty."[96]

As the discussion ensued, Secretary Herter broke into the conversation to ask Khrushchev to expand upon his withdrawal of the invitation to Eisenhower to visit the Soviet Union. "Please understand this . . . How can we invite as a dear guest the leader of a country which has committed an aggressive act against us?" Khrushchev responded. "No visit would be possible under present conditions. How could our people welcome him? Even my small grandson would ask his grandpa: 'How could we welcome [as] an honored guest one who represents a country that sends planes to overfly and which we shot down with a rocket?'"[97]

The meeting and, in effect, the Paris Summit Conference ended at 2 p.m. Khrushchev stood up from the table and strode from the room, accompanied by his delegation. After Khrushchev departed, the leaders of the Western powers gathered for a brief conversation in an adjacent room. Macmillan and de Gaulle offered Eisenhower their support. Firmly, de Gaulle told the president that "whatever happens, we are with you to the end." Eisenhower was seething inside. "I'm just fed up," he muttered, furious at Khrushchev's deliberate attempts to humiliate him. More angry still was Charles "Chip" Bohlen, Eisenhower's counselor for Soviet Affairs, who had listened to the premier's tirade and recognized it for what it was: a profane, obscene series of insults directed at Eisenhower, and delivered in Khrushchev's earthy, peasant idiom. Since Bohlen spoke excellent Russian, he recognized that Khrushchev's interpreters had deliberately "sanitized" much of the premier's remarks, making them less offensive in translation.[98]

Eisenhower returned to the American Embassy after the collapse of the talks at the Elysée where he blew off some more steam before conferring with his advisors, including his press secretary James C. Hagerty, about the content of a statement to be released to the press later that day. For his part, Macmillan conducted a series of shuttle meetings with de Gaulle, Khrushchev and Eisenhower, designed to salvage the conference. He found Khrushchev every bit as obstinate as earlier that morning; "polite but quite immovable," was Macmillan's description.[99]

Shortly after 7 p.m., Macmillan came to the American Embassy to have dinner with the president. Eisenhower was asking for some support from Macmillan but the prime minister merely voiced the opinion that Ike "could say he was sorry or, preferably [make] a formal diplomatic apology." Ike refused the suggestion and wanted a stronger expression of support from Macmillan.[100]

On 17 May, the summit reconvened at 10 a.m. at the Elysee Palace. Since Khrushchev had not received his apology from Eisenhower, he did not attend this session or the one later in the day. So the meeting consisted of Eisenhower, Macmillan, and de Gaulle. Remarking on the meeting of 16 May, Eisenhower "said that when Khrushchev had begun his personal attack on him he had been inclined to let his Dutch temper get the better of him but he had decided to say nothing and not even look at Khrushchev."[101] He then complimented de Gaulle for handling an awkward situation in a dignified manner. The meeting ended with little in the way of further discussion.

Following this second meeting, Eisenhower asked Macmillan to take him to the British Embassy and while en route, the two could confer in the car. After a brief visit to the Embassy, the two leaders drove outside of Paris to the small village of Marnes-la-Coquette, close to SHAPE headquarters. In the village, Eisenhower asked to see Mayor Jean Minot, a friend from Ike's days as NATO commander in 1951–52. Learning of Eisenhower's presence in the village, the mayor hastily found Ike and Macmillan and took them to his office for a pleasant conversation. Eisenhower made a special point of introducing Macmillan to the mayor. After finishing their brief visit in the French countryside, Macmillan and Eisenhower returned to Paris to see if Khrushchev would attend the meeting scheduled for 3 p.m.

The public drive in the countryside by Eisenhower and Macmillan has been subjected to some differing interpretations. In his memoirs, Macmillan explained that, by being seen together, between the breakup of the first and second meeting of the summit, Eisenhower and Macmillan were sending a message of Anglo-American solidarity to Khrushchev.[102] In his memoir, *Strictly Personal*, John Eisenhower conveyed a similar impression of the purpose of this casual interlude.[103]

It is instructive to note that Eisenhower wanted to show Macmillan the house where he lived while serving as NATO commander. In this home, Eisenhower received the delegations from the United States who wanted him to return to the United States and seek the presidency in 1952. This was also the house where he had decided to accept the pleas of his supporters and run for the GOP presidential nomination.[104]

However, British historian Richard Aldous views the visit by Eisenhower and Macmillan to Marnes-la-Coquette differently. Aldous contends that Eisenhower had been unimpressed with the relatively weak support which he had received from Macmillan by contrast with the unswerving loyalty he had received from de Gaulle. Taking Macmillan with him "out in public," so to speak, was Ike's way of preventing Macmillan from distancing himself from the president and avoiding responsibility for the collapse of the summit.[105]

Regarding the 10 a.m. meeting on 17 May, Eisenhower had become exceptionally skeptical about Khrushchev's erratic behavior and felt that the entire summit was in jeopardy. Macmillan still hoped to salvage something from the conference. As the notes of the meeting read, Macmillan expressed the hope that a statement giving Khrushchev an ultimatum, in effect, to attend the 3 p.m. meeting or else the summit would be adjourned, might enable the leaders to have a summit at some point in the future. "Mr. Macmillan expressed the hope that such a statement would indicate that the Paris meeting could not be held but not necessarily exclude the whole idea of future summits and that the [Paris] meeting was simply adjourned," the notes read.[106]

Promptly at 3 p.m., Eisenhower, Macmillan, and de Gaulle returned to the Elysée Palace, hoping that Khrushchev would appear and that the summit conference would resume. Khrushchev refused to attend this session, also. In fact, during the morning, while Eisenhower and Macmillan had traveled to Marnes-la-Coquette, the Soviet leader was on his own special outing. Walking about Paris, he repeated his demand in front of the press who accompanied him that Eisenhower needed to apologize for his "aggressive actions" or else he would refuse to attend any more meetings.[107] Following this impromptu news conference, Khrushchev, Andrei Gromyko, the Soviet foreign minister, and Malinovsky drove out of the city to visit the battlefield of the Marne, where Malinovsky had fought as a 16-year-old in World War I. While en route to their destination, the Russian party was stopped by a blocked tree in the road. Khrushchev left his car, took an axe from one of the workers who was clearing the road, and cut off part of the tree.[108]

Arriving at the site where Malinovsky had once fought, the Russians discovered that the property belonged to a French farmer, René Pignard. Startled to see the Russians, Pignard nevertheless did his best to be hospitable. Visiting the area brought back some poignant memories for Malinovsky who remembered that, during the Great War, he had fought along side the French, the British, and the Americans. Malinovsky said he preferred the Americans "because they seemed more like Russians."[109] In a week of strange comments, this was one of the strangest; the hard-line Malinovsky was attempting to soften the Soviet line toward the Americans.

During the sojourn, Malinovsky engaged in conversation with the villagers at Pleur-sur-Marne. Someone shouted out, "Of course, we remember you. You had a Russian bear in your outfit, didn't you?" Malinovsky nodded, and then told Khrushchev that his unit had indeed taken a bear cub with them on their way to France. Malinovsky also inquired about the whereabouts of a young woman whom he had met during the war. The woman no longer lived in the village; Malinovsky was disappointed.[110]

While the Russians met in the French barnyard, two of de Gaulle's couriers sped up and handed Khrushchev a written invitation from de Gaulle to attend the afternoon meeting. Khrushchev read the note and then he and his group sped back to Paris, ignoring highway safety in the process. But Khrushchev did not return to the Elysée; he simply went to the Soviet Embassy where he climbed into a hot bath.

At the Elysée Palace, Eisenhower, Macmillan, and de Gaulle debated as to what to do, given Khrushchev's absence. For his part, Khrushchev continued to postpone any inquiry about decisions, telephoning to ask "the purpose of the meeting. If the question was to discuss what had been discussed yesterday [16 May] then the meeting would be acceptable, but not before 5 p.m. because Mr. Khrushchev had had no lunch. However, if other questions were to be discussed, then Mr. Khrushchev could not attend."[111] So, the three leaders of the Western democracies were forced to wait, once again, on the whims of Khrushchev.

Eisenhower and de Gaulle recognized the stark reality of the situation; unless Eisenhower publicly issued an apology, thereby humiliating himself, the United States government, and his Administration, the summit was finished. In fact, the realistic possibility for a summit may have collapsed once the Soviets captured Francis Gary Powers. Macmillan believed differently, of course, and wanted to attempt another overture to Khrushchev. Macmillan proposed that de Gaulle offer to serve as a mediator between the three Western leaders and Khrushchev, the implication being that de Gaulle might be able to save the conference after he and Eisenhower had failed.[112] But de Gaulle was not convinced that Macmillan's plan had any reasonable chance of success.[113]

Macmillan persisted, holding open the prospect that the summit could resume the following day if Khrushchev were only to soften his attitude. By this point, Eisenhower's patience was sorely tested. Reminding both Macmillan and de Gaulle that "this morning it had been agreed to seek an early and graceful end" to the conference, Ike argued that "one should remember that not only the personal dignity of the participants but even more the dignity of the Governments represented here were involved. There would be no point in protracting the situation."[114] Bowing slightly to Macmillan's position, Eisenhower had no objection to a meeting between Khrushchev and de Gaulle but now "the situation seemed to be imposing on President de Gaulle's patience."[115]

Macmillan was isolated. Eisenhower wanted to bring down the curtain before the West received any more insults from Khrushchev. "The question was whether after two days of work and waiting we should give this man one more opportunity to change his mind," Eisenhower said. "Would we not look ridiculous in that case? If we continued waiting, our own press would start criticizing us."[116]

Then, the meeting was interrupted by a telephone message from Khrushchev, asking if the 3 p.m. meeting was to decide on the issues to be discussed at the meeting, instead of resuming formal negotiations between the opposing sides. Macmillan wanted to pursue the new message; de Gaulle stuck to his previous position; Eisenhower recognized the trap and was opposed. Eisenhower "emphasized that if there should be a meeting to discuss with Mr. Khrushchev only the possibility of holding the Conference, it would have to take place without the President because he was the object of Khrushchev's hatred and insults."[117] Macmillan fought back, saying that "President de Gaulle could reason with Khrushchev. It was necessary to exert every possible effort to prevent the leftist elements from saying that we have failed to do everything in our power to get the Conference going."[118]

Then came a second reply, by telephone, and then a third reply, in writing. Khrushchev's written message was the same: the United States must "condemn the treacherous incursion of American military aircraft into the airspace of the Soviet Union, publicly express regret ... and punish those responsible."[119] By this point, all that remained was for Eisenhower, Macmillan, and de Gaulle to agree on the language of a joint communiqué, and announce the end of their meetings.

Macmillan still wanted to hold off issuing a final communiqué in the event of a change of heart by Khrushchev. He bemoaned the fact "that this development was the collapse of a policy that had been pursued persistently by his Government for two years. The situation could have grave consequences and could even bring us closer to war."[120] For Macmillan, 17 May was "the most tragic day of my life."[121]

Talking to Herter, Eisenhower was inclined to agree with Macmillan on waiting until the following day before declaring the summit over. Sensing Macmillan's disappointment, Ike was willing to ask Herter to concede the point to Macmillan.[122] But de Gaulle was opposed to any further "emotional" appeals. In effect, Khrushchev had destroyed the summit conference by failing to attend the meetings at 10 a.m. and 3 p.m. on 17 May.[123] It was the summit conference that failed to meet, the summit conference that never was.[124]

The four leaders – Eisenhower, Macmillan, de Gaulle, and Khrushchev – never met again together. Khrushchev's demands placed another summit meeting out of Eisenhower's reach. Interestingly, however, it was de Gaulle who sensed some vulnerability on Khrushchev's part. He wondered aloud on 17 May that, by 21 January 1961, "Mr. Khrushchev himself may not be around."[125] Even so, the fireworks were hardly over. On 18 May, Khrushchev held another news conference at the Palais des Chaillot, attacking Eisenhower for the final time. Before leaving Paris, Khrushchev also paid a final visit to both Macmillan and de Gaulle.

On 19 May, Eisenhower, Macmillan, and Khrushchev left Paris. Eisenhower had scheduled a visit to Portugal which he moved up in his schedule because of the collapse of the summit. Khrushchev returned to Moscow via East Berlin. Macmillan returned to London, disconsolate. Macmillan appeared to take the collapse of the summit in personal terms. It was a "disappointment amounting almost to despair – so much attempted, so little achieved."[126]

Back in London, Macmillan had difficulty hiding his sense of defeat. As he later recalled:

> Well, these were the hopes of three years finished, or looked liked finished. I'd worked for this [summit] ever since I'd been to Russia, three years (sic). And to get everybody into agreement, to get actually to a date, and to get what was to be much more important than the date, the acceptance of the view that this would be an annual event and [then] ... everything went wrong ... [It was] not a great blow to de Gaulle, who didn't think much of the Summit. I don't think [it was] really a great blow to Eisenhower except to his prestige, because he didn't hope for much of it. But to me who had made this plan, especially the continuation of a new methodology by which the world might look toward peace, I am bound to say it was the most tragic moment of my life.[127]

Macmillan might have underestimated Eisenhower's sense of disappointment, however. An exhausted Eisenhower returned to Washington on 20 May, to a hero's welcome. He realized that the Cold War had reached a new and more dangerous level of intensity as a consequence of the lost U-2 and the aborted summit conference. Descending from his airplane at Andrews Air Force Base, Ike noticed Mamie "with tears in her eyes."[128] Ike looked away; it was too painful to watch. For a time afterward, he even entertained thoughts of resignation. He never believed that the arms control negotiations with the Soviets, either in the UN Subcommittee on Disarmament or at Geneva, would be productive, even though he had tried to nudge them along from time to time with some concessions. With time running out on his presidency, he had made a bold personal move for peace by inviting Khrushchev to the United States and then agreeing to the summit. It even looked like he was making some progress until the "stupid U-2 mess" came and ruined the entire effort. Now it was simply a question of counting down the days until the end of his presidency.[129]

A diplomatic failure of the magnitude of the Paris Summit Conference inevitably leads to recriminations and blame-casting. Shortly after the summit's collapse, two articles appeared which attempted to shed light on the events in Paris. One article, authored by Don Cook, was entitled "Summit Casualty – Macmillan" and appeared in the *New York Herald Tribune*. The second article, "West's Future Aims: Macmillan's Summit Role," appeared in the *New York Times* and was authored by Drew Middleton.[130] Neither article presented the efforts of either British or American diplomacy in the best possible light and it was obvious that officials on both sides had been critical of each other, both during the Paris meetings and then in the aftermath. According to Cook, Macmillan had pushed his "middleman" role "past the point of diplomatic usefulness." Macmillan's "stock has fallen sharply in Washington" while "de Gaulle's has risen." The article went on to speculate that it was unlikely that Macmillan's advice would be sought much in Washington. American officials, according to Cook, blamed Macmillan for "going on too long" with his "apology formula" to satisfy Khrushchev when it was obvious that the Soviet premier had his mind made up not to negotiate. Under these conditions, it was highly unlikely that the Americans would "be considering another summit conference approach to the Russians for months, if not years."[131]

For its part, Middleton's article was considerably more sympathetic to Macmillan. As Middleton wrote:

> Some members of the United States delegation did a good deal of talking around the newly relighted camp fires of the "cold war" after President Eisenhower left Paris last Thursday. The burden of their talk was that a conference of heads of government was

always a bad idea and that Mr. Macmillan had talked Mr. Eisenhower into it.[132]

The main argument which the Americans made was that the Russians took advantage of Macmillan's naïvety to force a major diplomatic humiliation upon the United States. It was, as Middleton wrote, a case of the British "tail" wagging the American "dog."[133]

But the British were convinced that Macmillan's approach was correct. "What were we supposed to do, sit around growling at each other until some ass blew the world apart?" asked one of Middleton's British sources.[134] Regardless of the apparent acrimony between the two delegations, both sides agreed that there was no evidence of any personal animosity between Eisenhower and Macmillan, or between Christian Herter and Selwyn Lloyd.

Both Eisenhower and Macmillan moved quickly to repair any strained diplomatic feelings which may have come from the effect of the Cook and Middleton articles. Following their returns to the United States and Great Britain, respectively, Eisenhower and Macmillan attempted to alleviate any stress in their relationship which was a residual effect of the collapsed summit conference. Before leaving Paris, Eisenhower sent Macmillan a brief note, acknowledging that "you did everything that you possibly could to bring about a degree of civilized behavior in the arrogant and intransigent man from Moscow."[135] Back in the United States, Eisenhower was especially chagrined to see the articles by Cook and Middleton which suggested some tension between the British and Americans and some lingering disenchantment with Macmillan. On 20 May, Macmillan wrote Eisenhower, thanking him for his letter of 18 May which "cheered me up a great deal."[136] Macmillan certainly wished to preserve his close relationship with Ike. "Of course, this is all very depressing, but I am now pretty sure, looking back on the course of the Paris meeting, that Khrushchev had determined before he arrived to break it up.[137] I cannot tell you how much I admired the magnanimity and restraint with which you acted throughout those trying few days."[138]

On 24 May, Ike responded to Macmillan. He spoke of being disturbed by "two newspaper stories, that came out of London, one written by a man named Cook, the other by Middleton, both Americans."[139] Ike deplored the reports of "some fancied rift" between the two leaders and their respective delegations. "All the people around me and with me heard me time and again refer to the ideal association between you and myself and, indeed, between the both of us with General de Gaulle."[140]

He also reassured Macmillan in words which must have sounded somewhat welcome that "you and I agreed long ago that a Summit meeting was advisable, particularly after Mr. K removed his alleged ultimatum on Berlin."[141]

V

The collapse of the summit meeting in Paris has led to an abundance of speculation about Khrushchev's motivations for using the U-2 incident as the reason for his unwillingness to negotiate at Paris. Numerous theories have been advanced. Khrushchev "wrecked" the summit because he felt personally "betrayed" by his "good friend" Eisenhower and refused to negotiate with him for that reason. Khrushchev was under heavy pressure from conservative elements in the military and in the Kremlin not to make concessions to the West, either on arms control or on the status of Berlin, and therefore used the U-2 incident as a reason not to discuss issues where he might be forced to make concessions. Khrushchev torpedoed the summit because he wanted to cancel Eisenhower's visit to the Soviet Union and thereby deprive the West and the United States in particular of a major public relations victory. Khrushchev acted suspiciously because he did not want any agreements to come out of the summit but simply craved the media opportunity to achieve diplomatic parity with the West, and with Eisenhower specifically. Simply appearing with Eisenhower at the Paris summit was sufficient for Khrushchev to achieve that objective; he did not need any agreements which might possibly detract from that achievement. Another possible reason was that Khrushchev was using the U-2 incident as an opportunity to "split the Allies," which the Americans saw as a major objective of Soviet foreign policy. Recognizing that the U-2 incident was an embarrassment for the Americans, Khrushchev hoped to use the British and French to bring pressure on the Americans for concessions. Finally, Khrushchev felt that the political environment would be more conducive to his purposes with a new administration in office, rather than attempt to extract some concessions from the Eisenhower Administration, which was only going to hold office for the next six months. The U-2 incident therefore served as a useful excuse to keep from engaging in useful discussions with a "lame-duck" administration.

Each of these theories has its supporters, of course. In his memoir, Sergei Khrushchev espoused the "Eisenhower as betrayer" theory. According to the son of the late Soviet premier, "Father's wounds never healed. The deception on the part of his 'friend' General Eisenhower, who had gone on walks with him at Camp David and agreed that nothing was more terrible than war, struck Father to the heart. He forgave neither Eisenhower the president nor Eisenhower the man for the U-2."[142]

Such sentiments convey a greater degree of intimacy between the two leaders than may have existed as well as calling into question the notion that personal relations between heads of state form the determining basis for their foreign policies. When Khrushchev visited the United States in September 1959, his visit appeared to the Eisenhower Administration to be a fine propaganda opportunity for the Soviet leader but certainly not the occasion for any serious diplomatic breakthroughs, although Khrushchev did drop his ultimatum on Berlin.[143] Otherwise, any mention of a solution to the Berlin controversy or of a reduction in the arms race was simply faced by Khrushchev's peculiar brand of rhetorical resistance.[144] Likewise, the "Spirit of Camp David" was largely the creation of Khrushchev.[145] In view of the U-2 incident, this view holds, Khrushchev should make no concession to the Americans unless they first made a humiliating apology.

The key indicator of this perception was the presence of Marshal Malinovsky with Khrushchev in Paris. Harold Macmillan believed that Malinovsky's presence signaled the relative weakness of Khrushchev's policy of détente within the councils of the Kremlin.[146]

Khrushchev himself added some fuel to support this belief, nine years after the U-2 incident and five years after his removal from power. According to the former premier, he was pursuing a policy of gradual détente in foreign policy and gradual liberalization at home until the U-2 incident. "From the time Gary Powers was shot down in a U-2 over the Soviet Union, I was no longer in full control. Decision-making powers were weakened after the U-2 crisis," Khrushchev wrote. "It scared the Kremlin militarists. My own ascendancy was over."[147]

That particular view has its critics, too, including Sergei Khrushchev, who disputed the notion that his father was not the master of the Soviet government. Just prior to the summit, Sergei Khrushchev noted, his father had made a series of personnel changes in the Presidium, hardly the work of someone who lacked the support of his party organization. Sergei Khrushchev has written: "Some Western authors who write about the Paris crisis argue that there were serious differences in the Soviet leadership at the time and that pressure on Father from the right led to the break-up of the conference. This viewpoint strikes me as profoundly mistaken."[148]

Marshal Malinovsky's presence at the conference seemed to be an indicator of an attempt by conservative elements in the Kremlin to "keep Khrushchev on a short leash" in Paris. But it now appears that both Malinovsky and Tom Gates were in Paris because of a misreading of some subtle diplomatic signals. On 16 May 1960, Ambassador Thompson recorded a conversation with "a member of the French delegation" who told him that the Soviets added Malinovsky to their delegation only after learning that the Americans intended to bring Secretary of Defense Gates to Paris. Since the Soviets had no civilian counterpart to the American secretary of defense, they added Malinovsky for that purpose.[149] In his memoirs, Sergei Khrushchev essentially confirmed Thompson's conversation.[150]

The Americans likewise had an understanding of Malinovsky's presence at the summit similar to the Russian understanding of Gates's presence. As Gates recalled:

> We found out that Khrushchev planned on bringing Marshal Malinovsky to the Summit. When we found out that Malinovsky was to be Khrushchev's principal assistant at this meeting, I was added to accompany the President to sort of offset the presence of Malinovsky. The Politburo had obviously hotly debated the U-2 incident. Malinovsky was not in on the Russian planning for the Summit conference [but] was an important factor in the Summit. Malinovsky was added only after the U-2.[151]

A third explanation for the collapse of the summit was that Khrushchev was looking for a convenient way to cancel Eisenhower's proposed trip to the Soviet Union. Robert Murphy was a strong proponent of this view. As Murphy wrote: "Khrushchev utilized the U-2 flight as an excuse to revoke the invitation to Eisenhower to visit the Soviet Union. The President's tour could have made a tremendously favorable impression on the Russian people. Communist leaders feared it."[152]

Presumably, communist leaders in China also feared the effects of an Eisenhower visit to the Soviet Union, while the United States and the Soviet Union were at least willing to discuss the subject of détente, the United States and China remained the most implacable of foes during the 1950s. Eisenhower's military response to the Chinese shelling of Taiwan's offshore islands in 1958 had angered the Chinese government, and Mao Zedong was challenging Khrushchev to pursue a harder line against the Americans. Canceling Eisenhower's visit provided Khrushchev with an opportunity to pursue some solidarity in the communist camp, particularly with the Chinese, who were becoming increasingly critical of the Soviet Union.[153]

A fifth reason for Khrushchev's behavior may have involved his desire to split the NATO allies. Certainly his personal conversations with Macmillan and de Gaulle, and not with Eisenhower, support this view. Likewise, British and American foreign policy specialists generally ascribed that motive to much of Soviet foreign policy.

After the collapse of the conference, however, much was said about how Khrushchev's behavior had tended to unify the Western allies, rather than to divide them. Admittedly, some of these statements could be interpreted as an attempt to put the best possible face on what was in reality a major diplomatic embarrassment. But, at their final meeting on 18 May before leaving Paris, Eisenhower, Macmillan, and de Gaulle attempted to harmonize their attitudes and actions. This meeting began with a brief explanation by Maurice Couve de Murville, the French foreign minister, of the discussions between the foreign ministers during the conference. Couve de Murville spoke about the need to inform the North Atlantic Council about developments at the summit as well as the impact of the summit's collapse upon the situation in Berlin. He also spoke about the position which the three nations would take when arms control negotiations began once again in June.

Eisenhower, Macmillan, and de Gaulle all expressed concern about possible Soviet moves in Berlin. Couve de Murville assured them that plans were in force to be able to supply West Berlin if it was cut off by the Russians or East Germans.[154]

As was customary, Eisenhower sought to play the role of unifier at the conference, but Macmillan and de Gaulle were likewise caught up in the valedictory sentiment of the meeting. The final notes of the meeting read poignantly:

> The President stated that he did not know what the future might hold. It might be that this would be the last meeting of the three while he was still President of the United States. If it were the last, he wanted to say that it had been a great privilege to work with two such colleagues and to express his esteem and admiration, even affection, toward them.
>
> Prime Minister Macmillan said that he associated himself with the remarks of the President. He wanted to express his thanks to President de Gaulle for the way he had brought them through these

disappointments. He believed that the experience had brought the three closer together.

President de Gaulle then terminated the meeting by saying goodbye to both *"mes amis."*[155]

Finally, a sixth reason for Khrushchev's behavior may have been his desire not to take any positions at Paris which might tend to strengthen the Republican Party in the upcoming presidential election. By this point, Khrushchev had developed a profound dislike for Richard Nixon, referring to him as the "shopkeeper."[156] Khrushchev and Nixon had, of course, verbally sparred in July 1959, at their famous "kitchen debate" in Moscow as well as when Khrushchev visited the United States in September.[157] In Khrushchev's memoirs, he linked Nixon with John Foster Dulles, the supreme anti-communist of the 1950s, as the Americans most despised within the Russian hierarchy.[158] In Khrushchev's mind, his enemies in America were clearly defined: John Foster Dulles, the anti-communist ideologue; Allen Dulles, the American spymaster; and Richard Nixon, the pugnacious rhetorician. For five years, Khrushchev had contended with such individuals; perhaps he wanted to deal with a different set of American leaders.

In that regard, an interesting conversation occurred in Paris on 18 May during a reception at the American Embassy. During the course of the evening, an American diplomat told of a conversation which he had had on the evening of 17 May with Quarles Van Ufford, a member of the Dutch embassy staff. Van Ufford related the story of a member of his staff who had spoken with Yvan Koudriatsev, the Soviet counselor of economic affairs, and inquired about the reasons why Khrushchev was "playing up the airplane incident so much and using it as a pretext for breaking off the Summit."[159] Koudriatsev agreed that the airplane incident was over-played "because the Soviets want to wait until there is a new administration in the United States before taking up the important problems which were to have been discussed at the Summit."[160] And, one must also remember that Khrushchev joked with John F. Kennedy the following spring in Vienna that he "voted for him" by waiting until after the election to release the American pilots who were captured when their RB-47 aircraft was shot down by the Soviets in July (see Epilogue).[161]

Nixon realized that the U-2 incident and the collapse of the summit conference in Paris had damaged him politically for his upcoming campaign against the Democrats. The failure of the summit conference led to the suspicion that the Cold War might continue indefinitely. As

Nixon later wrote, his use of the "peace issue [in the presidential campaign] was tarnished."[162] The U-2 incident may not have damaged Eisenhower and Macmillan in terms of their domestic standing, but it did long-term political damage to both Nikita Khrushchev and, ironically, to Richard Nixon.

Epilogue

On 18 May in Paris, following the collapse of the Four-Power Summit Conference, Dwight D. Eisenhower, Harold Macmillan, and Charles de Gaulle met together for the last time as national leaders. Eisenhower forecast a difficult road ahead for the Western alliance. "President Eisenhower said he thought the great problem we would face [in the post-summit period] would be a succession of little events, annoying but not important or dramatic enough in itself to arouse public opinion," read the notes of the meeting. "Such tactics would pose very difficult problems."[1] In Eisenhower's estimation, Khrushchev did not intend to provoke another crisis over Berlin but would attempt to take advantage of political instability in certain areas around the world in order to keep the allies off-balance.

Between June and November 1960, Eisenhower and Macmillan were forced to contend with several difficult situations as the rivalry between the great powers turned in a different direction. In July, the Soviets shot down an American RB-47 reconnaissance aircraft, capturing its two pilots, and for a moment it looked as though the world was about to witness another U-2 crisis. The situation was complicated by the fact that the RB-47 aircraft had taken off from a base in Great Britain and the British were implicated in the surveillance enterprise.[2] Unlike the U-2 crisis of May, however, both the Americans and the Soviets kept from inflaming the incident, and the two pilots were returned to the United States early in 1961.[3]

Other problems also began appearing around the world in the summer of 1960. In July and August, the Eisenhower Administration and the Macmillan government grew concerned about Russian meddling in the civil war in the mineral-rich African nation of the Congo. In the Caribbean, Fidel Castro and his pro-communist government in Cuba had solidified its power base and was threatening to export its revolutionary message throughout Latin America. Castro's anti-Americanism had become glaringly evident, as well as his decision to link the regime's fortunes with the Soviet Union. Finally, the communist-led insurrection in Southeast Asia had intensified, particularly in the small country of Laos. By the end of 1960, the violence in Laos concerned Eisenhower the most of all of these "succession of little events."

As these "little events" came to affect the world situation, Harold Macmillan functioned more as an advisor to Eisenhower than as a partner in the policy-making role which he had undertaken for the previous three years. In a sense, policy-making had become a casualty of the U-2 crisis and the failure of the summit conference as the Soviets showed little interest in further arms control negotiations or in discussions about Berlin.

Macmillan played a useful role in the final six months of the Eisenhower presidency. The increase in tensions during the summer of 1960 enabled Macmillan to press for more cooperation between the United States and Great Britain in the area of defense. Since 1956, the United States Department of Defense and the Navy Department had been working on the development of a submarine-launched ballistic missile system. The project which eventually became known as Polaris, the name for the missile, had surmounted a host of engineering, budgetary, and navigational problems to the point where it was ready for deployment by the end of 1960. The first Polaris-firing submarine, the *George Washington*, entered active service in December 1960, carrying 16 medium-range ballistic missiles, each with a range of 1,200 miles.[4]

Given the Eisenhower Administration's desire to strengthen NATO, and in particular NATO's nuclear component, it was logical that the British and the Americans would eventually cooperate on the submarine-launched ballistic missile program in the same fashion that they had cooperated on the land-based IRBM program in 1957. By the conclusion of Eisenhower's presidency, the two nations had concluded an agreement which enabled the Americans to base Polaris submarines in Scotland, another step along the path of strengthening Britain's contribution to the deterrent capability of the Western alliance.[5]

The increasing tensions between the Soviet Union and the Western alliance during summer 1960 carried over into the autumn. In September, Nikita Khrushchev once again came to the United States but not in the pursuit of détente. Instead, he visited the United Nations in New York to deliver a vigorous, theatrical anti-imperialist address. Macmillan accepted the challenge of responding to Khrushchev, on the floor of the United Nations, but Khrushchev deliberately interrupted him in his now-famous shoe-pounding episode. In one of the memorable events of the Cold War, however, Macmillan maintained his aplomb and delivered a devastating rhetorical blow to the Soviet premier.

During the UN sessions, Eisenhower and Macmillan met in New York for what were their last bilateral meetings of Ike's presidency.

By this point, the two leaders had re-established their customary candid and friendly relationship. Although both men certainly realized that the curtain was about to come down on their tenure together as national leaders, they nevertheless conducted their talks as though they intended to remain in office indefinitely. Discussion about the usual subjects – disarmament, European security, instability in the non-aligned world, the future of the United Nations, and other topics – dominated the agenda.[6] This time, however, Eisenhower was accompanied by Secretary of State Christian Herter instead of John Foster Dulles, and Macmillan was accompanied by Sir Alec Douglas-Home, who had been appointed Foreign Secretary in July to replace Selwyn Lloyd, who moved over to the Exchequer after Macmillan reshuffled his Cabinet. The personalities, on both sides, had changed markedly since the Americans and the British had met together at Bermuda in March 1957.

I

Eisenhower and Macmillan left Paris in late May with a sense of foreboding about the future. For Eisenhower, his hope for a graceful end to his presidency, culminating in an historic nuclear test-ban agreement, a reduction in the arms race, and strict controls on the enormous sums which were being spent on defense, had been smashed by the controversy surrounding the U-2 incident. For Macmillan, his hopes for a successful summit, and the acceptance by the great powers of a series of summits, held regularly, had also vanished. Like Eisenhower, Macmillan feared a future where the Soviet bloc and the Western alliance continued to be implacable foes, building weapons of mass destruction at an accelerated rate. As Macmillan confided to his diary about a month later: "We are now beginning to realize the full extent of the summit disaster in Paris. For me, it is the work of two or three years. For Eisenhower, it means an ignominious end to his Presidency. For Khrushchev, a set-back to his more conciliatory and sensible ideas. For the world, a step toward ultimate disaster."[7]

Under these circumstances, one could argue that the last event which Eisenhower and Macmillan, and perhaps even Khrushchev, wanted was another U-2 incident. In early July, however, it looked as though the recent past was about to repeat itself. On 1 July, the Soviets shot down an American RB-47 surveillance aircraft operating over international waters. The plane had taken off from a base in Britain with the purpose of obtaining electronic reconnaissance along the northern border of the

Soviet Union. For ten days, both sides played a "cat and mouse" game, with the Americans unwilling to admit that they had lost another surveillance aircraft while the Soviets, holding two pilots, waited for the Americans to issue another false "cover story." On 11 July, Khrushchev revealed that the Russians had once again shot down an American aircraft and were holding two survivors of the crash. True to form, Khrushchev lashed out at the "provocative acts" of the Americans and threatened the British for allowing the Americans to use their bases for espionage committed against the Soviet Union.[8]

With the Americans taking a deliberately low-key approach to the RB-47 matter, Macmillan became the cheerleader for the Western alliance against Khrushchev's tactics. It took a considerable amount of courage for Macmillan to align himself closely with the American government in view of the concern that the use of British bases by American reconnaissance aircraft made Great Britain a potential target for attack. Regardless, on 19 July, Macmillan read his response to Khrushchev in an "open letter" on the floor of the House of Commons. The response was a mixture of conciliation, a justification of Western policy in the non-aligned world after the collapse of the Summit, and concern over the trend in East–West relations.

In his letter to Khrushchev, Macmillan attempted to re-invoke the optimism which prevailed at the beginning of 1959. "I would like to remind you of the conversations which we have had from time to time when we have both agreed to seek methods by which the underlying tension in the world could be reduced," he wrote. "When I had the pleasure of being your guest in Moscow last year I think we succeeded in setting in motion a sequence of developments which appeared to have some great promise."[9] Despite the collapse of the summit, Macmillan suggested to Khrushchev that "some forward movement" might still be possible in reducing world tensions. Nevertheless, he still admonished Khrushchev about the RB-47 incident and the threats made upon Great Britain by the Soviet Union. "[Even] if the facts had been as stated by your government, I do not think that the Soviet authorities should have taken so grave an action and one so calculated to turn the incident into a major international dispute."[10]

Next, Macmillan moved into a justification of the West's policies regarding the non-aligned world, especially in Africa and Asia, where independence movements were in full motion. "For more than a century, it has been our [Great Britain's] purpose to guide our dependent territories toward freedom and independence," Macmillan stated.

> [Since] the second World War, India, Pakistan, Ceylon, Ghana, Malaya, comprising over 510 millions of people have, with our help, reached the goal of independent life and strength... Nor is this movement at an end. In October of this year, Nigeria, with, its 35 million people, will be another great independent country. Sierra Leone will become independent in April 1961. The West Indies Federation is moving rapidly in the same direction, and so the process goes on.

Finally, Macmillan firmly rebuked Khrushchev for this latest example of inflammatory rhetoric. "As I think you will agree, I have consistently welcomed and given much weight to your assurances of the Soviet government's desire for peaceful coexistence and détente in international relations. I have shown my sympathy with such purposes," Macmillan emphasized.

> It is, however, my firm opinion that these objectives cannot be successfully pursued without the exercise of patience and restraint. Much of my present anxiety derives from the fact that these elements seem to be absent from recent manifestation of Soviet Government policy. I write to you now so plainly because I have the memory of our frank discussions with you in my mind. I simply do not understand what your purpose is today.[11]

Macmillan sent a letter to Eisenhower on 18 July, one day before his appearance in the House of Commons, explaining why he wrote to Khrushchev. "I have attempted in my letter to make some counter-attack on Mr. Khrushchev," Macmillan wrote. "I hope you will think that this is wise. I felt that we should not attempt to answer his individual notes in detail but should also draw the attention of the world to the dangerous tendency presented by the Soviet attitude since the Summit Meeting."[12]

On 23 July, Eisenhower responded to Macmillan. "I thought the tone of the note [to Khrushchev] was fine and your letter was excellent," Ike wrote. "I feel you were entirely correct to make some sort of counter-attack, particularly about the dangerous trend of Soviet policy since the Summit meeting."[13] The two leaders appeared to be closing ranks after the disappointments of the Summit.

Khrushchev did not lose sight of his objectives, either. Realizing the political sensitivity of the espionage issue in America during a presidential election year, he responded by holding the two American RB-47 pilots until early 1961. Bowing to American pressure to release the pilots before the election would have been a political and public relations victory for both Eisenhower and Richard Nixon. Khrushchev had no desire to take any steps which benefited either man, especially Nixon. So both Francis Gary Powers and the RB-47 pilots remained in the Soviet Union until after the American presidential election, which John F. Kennedy won by the narrowest of margins. On 21 January 1961, the day after Kennedy's inauguration, Khrushchev informed Ambassador Llewelyn Thompson in Moscow of his intention to release the RB-47 pilots as a positive gesture toward the new Administration. Powers, however, was not released until 10 February 1962, when the United States and the Soviet Union exchanged him for the East German spy, Rudolf Abel.[14]

Eisenhower and Macmillan also discussed the worsening situation in Cuba. On 2 July, Macmillan mentioned the problem which Fidel Castro presented for Allied interests in the Western Hemisphere. Writing to Eisenhower on a number of topics, Macmillan mentioned that "I have been thinking a lot about our new troubles with Castro. Chris and Selwyn are in close touch about this, but do let me know if there is anything you think we should do. We will try to help you in any way we can over what might develop into a really serious Russian threat."[15]

In fact, the Cuban situation was one of the problems uppermost in Eisenhower's mind in the aftermath of the summit conference. Responding to Macmillan on 11 July, he thanked the prime minister for his interest and then outlined the American position. "Because the Cuban problem so profoundly affects not only the security of the United States but is also related to the security of the Free World as a whole, it might be well to review the dimension of the problem as we see it," Ike wrote.[16] Eisenhower divided the Administration's response to the Cuban problem into three phases: the testing phase, which occurred during the first six months of 1959; the "policy of restraint," which lasted from the middle of 1959 to the middle of 1960; and finally, a third phase (then in progress) designed "to bring home to the Cuban people the cost of Castro's policies and of his Soviet orientation and also to establish a climate in those who recognize the necessity of eventually beneficial relations between Cuba and the United States can assert themselves," essentially a time in which the Administration planned to institute a series of measures designed to bring internal and external pressure on the Castro regime.[17]

As for help from the British, Eisenhower was specific. First, he asked the British to support the United States if the Cubans protested the

American-supported trade embargo against the Castro regime and found support from the Soviet Union for that action. Second, Eisenhower was searching for ways to damage the Castro regime economically. A "more immediate problem concerns tankers," Ike wrote. "As of now, Castro's insistence on displacing Free World petroleum with Soviet oil led to the taking over of British and American refineries, despite the fact that the companies concerned had in effect previously extended substantial credits to finance continued petroleum exports to Cuba."[18] The Soviets were willing to ship oil to Cuba but were encountering difficulties finding tankers to transport the petroleum.

> We think that there is every reason discreetly to discourage the use of Free World tankers to bring Soviet oil to refineries which have been taken from our companies and yours and, more importantly, that a petroleum shortage in Cuba would not only raise questions there about Castro's capabilities but also crystallize doubts about the USSR. Your help, not only with respect to British tankers, but also in influencing other tanker-owning countries would be invaluable.[19]

Finally, Eisenhower wanted to restrict the sale of arms to Cuba, from whatever the source. He solicited British support for that effort, concerned that Castro intended to use these arms shipments to carry his revolution into other Latin American countries.[20]

Macmillan responded quickly to Eisenhower on 22 July, but he was obviously unwilling to be as forceful with Castro as Eisenhower had proposed. The tone of Macmillan's letter indicated a general sympathy with the American concern about Castro, but also a definite skepticism about British involvement in the Caribbean. "Let me first tell you how deeply interested I was by your long letter about Cuba and Castro," Macmillan told Ike.[21] "Castro is really the very Devil. He is your Nasser, and of course with Cuba sitting right at your doorstep the strategic implications are even more important than the economic. I fully understand and share your apprehensions."[22]

Beyond that expression of apprehension, however, Macmillan refused to go further, especially on the matter of denying tanker capacity to other nations. "Do let me know if there is any particular point where we are in a position to help, without embarking on measures which are only suitable in times of emergency," he continued.[23] "The tankers, for instance, we can only control by taking powers similar to those we take in wartime. However, I feel sure Castro has to be got rid of, but it is a tricky operation for you to continue and I only hope you will succeed."[24]

On 25 July, Macmillan sent another letter to Eisenhower which expanded on some of the points which he had raised in his earlier letter. Written in Macmillan's carefully constructed prose, the letter was a precise critique of the evolving American policy toward Cuba and toward Castro. "I need hardly say that we fully share your concern at the way in which Castro has allowed his country to become ever more open to communist and Soviet influence," Macmillan began.[25] "We are now inclined to agree with the view expressed in your letter that Castro and his Government are now so fully committed to the course they have chosen that the only hope for an improvement in the position must lie in the replacement of his regime. But it is not easy to see how this can be done."[26]

Macmillan then made it clear that he doubted the effectiveness of the presumptive American attempt to topple the Castro regime. "I must confess to some doubts as to the success of the new policy," he wrote.

> Although better off than many Latin American peoples, the mass of Cubans are poor and accustomed to hardship. Having tasted the flavour of revolution they are likely, it seems to me, seriously to react against a deterioration in the conditions of their life only if they are confident that this is in no way the work of "counterrevolutionaries" or of the United States Government against which they have been encouraged to feel so much resentment. There does seem to be some danger that if, as a result of the measures which you have taken, or may take in the coming months, conditions of economic hardship are created, many Cubans who might otherwise have gradually drifted into opposition to Castro will instead be inclined to regard him – and themselves – as martyrs.[27]

In this letter, Macmillan expressed a clear preference for a strategy of support for the "pro-reform," anti-Castro elements both inside and outside of Cuba. Castro's "revolution" increasingly showed signs of a closer attachment to Moscow and the perversion of reforms promised to the Cuban people. Castro's "spendthrift economic policy, his continued denial of the ordinary freedoms, and his refusal to allow the peasants to own the confiscated land all seemed likely to lead to great internal dissatisfaction," Macmillan wrote. In that scenario, Castro might be deposed if his revolution failed to meet popular expectations.[28] In that respect, Macmillan cautiously entertained the hope that "important defections" from Castro's revolution might develop, "bent on restoring the revolution to its intended course."[29] Under those circumstances, Macmillan surmised that "it might... be wiser to let the yeast rise of its own accord."[30]

Deferring to Eisenhower, Macmillan wrote that "you must clearly play the hand in this affair and we will certainly help you in any way we can."[31] But what, exactly, was the way in which the Eisenhower Administration could expect assistance from the British? Macmillan stated that the British would support American efforts in the United Nations to isolate Castro economically. Eisenhower could definitely expect British support in efforts to restrict the shipment of arms into Cuba. In other areas, however, support was not forthcoming. As Macmillan stated,

> I'm afraid the problem of tankers for the carriage of Soviet oil to Cuba is not easy. There is a considerable excess of tanker tonnage in the world at present, and much of it is in the hands of owners whom we cannot influence or even advise. I am told that it would not be possible in the way you propose so effectively to Cuba as to cause any really serious dislocation there. We – and you – would then be in the position of incurring maximum odium with the Cubans and perhaps encouraging them to turn still further to the Russians without achieving the aim which you have in mind. As I told you in my message of July 22, we have no legal power to compel tanker owners not to carry oil to Cuba.[32]

Macmillan found no simple course to follow regarding the problem of Castro. "I know, and fully sympathize with, your purpose – the unseating of Castro and his replacement by a more suitable regime – but I am not very clear how you really mean to achieve this aim," Macmillan wrote.[33] Obviously, the British were as unwilling, under Macmillan's leadership, to risk their status and credibility in the world community for American interests in the Caribbean as the Americans were to risk their status and credibility for British interests in the Middle East.

On 8 August, Eisenhower responded to Macmillan on the issue of Cuba. Noting Macmillan's comments that Castro had lost the support of middle-class, pro-reform elements in Cuba, Eisenhower also confirmed the hard reality that the "Castro regime's police control and Communist terror tactics have thoroughly intimidated the politically articulate Cubans, and that left undisturbed, the regime will increase its domination to the point that internal opposition is unlikely ever to attain sufficient strength and resolution to overthrow Castro."[34] Ike's main concern, beyond the Soviet Union's use of Cuba as a satellite, was the possible destabilizing effect of the Cuban revolution on the rest of Latin America. Many of the other Latin American nations, while concerned about the exporting of the Cuban revolution, nevertheless had "foundations [which] too often rest uneasily on outmoded societies ripe for change."[35] Hence the problem: "Should Castro manage to survive for another year or more, these nations run the risk of being overtaken by revolution with conditions such as [are] now existing in Cuba."[36]

So, what was to be the American policy in dealing with Castro? First, Eisenhower did not completely discount the possibility of some kind of popular discontent toward the Castro regime. Retelling an account of a story told him by an anti-Castro Cuban, Eisenhower wrote that

> the average Cuban sugar worker wants to receive his earnings in cash and go to the store, buy a white *guayabera*, white shoes, a bottle of rum and go to a dance; not be paid in script redeemable at the people's [government] store where only work clothing and rice are to be had and a lecture by a government official is the only entertainment offered.[37]

Even so, the United States faced a long and difficult task in trying to build on anti-Castro sentiments in Cuba, given the growing strength of the regime. In his final comments to Macmillan, having ruled out even the suggestion of intervention against Castro, Eisenhower confessed that economic pressure was about the only recourse which the Americans had. "I wish to stress that we shall also be substantially increasing our efforts on the positive side by way of economic, financial, and technical assistance to the countries of Latin America," Eisenhower wrote.[38]

> As we have so often said to the Cubans to no avail, we recognized the need for major changes, revolution if you will, in the Cuban social and economic structure, and were and are prepared, if asked, to assist Cuba and anyone of the other countries in bringing about needed improvements carried out legally and responsibly under democratic regimes. Although we must make sure of the ultimate achievement of our aim, I fully agree that our course is fraught with difficulties and dangers.[39]

II

The collapse of the summit conference in Paris and the tensions in the international environment which followed it, led the Eisenhower Administration and the Macmillan government back onto some familiar territory: a resumption of the cooperation on defense policy which had characterized the previous three years. In 1960, however, the area of cooperation involved the development of the fleet ballistic missile system (FBM) by the United States, culminating in the deployment of the Polaris class nuclear submarine program in 1959–60 and the subsequent agreement by the Macmillan government to provide berthing facilities for Polaris submarines in Scotland. By the time Eisenhower left office in 1961, these agreements had been completed. The Americans had achieved their objective of securing a base, in the most friendly of hands, within the range of the Soviet Union, and the British had achieved their objective of acquiring advanced American missile technology and integrating it into British forces to strengthen Britain's independent nuclear deterrent.

The joint United States–United Kingdom agreement on the Polaris missile system satisfied several major defense objectives of both countries, but it nevertheless wound a tortuous negotiating path before the United States and Britain concluded their agreement. Some background is necessary. For the United States, defense planners and missile technologists in the Pentagon as well as in the armed services began a search in the mid-1950s for a missile capability which could offset the presumed advantage which the Soviets would soon enjoy in long-range intercontinental ballistic missiles. In fact, the agreement in March 1957 between the United States and Great Britain at the Bermuda Conference involving the transfer of Thor IRBM technology to Britain as well as the adoption of the Norstad Plan at the North Atlantic Council meeting in December 1957 were steps in that direction.

Even so, the Americans were still searching for a more effective system to add to their deterrent capability and, in 1957, the Navy Department provided the Administration with an answer in the form of an intermediate-range missile which could be fired from a nuclear-powered submarine. Thus was created the Fleet Ballistic Missile program with the objective of deploying these submarines, known by the acronym SSBN, by 1963. To expedite the entire process, and also to give the Navy an edge in developing the missile, which became known as the Polaris, ahead of the missile programs in the Army and in the Air Force, Admiral Arleigh A. Burke, the chief of naval operations, and Thomas S. Gates, then secretary of the navy, created the Special Projects Office (SPO) and placed Vice Admiral William "Red" Raborn in charge of it. Essentially, the Navy Department took the development of the Polaris missile out of the normal channels of its bureau system and placed it on a "fast-track" basis in order to expedite the program.[40]

Raborn and his team of Navy officers, Pentagon planners, and thousands of contractors succeeded in an unprecedented fashion. By reallocating hundreds of millions of dollars within the Navy Department's budget, by altering the design and construction of submarines, and by revising the range of the Polaris missile, the Navy managed to complete the construction of its first nuclear-powered fleet ballistic missile submarine, named the *George Washington* (SSBN-598), on 6 June 1959. The Navy completed the construction of three more SSBN-class submarines, the *Patrick Henry*, the *Robert E. Lee*, and the *Theodore Roosevelt*, by the end of 1959.[41] Then, on 20 July 1960, two Polaris missiles fired from the *George Washington* successfully hit their targets at a distance of 1,155 miles.[42] The Fleet Ballistic Missile system had become a reality.

On 15 November 1960, the *George Washington* entered active service, followed by the *Patrick Henry* on 30 December 1960.[43] Eisenhower was enthusiastic about the capability and versatility of the FBM system. "Roving and hidden under the seas with 16 thermonuclear missiles apiece, the *George Washington* and her sister ships possess a power and relative invulnerability which will make suicidal any attempt by an aggressor to attack the free world by surprise," he said.[44]

If American defense planners were searching for more invulnerability for their nuclear capability, the British entertained similar ambitions. Macmillan wanted to phase out Britain's reliance on fixed sites for missile installations, which he believed were becoming technologically obsolescent and, more importantly, made Britain too much of a target of the Soviet Union. As Macmillan stated in a letter to Queen Elizabeth II: "[For] political and morale reasons I am very anxious to get rid of these fixed rockets. This is a very small country, and to put these installations near the large centers of population – where they have to be – would cause anxiety to Your Majesty's subjects."[45]

During the 1950s, the British had attempted to develop their own surface-to-surface missile, called Blue Streak. In addition to being launched from a fixed site, the Blue Streak had the disadvantage of being increasingly expensive with costs that were getting harder to justify. The answer to Macmillan's concern about cost overruns and immobility on the part of Blue Streak could be resolved if the British decided to purchase the American Skybolt missile, then under development by the United States Air Force. The Skybolt was a long-range, air-to-surface missile which was designed for compatibility with the British V-bomber fleet. Purchase of these missiles would solve two problems for Macmillan; it would address the matter of immobility since aircraft could be dispersed throughout the country or, if necessary, remain aloft during a military emergency, and it would maintain a strategic role for the British bomber fleet.

As the two countries began discussions about their defense policies early in 1960, Britain clearly was prepared to abandon its Blue Streak project in favor of acquiring the American Skybolt missile.[46] As might be expected, the American interest in obtaining a base in Britain for its Polaris submarines and the British interest in obtaining American Skybolt missiles intersected with each other and led to some worries and concerns on both sides before those anxieties were ultimately resolved.

Discussions between the United States and Great Britain on the Skybolt–Polaris issues began in January 1960, and involved Secretary of Defense Thomas Gates and British Defense Minister Harold Watkinson. Gates wanted an agreement with the British to provide a submarine tender in the Gare Loch site on the River Clyde in Scotland. Such a location was especially advantageous for the Americans because the United States expected to have the Polaris submarines patrol in the Norwegian Sea and the North Sea.[47] But Watkinson and Gates reached no final agreement.

The Skybolt–Polaris issue was next discussed in a bilateral setting between Eisenhower and Macmillan at Camp David between 27 and 31 March 1960. Macmillan and Eisenhower left these discussions with the vaguest outline of an agreement: the British would be able to purchase American Skybolt missiles for their bomber force while (eventually) the British would supply the Americans with berthing facilities for Polaris submarines in Scotland.[48]

A major reason for the ambiguity involved the fact that the State Department and Defense Department were divided over whether or not to involve the British in the Polaris deployment. Regardless, the British believed that they had sufficient assurances from the Americans for the future acquisition of the Skybolt missiles that they could safely announce the termination of the Blue Streak project, an action taken in mid-April.[49]

Within weeks of the collapse of the Paris summit conference, Gates and Watkinson resumed their discussion of the Skybolt–Polaris issue. As historian Ronald Landa has observed, Watkinson hoped to achieve four objectives from his conversation with Gates at the Pentagon on 1 June and then again on 6 June: to negotiate an agreement for Britain's purchase of 100 Skybolt missiles; to arrange for British financing of the purchase; to "disconnect" the purchase of Skybolt missiles from the establishment of a Polaris submarine facility in Scotland; and finally, if the two issues could be separated and Britain would eventually participate in support of the Polaris venture, that it would come in as a "joint" partner of the United States in order to satisfy domestic constituencies in Britain about the placement of another American nuclear weapons system in the United Kingdom. Included in this fourth item was the suggestion that Britain might even purchase some submarines from the Americans.[50] On 6 June, in talks between Gates and Watkinson, Gates accepted the point that the British would be able to purchase two Polaris submarines as part of a berthing formula.[51]

Then suddenly the pressure of time became a factor. Watkinson wanted an agreement before Congress adjourned in August. Admiral Arleigh Burke wanted approval for the placement of Polaris facilities in Britain by the fall. The British wanted to ensure that the development of the Skybolt missile was proceeding satisfactorily. And, in Macmillan's view, anti-nuclear sentiment in Britain had now called into question the location of the berthing facility.

On 24 June 1960, Macmillan wrote to Eisenhower expressing his convictions on the subject. "We shall do all we can to assist you in this enterprise, and we hope that its success will further strengthen the partnership between our two countries and the whole Western alliance," Macmillan wrote.

> At the same time, I am sure you realize that this proposal must cause serious controversy in our country at this time. There are here, and we have to face it, difficult cross-currents of opinion on the nuclear problem; and opposition is kept alive by all kinds of forces, some of them traditional, such as the true pacifists and some of them less worthy. Ours is a small and densely populated island, and we already provide facilities for a substantial share of the strategic striking force of the West. Our people are inevitably conscious that this duty of providing the advance bases exposes them to special risks.[52]

Macmillan continued by asserting to Eisenhower that the British needed to have three concerns satisfied: the matter of location for the berthing facility; the implementation of the program as a joint "enterprise" between the British and Americans; and third, some British safeguards on the matter of controlling the use of the weapons. First, regarding the location, Macmillan wanted to move the berthing facility from the Gare Loch site to a more remote site, called Loch Linnhe. Since Macmillan and Eisenhower had discussed the subject at Camp David in March, Macmillan wrote he had "gone into this very carefully" and concluded that it would "be a serious mistake, from your point of view as well as ours, to use the Clyde for this purpose." The problem with the Gare Loch site was its proximity to Glasgow, the third largest city in Britain. "As soon as the announcement was made, Malinovsky would threaten to aim his rockets at Glasgow and there would be not only the usual agitation of the defeatists and the pacifists but also genuine apprehension among the ordinary folk," Macmillan wrote. He added, "One of the reasons why your bomber bases have worked so well is that they have been mainly in rural areas where they attract less attention and the population is steadier."[53]

Macmillan also wanted the British to be able to operate Polaris submarines of their own at some point in the future. "I think it must be made publicly clear from the outset that we shall have an option to come in ourselves on the operation of the Polaris submarines," Macmillan wrote. "In other words, we give you the facilities for the floating dock and the tender and we get in return the option of buying from you and/or building submarines so that we can make in the years to come a contribution to the Western deterrent as effective as our bomber force now is."[54] Third, Macmillan proposed to Eisenhower that the British be involved in the decision to launch Polaris missiles, not only from sites in the United Kingdom, but also from as far out as 100 miles into international waters.[55]

Macmillan's letter created serious problems in Washington, at both the State Department and the Pentagon. The objections concerned the fear that any agreement to Macmillan's terms would jeopardize American attempts to develop a medium-range ballistic missile (MRBM) capability within NATO and also anger French President Charles de Gaulle, who would view the agreement as another attempt by the Americans and British to dictate policy to the other members of the NATO alliance.

Writing to Eisenhower on 30 June, Secretary of State Herter outlined the combined State/Defense opposition to Macmillan's proposals. First, regarding location, the "proposed change in location to Loch Linnhe in Northern Scotland is unacceptable due to the lack of adequate shore facilities and to the long and hazardous entry."[56]

Second, the joint nature of the project, as proposed by Macmillan, threatened American relations with its other NATO allies, especially the

French. "Any bilateral deal ... of the sort proposed by the British ... would have a particularly serious impact on our relations with de Gaulle, who would see in this convincing proof of what he considers to be the 'inner circle' US–UK relationship in the defense and nuclear field."[57]

Finally, Herter questioned why Macmillan was attaching conditions to this subject when none had been mentioned at Camp David in March. "Finally, it will be recalled that Prime Minister Macmillan agreed with you at Camp David to the principle of granting tender facilities in the U.K. for Polaris submarines. There was no indication that any conditions would be attached."[58] If the British insisted that the Americans meet these conditions, Herter argued that the United States needed "to turn elsewhere for berthing facilities either in Europe or temporarily in the U.S."[59]

Eisenhower accepted the views of his advisors and responded to Macmillan on 30 June. Referring to the previous discussions at Camp David in March, Eisenhower expressed some surprise that some new conditions were being added. "Although I had not realized that there were such [political] considerations when we discussed the matter at Camp David, I must of course recognize that they do exist for you," Ike stated.[60] Nevertheless, Macmillan's suggestions were unacceptable to the Americans. The site of Loch Linnhe was unsatisfactory to the Navy and "the other points raised in your letter [regarding joint operation and control of the Polaris submarines] would present difficulties."[61] As a result, Eisenhower declared that the Navy intended to "keep the dry dock in the United States for another year, and to delay deployment of the tender until other arrangements can be made."[62]

With the matter now dangerously deadlocked, the British and the Americans spent the summer months trying to resolve their differences. By 27 September, when Eisenhower and Macmillan conferred in New York during the session of the United Nations, the two sides had selected a third location, Holy Loch, near Gare Loch, as the site for the Polaris facility. But they had not resolved the issue of dual control of missile launching.[63]

Given domestic considerations, Macmillan wanted the maximum amount of latitude in assuring the British people that the Americans could not provoke a nuclear exchange, independent of consultation with the British. Eventually, both sides agreed on language which stipulated that no decision to launch the Polaris missiles by the Americans would be made "without the fullest possible previous consultation."[64] Nevertheless, the Americans felt that they had been misled by the various statements that Macmillan had made, in the House of Commons and elsewhere, which differed from his statements to Eisenhower.

The British were also skeptical of American assurances about Skybolt, even though the Americans maintained that they had never made absolute assurances about the future of the Skybolt missile. On 25 October, Macmillan wrote to Eisenhower, seeking reassurance that the Skybolt program remained in effect. "Dear Friend," Macmillan wrote,

> I have been disturbed to hear that there is some talk of the possibility that you might reconsider your Skybolt program... you will remember that we canceled our Blue Streak Rocket... on the understanding that (so long as it proved technically feasible) Skybolt would be available for our V-Bomber Force. We are therefore relying very heavily on you in this.[65]

On 31 October, Eisenhower responded, in language which indicated that the Americans intended to press ahead with the Skybolt program: "I can at least assure you that we are still proceeding with the project as outlined in my Camp David memorandum to you of March 29, the Gates–Watkinson memorandum of 6 June, and the subsequent technical and financial agreement of September 27."[66]

Despite such statements, the fact remained that the Skybolt program had become a disappointment and faced an uncertain future. The British believed that the Americans had a definite obligation to supply the Skybolt missiles while the American insisted that the missiles would only become available if they proved successful. By the end of 1960, the two nations were in a curious state of limbo about this latest episode in defense cooperation. As historian Robert Watson has written, "The United States had obtained a promise of Polaris submarine facilities in Britain. The British believed they had a firm commitment on Skybolt but that weapon did not yet exist and faced an uncertain future."[67]

Once it was announced, the British–American agreement to establish a facility for Polaris submarines in Scotland led to protests against the government over the dread possibility of a nuclear accident. Fortunately for Macmillan, the Labour Party was unable to mount an effective opposition to the agreement. Political to the core, Macmillan realized that some "economic development" issues might make the agreement more attractive, over the long term. As he wrote in *Pointing the Way*,

> [The] arrival of a large number of American sailors and the permanent installation of the mother ship and all its accessories would

bring not only work but quite considerable sums of money to be spent in the neighborhood. These I believed would in due course act as compensation for either moral objections or physical alarm.[68]

Macmillan also spent considerable energy calming the fears of members of Parliament. When Labour MP Arthur Skeffington expressed concern that the berthing of Polaris submarines in Scotland might increase the possibility of nuclear war, Macmillan countered, "The provision of facilities in this country to our American allies increases the deterrent effect of the West's forces and thereby decreases the likelihood of war."[69] Judith Hart, one of Skeffington's Labour colleagues, was more concerned about issues of command and control. When she indicated her fear that the Americans might launch missiles without prior consultations with the British government, Macmillan calmly replied, "I am perfectly content to rely on our general understandings with the Americans on these matters."[70]

III

On 19 September, Nikita Khrushchev arrived in New York to attend a specially-called meeting of the United Nations General Assembly. The purpose of the session was to consider the explosive situation in the Congo and also to admit new members to the UN. Through diplomatic channels, the United States government forbade Khrushchev and his delegation from traveling outside of New York City without receiving permission from the police.[71] Khrushchev interpreted these orders as another attempt by Eisenhower to humiliate him. A more charitable view is that the United States government wanted to make sure that Khrushchev did not become the victim of any foul play should he travel outside the city. Regardless, these restrictions annoyed Khrushchev, and he responded by embracing Fidel Castro publicly in a noted photo opportunity at Castro's hotel in Harlem.

Eisenhower and Khrushchev both spoke at the United Nations. At the opening session on 22 September, Eisenhower spoke to the delegates and asked for support of the UN's efforts to restore stability to the Congo. On 23 September, Khrushchev gave a passionate anti-colonial speech, castigating both Eisenhower and especially Dag Hammarskjöld, the secretary general of the UN, who had opposed the Soviets on the Congolese issue.[72]

Harold Macmillan also attended. As Alistair Horne has written: "Macmillan decided to go himself to New York to confront Khrushchev

– 'if only to rally the West.' "[73] Before speaking to the General Assembly, however, Macmillan met with Eisenhower on 27 September. Eisenhower was accompanied by Secretary of State Herter and Andrew Goodpaster. Macmillan brought Foreign Secretary Home and Philip de Zulueta. After breakfast, the two leaders had a general conversation about a host of issues confronting the Western alliance, including relations with France, the Polaris negotiations, reconnaissance flights emanating from bases in Britain, the situation in the Congo, and other problems in Africa. Like the Americans, the British appeared to be particularly concerned about the Congo, especially with the prospect that the Marxist Congolese leader Patrice Lumumba might attempt to steer the Congo into the communist camp. According to Goodpaster's notes of the meeting, "Lord Home raised the question why we are not getting rid of Lumumba at the present time. He stressed that now is the time to get rid of Lumumba."[74]

On 29 September, it was Macmillan's turn to address the General Assembly. In his speech, which was a far-ranging commentary on the contemporary world situation, Macmillan referred to many of the points which he had made in his letter to Khrushchev at the time of the RB-47 incident in July, focusing particularly on how Britain had helped many of its former African colonies begin making the transition to independence and self-rule.[75]

During the speech, Macmillan discovered that he also was not immune from public attack by Khrushchev, who repeatedly interrupted and shouted at the podium, demanding to be heard. Then, in the most celebrated incident of the session, Khrushchev removed his shoe and began pounding it on his desk. Macmillan responded to this outburst by saying simply: "Mr. President, perhaps we could have a translation, I could not quite follow." Macmillan's humor and "unflappability" (the operative word at the time) served as an effective rhetorical counterpoint to Khrushchev's obstreperousness and became the single most remembered speech of the session.[76]

On 2 October, Eisenhower, Macmillan, and their advisors held their last meeting of Eisenhower's presidency. Given Khrushchev's behavior at the UN, the British and American leaders wondered if the Soviet premier was bent on destroying that organization in the same fashion that he had broken up the summit conference in Paris. Khrushchev's views had no flexibility: not on disarmament, Berlin, or relations with non-aligned countries.[77] Prior to returning to Britain, however, Macmillan met briefly with Khrushchev on 4 October, finding him more subdued but still unwilling to engage in substantive negotiations.

Macmillan and Eisenhower recognized the obvious: there would be no further movement toward détente while Eisenhower was president.[78] In fact, Macmillan probably had the situation sized up best when he observed in a letter to Eisenhower on 7 October that Khrushchev's "rhetoric is a cover for inactivity."[79]

IV

After the conclusion of the UN meetings, Dwight D. Eisenhower realized that the end of his diplomatic partnership with Harold Macmillan was approaching rapidly. On 14 October, he wrote to Macmillan that "while in some ways I will be glad to set down the burden of this office on January twentieth next, I will miss the great satisfaction I have had from our close relationship which will of course lose its official nature."[80] On 8 November 1960, John F. Kennedy defeated Richard M. Nixon in the closest presidential election in American history. The Eisenhower presidency had reached its de facto conclusion, although Kennedy would not assume office for another ten weeks. On 10 November, Macmillan wrote a letter to Eisenhower, the one that he knew was inevitable.

> Dear Friend-
> I feel I must write a few words to you on a purely personal basis at this time. The election of a new president has brought home to me the situation which of course I knew must come, that the period of our close cooperation together in many fields is drawing to an end. When I look back on the first time we met in the Hotel St. George, nearly 20 years ago, I realize how long this friendship has been. I know that nothing will ever impair its strength or its usefulness to our two countries.
> As a soldier, you had under your command the largest forces that Britain has ever put into action by air, sea or land: as President you have done everything to maintain the close friendship of our two countries. I think you must have realized when you drove from London airport last year what the British people feel about you.
> I can only assure you that I will try my best to keep our Governments and our countries on the same course. But I cannot of course ever hope to have anything to replace the sort of relations that we have had.[81]

The end of the 1950s also brought the Eisenhower–Macmillan diplomatic partnership to a conclusion. Questions obviously have been raised as to the effectiveness of the relationship and whether British–American relations were on a more positive footing after Eisenhower left office than they were when Macmillan became prime minister in 1957. On this point, Macmillan's supporters have stated their case, arguing that Macmillan played the crucial role in preserving Britain's "special relationship" with America, an absolutely indispensable prerequisite for maintaining Britain's position as a factor in international relations. In his biography of Macmillan, Alistair Horne quoted the British author Randolph Churchill who gave Macmillan virtually all the credit for restoring the diplomatic alliance with the Americans.[82]

According to other writers, the mere restoration of the "special relationship" between Britain and America was not necessarily positive, however. For example, Richard Aldous and Sabine Lee believed that Macmillan's emphasis on the purely personal aspects of his relationship with Eisenhower damaged the independent conduct of British foreign policy by alienating Charles de Gaulle, who was left out of the "special relationship," and that the close connection to Washington "was generally interpreted as British servility toward Washington."[83]

A more realistic assessment of the effectiveness of the Eisenhower–Macmillan partnership lies in an analysis of how each leader managed to use the partnership to achieve his own objectives. For Macmillan, the relationship with Ike enabled him to realize at least three goals. First, he was able to negotiate a series of cooperative agreements with the Americans in the defense field which enabled Britain to "stay in the game" as a participant in international diplomacy. As historian John Baylis has written:

> The main trend within the [British–American] alliance during the final years of the Eisenhower Administration was one of growing intimacy ... In this close partnership Britain undoubtedly received more than she gave but her own contribution was far from negligible. She provided the benefit of her independent research in the nuclear field, bases for US aircraft and missiles facilities at Christmas Island in the Pacific for hydrogen bomb tests, and inventions in the more conventional areas of defense ... Britain also provided invaluable diplomatic support for the United States at a very difficult time in the cold war.[84]

Second, Macmillan's close relationship with Eisenhower enabled him to play a complementary role to Ike in international relations, and to attempt new initiatives without endangering the structure of the alliance. Thus, Macmillan was able to pursue a somewhat independent course with Khrushchev in order to begin a dialogue between East and West with the ultimate goal of reducing world tensions. The fact that the U-2 crisis ultimately negated this effort should not detract from its worthiness.

Third, Macmillan's personal relationship with Eisenhower was a tremendous source of domestic political strength. Most British voters had powerful memories of World War II and the strong attachment between their country and Eisenhower. Of all the British politicians, except Winston Churchill, Macmillan was the one who could lay the best claim to being able to work effectively with Eisenhower. Moreover, such a claim was hardly an empty political boast for Macmillan, as his frequent consultations with Eisenhower between 1957 and 1960 demonstrated. For his part, Eisenhower considered Macmillan a worthy successor to the Churchill tradition and sought to maintain Macmillan's stature with the British electorate, as his trip to London prior to the general election in 1959 showed.

For Eisenhower, the benefit of the partnership with Macmillan came in two forms. First, Ike wanted to guarantee the strength and endurance of NATO. The program of defense cooperation with Great Britain enabled Eisenhower to establish a firm foundation in that respect. By the time he left office in 1961, NATO was considerably stronger than it had been in the early 1950s. The decision to sell American IRBMs to Britain and also to establish a berthing facility for Polaris submarines were two such examples.

Second, it was obvious that in his second term Eisenhower had grown increasingly concerned about an impending explosion in defense spending, a concern which commenced shortly after the Russians launched their first Sputnik satellite in October 1957. In the post-Sputnik political environment, the clamor for increased defense spending gained momentum, and Eisenhower grew apprehensive. Evidence of Ike's concern is not hard to find. As early as 20 August 1956, Eisenhower wrote to his friend Swede Hazlett:

> [Some] day there is going to be a man sitting in my present chair who has not been raised in the military services and who will have little understanding of where slashes in their estimates can be made with little or no damage . . . If that should happen while we still have the state of tension that now exists in the world, I shudder to think of what would happen in this country.[85]

Then, on 1 January 1957, while contemplating his second term as president, Eisenhower confided to his diary that he intended to hold the line on defense spending: "During my term of office, unless there is some technical or political development that I do not foresee – or a marked inflationary trend in the economy (which I will battle to the death) – I will not approve any obligational or expenditure authorities for the Defense Department that exceed something on the order of [the] 38.5 billion dollar mark," he wrote.[86]

Nevertheless, in 1957–58, the Soviet launching of Sputnik and the dissemination of the Gaither Report within the government placed the Administration on the defensive in regard to military spending during Ike's second term. Then, once the Democrats expanded their majorities in the 1958 Congressional elections, prominent Democratic senators found it politically advantageous to advocate increased defense spending in order to counter advances in Soviet missile technology. Lyndon B. Johnson used his chairmanship of the Senate Subcommittee on Preparedness to call for a greater effort on defense. Stuart Symington, Democratic senator from Missouri and former secretary of the air force in the Truman Administration, forecast a "missile gap" between the United States and the Soviet Union if more funds were not appropriated for missile technology.[87]

Moreover, by the beginning of 1960, Eisenhower faced a double-barreled, bipartisan effort to boost defense spending when Nelson A. Rockefeller, the Republican governor of New York, used the results of a recent Rockefeller Brothers study to recommend spending an additional $3.5 billion annually on defense. Entertaining thoughts of a run for the Republican presidential nomination, Rockefeller hoped to use the defense issue as the means of promoting his candidacy. Rockefeller's rumblings on the issue had their desired effect: even Richard Nixon moved away from wholehearted support of Ike's defense budgets in an effort to placate Rockefeller.[88]

Despite the views of his critics, Eisenhower continued to feel so strongly about proper restraints on defense spending that he pressed the issue with prominent individuals outside of the Administration. For example, on 6 July 1960 he wrote to Henry R. Luce, the chairman of Time-Life publications and an advocate for increased defense spending, warning him about the dangers of such a course. "I have always tried to lean toward the side of generosity in these decisions [on defense spending] and have invariably allowed more than is allowed by the Budget Bureau studies and analyses," Ike told Luce. "One political individual who has lately been urging a three billion dollar additional expenditure gives this as his cost estimate of the additional programs he recommends. Some of my people are estimating that his programming would cost ten rather than three billion dollars additional."[89]

With pressure building for more defense spending throughout his second term, Eisenhower's movement toward Macmillan's position on the advisability of a summit with Nikita Khrushchev becomes more understandable. By standing united with Macmillan at the summit, and also with de Gaulle, it was more likely that Eisenhower could achieve a meaningful nuclear test agreement than if the allies were divided. A workable nuclear test agreement might slow the arms race sufficiently to prevent Ike's successor, be it Richard Nixon or his Democratic opponent, from going on a post-Eisenhower defense spending spree. After all, in Ike's meetings with Khrushchev at Camp David, a main topic of conversation between the two men was how to resist the pressures from their military services to spend more on weapons.

During his second term, Eisenhower was not overly concerned about the Soviet Union's military capability, because the success of the U-2 flights had provided him with sufficient intelligence to make a valid judgment about Soviet military strength. Ike also reasoned, accurately, that Khrushchev's threats on Berlin would not result in any military conflict between the great powers. But an unrestrained arms race was another matter. Such a development could only increase world tensions and undermine the economies of the Western allies. That was a prospect to be avoided, if at all possible.

Finally, as a pair of statesmen, Eisenhower and Macmillan achieved a great deal. First, the diplomatic partnership between the two men and the military alliance between the United States and Great Britain helped to strengthen NATO as a viable counterweight to the enormous advantage in conventional strength which the Soviet bloc enjoyed in Eastern Europe. Eisenhower was probably not thinking of Macmillan when he observed, after leaving office: "The United States never lost a soldier or a foot of ground in my administration. We kept the peace. People ask how it happened – by God, it didn't just happen, I'll tell you that."[90] But, if Roosevelt and Churchill succeeded in their objective of winning World War II in the 1940s, so also did Eisenhower and Macmillan succeed in their objective of keeping the peace in the 1950s, or at least maintaining a measure of stability in the world situation.

Second, Eisenhower and Macmillan also introduced the important concept of moving gradually from an era of confrontation to an era of negotiation with the Soviet Union. To be sure, they did not succeed in bringing any peaceful resolution to the issues which divided East and

West nor did they abandon their predecessors' policy of containment vis-à-vis the communist world. Nevertheless, neither Eisenhower nor Macmillan was satisfied with pursuing a foreign policy characterized only by endless recrimination, mistrust, and hostility toward their adversaries. In some respects, they even planted the seeds of the policy of détente, and its various components: direct, personal negotiations between heads of state and their chief foreign policy advisors (or "summitry"), negotiations which would ultimately lead to verifiable arms control agreements, and restraint on involvement in conflicts in the non-aligned world. Eventually, of course, the foreign policy of détente became the accepted diplomatic norm in both the United States and the Soviet Union. But the first, faint movement in the direction of détente occurred in the late 1950s.

In conclusion, the friendship between Eisenhower and Macmillan survived their years in office. Macmillan, who outlived Ike by 17 years, developed a greater admiration for Eisenhower as the men lived out their post-leadership years. During the late 1950s, Macmillan often considered Eisenhower a weak leader, one who was too easily influenced by John Foster Dulles or by the consensus views of his advisors. Macmillan believed that Eisenhower was too prone to lead by his natural instincts of fairness, respect for the opposing point of view, and his anti-communist philosophy instead of seeing the world and its numerous conflicts in more subtle terms. Furthermore, Macmillan never outgrew his slightly patronizing attitude toward the way in which the Americans practiced diplomacy.

But the passage of time brought Macmillan to a greater appreciation for Eisenhower's style of leadership and how the president even made Macmillan's job easier. After Eisenhower's health began to fail after a series of heart attacks, beginning in 1965, Macmillan visited Ike in California in 1968, a year before Eisenhower's death in 1969. "I think people now realize what a fine man Ike was," Macmillan once said. "He was a sort of Duke of Wellington of America. I was lucky to have him."[91]

For his part, Eisenhower listed Macmillan in his memoirs as one "of the towering figures of the West" with whom he had worked since 1942.[92] But Ike included Macmillan in a lengthy list which consisted of the other major British politicians of the era – Churchill, Eden, and Clement Attlee – as well as a number of British military officers. Did Eisenhower consider Macmillan simply another British political leader who had crossed his path? Given the number of world leaders who Eisenhower dealt with during the course of his career, it is difficult to say where Ike ranked Macmillan in that collection of notables. In his memoirs, though, Eisenhower spoke about "his high regard" for Macmillan which "he expressed both publicly and privately."[93] Those words convey the basis for their diplomatic partnership between 1957 and 1961.

Notes and References

Prologue

1. Eisenhower to Macmillan, 10 January 1957, Dwight D. Eisenhower Library, Papers as President, 1953–1961, Ann C. Whitman File, International Series, Box 22, "Harold Macmillan," folder 7. Hereinafter cited as EL, PP (AWF-IS), box, title, and folder.
2. Macmillan to Eisenhower, 14 January 1957, EL, PP (AWF-IS), Box 22, "Harold Macmillan," folder 1.
3. Robert J. Watson, *Into the Missile Age, 1956–1960. Vol. IV, History of the Office of the Secretary of Defense* (Washington, DC: Historical Office of the Secretary of Defense, 1998), 1–2. Watson's study is an exhaustive and comprehensive account of defense policy in the last five years of the Eisenhower presidency.
4. "Memorandum of Conversation: Closer U.S.–U.K. Relations and Free World Cooperation," 23 October 1957, EL, PP (AWF-IS), Box 23, "Harold Macmillan, October 23–25, 1957," folder 1.
5. Address by Prime Minister Stanley Baldwin at Albert Hall, 27 May 1935, reported in *The Times* (London), 28 May 1935, in Henry A. Kissinger, *Diplomacy* (New York: Simon & Schuster, 1994), 537.
6. Ibid.
7. The distinctions between the Roosevelt–Churchill relationship and the Eisenhower–Macmillan one were outlined carefully by Alexander Macmillan, second Earl of Stockton and grandson of Harold Macmillan, in an interview in London with Bruce Geelhoed, 8 May 1987. Lord Stockton argued that the Eisenhower–Macmillan relationship, begun when both were subordinates, had an intimacy which was lacking in the Roosevelt–Churchill relationship.
8. See Joseph Lash, *Roosevelt and Churchill, 1939–1941: the Partnership That Saved the West* (New York: W.W. Norton, 1976) and Warren G. Kimball, *Roosevelt, Churchill, and World War II* (New York: Morrow, 1997), for two studies which detail the Roosevelt–Churchill diplomatic partnership. See also James MacGregor Burns, *Roosevelt: the Soldier of Freedom* (New York: Harcourt, Brace, Jovanovich, 1970), 163, for an explanation of Churchill's relief when the United States finally entered World War II after the Japanese attack on Pearl Harbor.
9. Andrew J. Goodpaster, interview with Bruce Geelhoed, 13 June 1996, Washington, DC.
10. See Steve Neal, *The Eisenhowers: Reluctant Dynasty* (Garden City, NY: Doubleday, 1978), 9–13, for a profile of the family.
11. John Keegan. "Eisenhower and the American Dream," from "The Dwight D. Eisenhower Lectures in War and Peace," 28 October 1986, Kansas State University, Manhattan, Kansas. The lecture may be obtained via the Internet at http://www.ksuedu/history/specialevents/Eisenhowerlecture/eisenhower2.htm.

12. Norman Gelb, *Ike and Monty* (New York: William Morrow and Company, 1994), 30–1; David Kennedy, *Freedom from Fear: the American People in Depression and War, 1929–1945* (New York: Oxford University Press, 1999), 688.
13. Gelb, *Ike and Monty*, 32–8.
14. Ibid., 33. See also Steve Neal, *Harry and Ike: the Partnership That Remade the Postwar World* (New York: Scribner, 2001), 28, and James C. Humes, *Eisenhower and Churchill: the Partnership That Saved the World* (New York: Forum, a division of Random House, Inc., 2001), 85.
15. Kennedy, *Freedom from Fear*, 688.
16. Ibid., 688–9.
17. Gelb, *Ike and Monty*, 88.
18. When *Time* magazine published its commemorative issue for the 50th anniversary of D-Day, 6 June 1994, the magazine cover carried a picture of Eisenhower with the caption, "The Man Who Beat Hitler." See also Bruce W. Nelan, "Ike's Invasion," *Time*, vol. 143, no. 23 (6 June 1994), 36–49. See also Neal, *Harry and Ike*, 37.
19. Kennedy, *Freedom from Fear*, 689–90.
20. Interview, Alexander Macmillan.
21. Stephen E. Ambrose, "EPILOGUE: Eisenhower's Legacy," in Guenter Bischof and Stephen E. Ambrose, eds, *Eisenhower* (Baton Rouge, LA: Louisiana State University Press, 1995), 246–7.
22. Herbert S. Parmet, *Eisenhower and the American Crusades* (New York: Macmillan, 1972), 13; Neal, *Harry and Ike*, 110–17.
23. Theodore H. White, *In Search of History: a Personal Adventure* (New York: Harper & Row, 1978), 349–52. For an excellent discussion of Eisenhower's tenure as NATO Commander, see Thomas M. Sisk, "Forging the Weapon: Eisenhower as NATO's Supreme Allied Commander, 1950–1952," in Bischof and Ambrose, eds, *Eisenhower*, 64–83.
24. Stephen E. Ambrose, *Eisenhower: Vol. I. Soldier, General, President-Elect, 1890–1952* (New York: Simon & Schuster, 1983), 571; Parmet, *Eisenhower and the American Crusades*, 144; Neal, *Harry and Ike*, 242–54.
25. Richard Davenport-Hines, *The Macmillans* (London: Heinemann, 1992), 127–8. There is some disagreement as to Nellie Macmillan's place of birth. In *Macmillan, Vol. I, 1894–1956* (London: Macmillan, 1988), 5–9, Macmillan's official biographer Alistair Horne records Spencer as Nellie's birthplace. Horne's conclusions are based on conversations with Macmillan. Davenport-Hines bases his conclusions on research in county records of Owen County, Indiana, where Spencer is the county seat, as well as on Gayle Thornbrough's nine-volume edition of *The Diary of Calvin Fletcher* (Indianapolis: Indiana Historical Society, 1972–83).
26. Davenport-Hines, *The Macmillans*, 129.
27. Address, Harold Macmillan at a Special Convocation, Indiana University, 22 September 1956, in Archives, Indiana University Library, Bloomington, Indiana.
28. Richard Aldous, "'A Family Affair': the Art of Personal Diplomacy," in Richard Aldous and Sabine Lee, eds, *Harold Macmillan and Britain's World Role* (London: Macmillan, 1995), 11–12.
29. Horne, *Macmillan*, I, 11.
30. Ibid., 19.

31. Lester M. Hunt, "Nasser Called World Peril," *The Indianapolis Star*, 23 September 1956, 1, 16; Address by Macmillan at a Special Convocation, Indiana University, 22 September 1956.
32. Obituary of Harold Macmillan, *New York Times*, 30 December 1986, 1, 14.
33. Davenport-Hines, *The Macmillans*, 158; Horne, *Macmillan, I*, 41–9.
34. Davenport-Hines, *The Macmillans*, 158; Horne, *Macmillan, I*, 47–9. Also, in his interview, Alexander Macmillan explained that the wounds that his grandfather suffered during World War I caused him to shake hands with a "fishlike" grip and to shuffle as he walked.
35. Macmillan spoke about his survival in World War I in his speech at Indiana University, 22 September 1956; see also Richard Aldous and Sabine Lee, "Staying in the Game: Harold Macmillan and Britain's World Role," in Aldous and Lee, eds, *Harold Macmillan and Britain's World Role*, 158.
36. Robert Rhodes James, "Harold Macmillan: an Introduction", in Aldous and Lee, eds, *Harold Macmillan and Britain's World Role*, 3.
37. Aldous, "'A Family Affair:' Macmillan and the Art of Personal Diplomacy," in Aldous and Lee, eds, *Harold Macmillan and Britain's World Role*, 13–14.
38. Robert Murphy, *Diplomat Among Warriors* (Garden City, NY: Doubleday, 1964), 163–4. See also H.W. Brands, *Cold Warriors: Eisenhower's Generation and American Foreign Policy* (New York: Columbia University Press, 1988), 97–8; Winston S. Churchill, *The Hinge of Fate* (Boston: Houghton-Mifflin, 1950), 669–70.
39. Harold Macmillan, *The Blast of War, 1939–45* (London: Macmillan, 1968), 226–7; see also Horne, *Macmillan, I*, 156–8; Stephen E. Ambrose, *The Supreme Commander* (Garden City, NY: Doubleday, 1970), 155–6; and Murphy, *Diplomat Among Warriors*, 162. Hal Mack was an official from the British Foreign Office who was already posted to AFHQ. See Gelb, *Ike and Monty*, 175.
40. Macmillan, *The Blast of War*, 220–1; Horne, *Macmillan, I*, 156–8. See also M.R.D. Foot, "Eisenhower and the British," in Bischof and Ambrose, eds, *Eisenhower*, 45–6.
41. Macmillan, The *Blast of War*, 220–1; Horne, *Macmillan, I*, 158; Ambrose, *The Supreme Commander*, 134n; Blanche Wiesen Cook, *The Declassified Eisenhower* (Garden City, NY: Doubleday, 1981), 16; Brands, *Cold Warriors*, 96. See also Stephen E. Ambrose, *Ike's Spies: Eisenhower and the Intelligence Establishment* (Garden City, NY: Doubleday, 1981), 46–7.
42. Harold Macmillan, interview with Robert McKenzie, British Broadcasting Corporation, regarding his book, *Pointing the Way*, 1972, Conservative Central Office Papers, 20/8/6, 14, Bodleian Library, Oxford, UK.
43. Horne, *Macmillan, I*, 158–9.
44. Alexander Macmillan, interview. See also Horne, *Macmillan, I*, 165–6, for a slightly different version of this encounter between Eisenhower and Macmillan.
45. Horne, *Macmillan, I*, 183–4; Ambrose, *Eisenhower, I*, 237; Humes, *Eisenhower and Churchill*, 173.
46. James, "Harold Macmillan: an Introduction," in Aldous and Lee, eds, *Harold Macmillan and Britain's World Role*, 3.
47. Horne, *Macmillan, I*, 160. A slightly different version of this story may be found in Murphy, *Diplomat Among Warriors*, 164.

48. Horne, *Macmillan, I*, 160.
49. Ibid., 286–7.
50. James, "Harold Macmillan: an Introduction," in Aldous and Lee, eds, *Harold Macmillan and Britain's Modern Role*, 2–3.
51. Harold Macmillan, interview by Robert McKenzie, 14.
52. Harold Macmillan, *Riding the Storm* (London: Macmillan, 1972), 257.
53. EL, PP (AWF-IS), Box 25A, "Macmillan," folders 1–6; EL, PP (AWF-IS), Box 25 B, "Macmillan," folders 1–6.
54. Peter Boyle, ed., *The Churchill–Eisenhower Correspondence, 1953–55* (Chapel Hill: University of North Carolina Press, 1990), 2.
55. Eisenhower to Macmillan, 6 January 1958, EL, PP (AWF-IS), Box 23, "President, Macmillan, December 1957–May 1958," Department of State, cable.
56. Macmillan to Eisenhower, 5 May 1959, EL, PP (AWF-IS), Box 25A, "Macmillan, 3/23/59–6/30/59," folder 2.
57. Anna K. Nelson, "The Importance of Foreign Policy Process: Eisenhower and the National Security Council," in Bischof and Ambrose, eds, *Eisenhower*, 111–25.
58. C. Douglas Dillon, interview with Bruce Geelhoed, 21 October 1981, New York.
59. John S.D. Eisenhower, interview with Bruce Geelhoed, 15 March 1982, Phoenixville, Pennsylvania.
60. "Excerpts of Remarks by Secretary of Defense Thomas S. Gates to the Annual Convention of the U.S. Postmasters of America, Miami, Florida, 2 October 1960," 4. Dwight D. Eisenhower Library, Papers as President, 1953–1961, Ann Whitman File, Administration Series, Box 15, folder 2. Hereinafter cited as DD, PP (AWF-AS), box, title, folder.
61. Ambrose, "Eisenhower's Legacy," in Bischof and Ambrose, eds, *Eisenhower*, 251–2.
62. Simon Ball, "Macmillan and Defense Policy," in Aldous and Lee, eds, *Harold Macmillan and Britain's World Role*, 67–9.
63. Richard M. Leighton, *Strategy, Money, and the New Look, 1953–1956. Vol III: History of the Office of the Secretary of Defense* (Washington: Historical Office of the Office of the Secretary of Defense, 2001), 88–91. Leighton provides a convincing explanation of the Eisenhower Administration's effort to reduce the Truman defense estimates. See also E. Bruce Geelhoed, *Charles E. Wilson and Controversy at the Pentagon, 1953–1957* (Detroit: Wayne State University Press, 1979), 76–9; and Robert R. Bowie and Richard H. Immerman, *Waging Peace: How Eisenhower Shaped An Enduring Cold War Strategy* (New York: Oxford University Press, 1998), 105–8.
64. Robert B. Anderson, interview with Bruce Geelhoed, 6 October 1981, New York.
65. "Excerpts of Remarks by Secretary of Defense Thomas S. Gates to the Annual Convention of the U.S. Postmasters of America, Miami, Florida, 2 October 1960," EL, PP (AWF-AS), Box 15, folder 2.
66. Obituary for Harold Macmillan, *New York Times*, 30 December 1986, 1, 14.
67. Robert M. Hathaway, *Great Britain and the United States: Special Relations Since World War II* (Boston: Twayne, 1990), 14–15, 51–3, 118–20. See also Ritchie

Ovendale, *Anglo-American Relations in the Twentieth Century* (New York: St Martin's Press, 1998), 144–6; and Sir Robin Renwick, *Fighting with Allies: America and Britain in Peace and War* (New York: Times Books, 1996) 355–66.

1   1957: Bermuda, Washington, Paris

1. Dwight D. Eisenhower, *Waging Peace: White House Years, 1956–1961* (Garden City, NY: Doubleday, 1965), 19. For a useful discussion of the 1956 presidential campaign, see Neal, *Harry and Ike*, 298–9.
2. William Bragg Ewald, *Eisenhower the President: Crucial Years, 1951–1960* (Englewood Cliffs, NJ: Prentice-Hall, 1981), 29.
3. Stephen E. Ambrose, *Eisenhower: Vol. II. The President, 1953–1961* (New York: Simon & Schuster, 1984), 366–7. See also Michael Beschloss, *Eisenhower: a Centennial Life* (New York: Edward Burlingame, 1990), 146.
4. Ambrose, *Eisenhower, II*, 367–8.
5. Cole C. Kingseed, *Eisenhower and the Suez Crisis of 1956* (Baton Rouge, LA: Louisiana State University Press, 1995), 117.
6. Regarding the historiography of the Suez crisis, one can only say that there is an embarrassment of riches. Each of the national leaders discussed Suez in their respective memoirs. See Eisenhower, *Waging Peace*, 20–99; Anthony Eden, *Full Circle* (Boston: Houghton-Mifflin, 1960), 427–657; and Harold Macmillan, *Riding the Storm, 1955–1959* (London: Macmillan, 1971), 89–239. Biographers of each leader also discuss the Suez crisis. For Eisenhower, see Ambrose, *Eisenhower, II*, 366–8; for Eden, see Robert Rhodes James, *Anthony Eden* (New York: McGraw-Hill, 1987), 442–94; and for Macmillan, see Horne, *Macmillan, I*, 418–7. For the role played by John Foster Dulles, see Richard H. Immerman, *John Foster Dulles: Piety, Pragmatism, and Power* (New York: Scholarly Resources, 1999), 149–57; and Townsend Hoopes, *The Devil and John Foster Dulles* (Boston: Little, Brown, 1974), 383–93. Three excellent studies which deal exclusively with the Suez crisis are Donald Neff, *Warriors at Suez: Eisenhower Takes America Into the Middle East* (New York: The Linden Press/Simon & Schuster, 1981); Steven Z. Freiburger, *Dawn Over Suez* (Chicago: Ivan R. Dees, 1992), and Kingseed, *Eisenhower and the Suez Crisis of 1956*. Another useful discussion may be found in Kissinger, *Diplomacy*, 522–49. From the British perspective, see Nigel J. Ashton's outstanding work, *Eisenhower, Macmillan, and the Problem of Nasser* (Basingstoke: Macmillan Press – now Palgrave Macmillan, 1996), 81–102, and Renwick, *Fighting with Allies*, 199–229.
7. Alexander Macmillan, interview.
8. M.R.D. Foot, "Eisenhower and the British," in Bischoff and Ambrose, eds, *Eisenhower*, 53. See also Ovendale, *British–American Relations in the Twentieth Century*, 112–19.
9. Eisenhower to Dulles, 1 November 1956, in Louis Galambos and Daun van Ee, eds, *The Papers of Dwight D. Eisenhower*, XVII, 2346.
10. Kingseed, *Eisenhower and the Suez Crisis of 1956*, 113.
11. Hoopes, *The Devil and John Foster Dulles*, 380–1; Immerman, *Dulles*, 156–7.
12. James, *Anthony Eden*, 594–5.

13. Kingseed, *Eisenhower and the Suez Crisis of 1956*, 118. The Russians believed that it was their threat of intervention, with the potential for nuclear war, that caused the British and French to accept the ceasefire. This view, of course, discounts the effect of American economic pressure. See Sergei Khrushchev, *Nikita S. Khrushchev and the Creation of a Superpower* (College Park: Penn State University Press, 2000), 211–12. Whether the threat of Russian intervention was the major reason behind the British and French decision to accept the ceasefire is debatable. In his interview with Bruce Geelhoed, Andrew Goodpaster expressed his belief that the British and French were concerned about the Soviet rhetoric, however.
14. Ibid., 130. See also Neff, *Warriors at Suez*, 409–10. Neff has Rab Butler, not Macmillan, making the call to Humphrey, for economic assistance.
15. Lester M. Hunt, "Nasser Called World Peril," *Indianapolis Star*, 23 September 1956, 1, 16.
16. Horne, *Macmillan, I*, 419.
17. Ibid., See also Nigel J. Ashton, "Macmillan and the Middle East," in Aldous and Lee, eds, *Harold Macmillan and Britain's World Role*, 43–4. Also, in an interview with Bruce Geelhoed in London on 8 May 1987, Sir Philip de Zulueta commented that the conversation between Eisenhower and Macmillan on 25 September 1956 must have been elusive. "Ike wasn't the quickest man in the world on the uptake [sic] and Macmillan was very bad at explaining things that were embarrassing to him," de Zulueta said.
18. Neff, *Warriors at Suez*, 410.
19. James, "Harold Macmillan: an Introduction," in Aldous and Lee, eds, *Harold Macmillan and Britain's World Role*, 3.
20. Kingseed, *Eisenhower and the Suez Crisis of 1956*, 128.
21. Aldrich Oral History, 11.
22. Kingseed, *Eisenhower and the Suez Crisis of 1956*, 140; Freiburger, *Dawn Over Suez*, 198–9; Neff, *Warriors at Suez*, 424–6.
23. Peter Collier and David Horowitz, *The Rockefellers* (New York: Holt, Rinehart, and Winston, 1976), Signet paperback edition, 156–60.
24. Aldrich Oral History, 1–2.
25. Ibid., 5.
26. Ibid. Aldrich, "The Suez Crisis: a Footnote to History," *Foreign Affairs*, vol. 45, no. 3 (April 1967), 541.
27. Aldrich Oral History, 11.
28. Aldrich, "The Suez Crisis: a Footnote to History," *Foreign Affairs*, 548.
29. Neff, *Warriors At Suez*, 426.
30. Ibid., 426–7.
31. Freiburger, *Dawn Over Suez*, 200–1.
32. Kingseed, *Eisenhower and the Suez Crisis of 1956*, 140; Horne, *Macmillan, I*, 450–3.
33. Aldrich, "The Suez Crisis: a Footnote to History," *Foreign Affairs*, 547; Neff, *Warriors at Suez*, 427.
34. Neff, *Warriors at Suez*, 425.
35. Ibid., 425–6. See also Eisenhower Diary, 20 November 1956, in Galambos and van Ee, *Papers of Dwight D. Eisenhower, XVII*, 2403; Kingseed, *Eisenhower and the Suez Crisis of 1956*, 140; Freiburger, *Dawn Over Suez*, 200–1.

36. Brendan Evans and Andrew Taylor, *From Salisbury To Major: Continuity and Change in Conservative Politics* (Manchester: University of Manchester Press, 1996), 106–7.
37. James, "Harold Macmillan, an Introduction" in Aldous and Lee, eds, *Harold Macmillan and Britain's World Role*, 3–4.
38. James, *Anthony Eden*, 595.
39. Ibid., 595–6.
40. Richard Austen Butler, Baron Butler of Saffron Walden, *The Art of the Possible* (London: Hamish Hamilton, 1971), 195–6.
41. Neff, *Warriors at Suez*, 425; Freiburger, *Dawn Over Suez*, 199–204.
42. Andrew J. Goodpaster, interview.
43. Horne, *Macmillan, II*, 4–5; Eisenhower Diary, 20 November 1956, in Galambos and Van Ee, *The Papers of Dwight D. Eisenhower, XVII*, 2403.
44. Neff, *Warriors at Suez*, 427–8; Chester J. Pach, Jr. and Elmo Richardson, *The Presidency of Dwight D. Eisenhower* (Lawrence: University Press of Kansas, 1991), 132–5.
45. Aldrich, "The Suez Crisis," *Foreign Affairs*, 548; Freiburger, *Dawn Over Suez*, 199–200; Neff, *Warriors at Suez*, 428–9.
46. Aldrich, "The Suez Crisis: a Footnote to History," *Foreign Affairs*, 548.
47. Philip de Zulueta, interview.
48. Paul Greenberg, "Blunt Talk from the Iron Lady," *Indianapolis Star*, 3 November 1995.
49. Aldous, "'A Family Affair': the Art of Personal Diplomacy," in Aldous and Lee, eds, *Harold Macmillan and Britain's World Role*, 14.
50. Ashton, "Macmillan and the Middle East," in Aldous and Lee, *Harold Macmillan and Britain's World Role*, 43–4.
51. Kissinger, *Diplomacy*, 594–5.
52. Evans and Taylor, *From Salisbury To Major*, 107.
53. Horne, *Macmillan, II*, 21. See also Cecil James, "The Role of Missiles in British Concepts of Defense: the Influence of Duncan Sandys," in Roger G. Miller, ed., *Seeing Off The Bear: Anglo/American Airpower Cooperation in the Cold War* (Colorado Springs, CO: United States Airforce Academy, 1991), 25–37.
54. Watson, *Into the Missile Age*, 513–14.
55. Horne, *Macmillan, II*, 21–2.
56. Alexander Macmillan, interview.
57. Macmillan to Eisenhower, 23 January 1957, in EL, PP (AWF-IS), Box 22, "Harold Macmillan," folder 1.
58. Macmillan, *Riding the Storm*, 241–3.
59. Memorandum of telephone conversation between Eisenhower and Macmillan, 5 March 1957; EL, PP (AWF-IS), "Harold Macmillan," folder 7; Macmillan to Eisenhower, 5 March 1957, EL, PP (AWF-IS), Box 22, "Harold Macmillan," folder 1.
60. Macmillan, *Riding the Storm*, 263–8; Horne, *Macmillan, II*, 50.
61. Horne, *Macmillan, II*, 21.
62. Macmillan, *Riding the Storm*, 249.
63. Harold Macmillan to Viscount Montgomery, 22 February 1957, Macmillan Papers, c. 320, Bodleian Library, Oxford, UK.
64. Horne, *Macmillan, II*, 22.

65. Macmillan, *Riding the Storm*, 251–4.
66. Ibid.
67. Dwight D. Eisenhower, *Waging Peace*, 122–5; Ashton, "Macmillan and the Middle East," in Aldous and Lee, eds, *Harold Macmillan and Britain's World Role*, 48.
68. Alexander Macmillan, interview.
69. Macmillan, *Riding the Storm*, 250–1; Horne, *Macmillan, II*, 23–4.
70. Macmillan, *Riding the Storm*, 253.
71. Eisenhower, *Waging Peace*, 122–5.
72. Macmillan, *Riding the Storm*, 260.
73. Ibid., 258.
74. Ambrose, *Eisenhower, II*, 405.
75. Eisenhower, *Waging Peace*, 124–5.
76. Horne, *Macmillan, II*, 27.
77. Eisenhower, *Waging Peace*, 124–5.
78. Horne, *Macmillan, II*, 27.
79. Drew Middleton, "U.S. and Britain to Pool Planning and Intelligence," *New York Times*, 26 March 1957. See also M.R.D. Foot, "Eisenhower and the British," in Bischof and Ambrose, eds, *Eisenhower*, 54. Foot referred to Macmillan's re-establishment of a "quiet and extremely efficient worldwide cooperation on signals and electrical intelligence that has flourished unobtrusively down to the present day."
80. Middleton, "Planning and Intelligence," *New York Times*.
81. Ibid.
82. Eisenhower to Macmillan, 26 March 1957, EL, PP (AWF-IS), Box 22, "Harold Macmillan," folder 6.
83. Eisenhower to Macmillan, 26 March 1957, EL, PP (AWF-IS), "Harold Macmillan," folder 6.
84. Ibid.
85. Macmillan to Eisenhower, 27 March 1957, EL, PP (AWF-IS), Box 22, "Harold Macmillan," folder 6.
86. Macmillan to Eisenhower, 29 March 1957, EL, PP (AWF-IS), Box 22, "Harold Macmillan," folder 2.
87. Eisenhower to Macmillan, 29 March 1957, EL, PP (AWF-IS), Box 22, "Harold Macmillan."
88. Whitney to Eisenhower, 13 April 1957, in Galambos and van Ee, *The Papers of Dwight D. Eisenhower, XVII*, 120n.
89. Harold Macmillan to Selwyn Lloyd, 2 April 1957, Macmillan Papers, c. 320.
90. Macmillan to Eisenhower, 15 April 1957, EL, PP (AWF-IS), Box 22, "Harold Macmillan," folder 2.
91. Ibid., 5.
92. Ibid., 6.
93. Eisenhower to Macmillan, 28 April 1957, EL, PP (AWF-IS), Box 22, "Harold Macmillan," folder 5.
94. Ibid.
95. Harold Macmillan to Anthony Eden, 28 April 1957, Macmillan Papers, c. 310.
96. Paul Dickson, *Sputnik: the Shock of the Century* (New York: Walker Books, 2001), 111–12, 120.

166 Notes and References

97. Robert B. Anderson, interview.
98. Dickson, *Sputnik*, 85–6; John Eisenhower, *Strictly Personal*, 199–200.
99. John S.D. Eisenhower, interview, 22 February 1982.
100. Macmillan to Eisenhower, 10 October 1957, EL, PP (AWF-IS), Box 23, "Harold Macmillan, May 29, 1957–November 30, 1957."
101. Memorandum of Conversation, 23 October 1957, British Embassy, EL, PP (AWF-IS), Box 23, "Harold Macmillan, October 23–25, 1957," folder 1.
102. Ibid.
103. Ibid., 2.
104. Ibid., 4.
105. Memorandum of Conversation, "Free World Cooperation," Meeting Presided Over by the President and Prime Minister Macmillan," 10.30 a.m., The White House, 4–5, EL, PP (AWF-IS), Box 23, "Harold Macmillan, October 23–25, 1957," folder 2.
106. Ibid., 5
107. Ibid.
108. Ibid., 2.
109. Ibid., 3.
110. Memorandum of Conversation, Conversation at President's Dinner for Prime Macmillan, 24 October 1957, EL, PP (AWF-IS), Box 23, "Harold Macmillan, October 23–25, 1957," folder 2
111. Memorandum of Understanding (Eisenhower and Macmillan), 25 October 1957, EL, PP (AWF-IS), Box 23, "Harold Macmillan, October 23–25, 1957," folder 4.
112. Ibid.
113. News Release, Declaration of Common Purpose, 25 October 1957, The White House, EL, PP (AWF-IS), Box 23, "Harold Macmillan, October 23–25, 1957," folder 4.
114. Andrew Goodpaster, interview. See also Eisenhower, *Waging Peace*, 219; and Horne, *Macmillan, II*, 57.
115. Horne, *Macmillan, II*, 57–8. For Macmillan's reaction to Congressional passage of the revision of the McMahon Act, see Macmillan to Eisenhower, 7 July 1958, EL, PP(AWF-IS), Box 23, "Macmillan–President, 6/1/58–9/30/59," folder 1.
116. Ibid., 59.
117. Macmillan to Eisenhower, 25 October 1957, EL, PP (AWF-IS), Box 23, "Harold Macmillan, October 23–25, 1957, folder 3.
118. Memorandum of Conversation, Conversation at President's Dinner for Prime Minister, 24 October 1957, 7.00 p.m., the White House, 2, EL, PP (AWF-IS), Box 23, "Harold Macmillan, October 23–25, 1957," folder 2.
119. Memorandum of Conversation, NATO Heads of Government, 25 October 1957, EL, PP (AWF-IS), Box 23, "Harold Macmillan, October 23–25, 1957," folder 3.
120. Harold Macmillan to the American Ambassador, 31 October 1957, Macmillan Papers, c. 222.
121. Ambrose, *Eisenhower, II*, 435.
122. Ibid., 438. Several of Eisenhower's closest advisors and officials believed that the stress from the Sputnik hysteria may have contributed to Eisenhower's stroke. John Foster Dulles and Richard M. Nixon were two individuals who

held that opinion. See Michael Beschloss, *Mayday: Eisenhower, Khrushchev and the U-2 Crisis* (New York: Harper & Row, 1986), 149; Dickson, *Sputnik*, 151; and John Eisenhower, *Strictly Personal*, 199.
123. Macmillan to Eisenhower, 26 November 1957, EL, PP (AWF-IS), Box 23, "Harold Macmillan, May 29, 1957–November 30, 1957," folder 3.
124. Eisenhower to Macmillan, 30 November 1957, EL, PP (AWF-IS), Box 23, "Harold Macmillan, May 29, 1957–November 30, 1957," folder 4.
125. Eisenhower to Macmillan, 4 December 1957, EL, PP (AWF-IS), Box 23, "President, Macmillan, May 30, 1958."
126. Eisenhower, *Waging Peace*, 227.
127. Ibid., 230.
128. Watson, *Into the Missile Age*, 517.
129. Ibid., 518; Macmillan, *Riding the Storm*, 333–5. See also Lauris Norstad Oral History, Eisenhower Library.
130. Macmillan, *Riding the Storm*, 338.
131. Horne, *Macmillan, II*, 58.
132. Ibid.
133. McGeorge Bundy, *Danger and Survival: Choices About the Bomb in the First Fifty Years* (New York: Random House, 1988), 488. See also Robert S. Jordan, "Norstad: Can the SACEUR Be Both European and American?," in Robert S. Jordan, ed., *Generals in International Politics: NATO's Supreme Allied Commander, Europe* (Lexington, KY: University Press of Kentucky, 1987), 82.
134. Richard Aldous and Sabine Lee, "Staying In the Game: Harold Macmillan and Britain's World Role," in Aldous and Lee, eds, *Harold Macmillan and Britain's World Role*, 155.
135. Aldous, "A Family Affair?: the Art of Personal Diplomacy," in Aldous and Lee, eds, *Harold Macmillan and Britain's World Role*, 13.
136. Dwight Eisenhower to Harold Macmillan, 27 December 1957, PM's Personal Telegrams, Macmillan Papers, c. 340.

2 1958: Arms Control, Washington and Lebanon

1. Charles C. Alexander, *Holding the Line: the Eisenhower Era, 1952–1961* (Bloomington, IN: Indiana University Press, 1975), 202–6.
2. Ibid., 203.
3. Ibid., 205; Watson, *Into the Missile Age*, 689–90.
4. Watson, *Into the Missile Age*, 696–7.
5. Alexander, *Holding the Line*, 207–9; see also Robert A. Divine, *Blowing on the Wind: the Nuclear Test-Ban Debate, 1954–1960* (New York: Oxford University Press, 1978).
6. Harold Macmillan, *Pointing the Way, 1959–1961* (London: Macmillan, 1972), 102–3.
7. Robert Blake, *The Conservative Party From Peel to Thatcher* (London: Fontana, 1985), 281–2.
8. Ibid.
9. Macmillan, *Riding the Storm*, 298.
10. Macmillan to Eisenhower, 18 September 1957, EL, PP (AWF-IS), Box 23, "Harold Macmillan, May 29, 1957–December 30, 1957," folder 2.

168 *Notes and References*

11. Aldous, "'A Family Affair': the Art of Personal Diplomacy," in Aldous and Lee, eds, *Harold Macmillan and Britain's World Role*, 18.
12. Watson, *Into the Missile Age*, 588.
13. Robert B. Anderson, interview.
14. Ibid. Dickson, *Sputnik*, 135–8.
15. Lauris Norstad Oral History, 47–8, Number 385, Dwight D. Eisenhower Library.
16. Memorandum of Conference with the President, 20 March 1959, 7 p.m. (recorded 23 March 1959), EL, PP (AWF-IS), Box 24, "Macmillan Visit, March 20–22, 1959," folder 4.
17. Ewald, *Eisenhower the President*, 243.
18. Macmillan to Eisenhower, 2 January 1958, EL, PP (AWF-IS), Box 23, "Macmillan, President, Dec. 1, 1957–May 30, 1958," folder 2. This letter is also published in Ronald D. Landa, James E. Miller, David S. Patterson, Charles S. Sampson, eds, *Foreign Relations of the United States, 1958–1960, Vol. VII*, Part 1, "Western European Security and Integration, Canada" (Washington: Government Printing Office, 1993), 794–9. Hereinafter cited as *FRUS, VII*, page.
19. Ibid.
20. Ibid., 3–4.
21. Ibid., 5–6.
22. Ibid.
23. Ibid., 10.
24. "Prime Minister's Broadcast," *New York Times*, 5 January 1958.
25. Ibid.
26. Ibid.
27. Ibid.
28. Macmillan to Eisenhower, 2 January 1958, 9.
29. Memorandum of Letter of Prime Minister Macmillan Dated 1/2/58, 3 January 1958, EL, PP (AWF-IS), Box 23, "President, Macmillan, December 1957–May 30, 1958," folder 6.
30. Ibid.
31. Eisenhower to Macmillan, 6 January 1958, EL, PP (AWF-IS), Box 23, "President, Macmillan, December 1, 1957–May 30, 1958."
32. Macmillan to Eisenhower, February 19, 1958, 2, EL, PP (AWF-IS), Box 23, "President, Macmillan, December 1, 1957–May 30, 1958," folder 2.
33. Ibid., 2.
34. Ibid., 3.
35. Harold Macmillan to E. Shinwell, MP, 28 February 1958, PM's Personal Correspondence, Macmillan Papers, c. 312.
36. Eisenhower to Macmillan, 26 February 1958, 2, EL, PP (AWF-IS), Box 23, "President, Macmillan, December 1, 1957–May 30, 1958," folder 5.
37. Ibid.
38. Macmillan to Eisenhower, 3 March 1958, EL, PP (AWF-IS), Box 23, "President, Macmillan, December 1, 1957–May 30, 1958," folder 2.
39. Dulles to American Embassy, London, 4 March 1958, 1–2, EL, PP (AWF-IS), Box 23, "President, Macmillan, December 1, 1957–May 30, 1957," folder 5.
40. Ibid., 3. The Republicans made a dismal showing in the 1958 Congressional elections, winding up with only 34 seats in the Senate and 153 seats in the House of Representatives. See Ewald, *Eisenhower the President*, 292.

41. Eisenhower to Macmillan, 4 March 1958, EL, PP (AWF-IS), Box 23, "President, Macmillan, December 1, 1957–May 30, 1958," folder 5.
42. William Elliott to Harold Macmillan, 17 April 1958, PM's Personal Correspondence, Macmillan Papers, c. 312.
43. Eisenhower to Macmillan, 24 June 1957, EL, PP (AWF-IS), Box 23, "Macmillan, President, May 29, 1957–November 30, 1957," folder 6.
44. Eisenhower to Macmillan, 3 April 1958, in Louis Galambos and Daun van Ee, eds, *The Papers of Dwight D. Eisenhower. The Presidency: Keeping the Peace, vol. XIX* (Baltimore: Johns Hopkins Press, 2001), 815–16.
45. Ibid.
46. Address by the Rt. Hon. Harold Macmillan at a Special Convocation, Indiana University, 22 September 1956, 1–2.
47. Macmillan, *Riding the Storm*, 322.
48. Ibid., 492–3.
49. Ibid., 493–4.
50. Alexander Macmillan, interview.
51. "Meetings Between the President and the Prime Minister," EL, PP (AWF-IS), Box 24, "Macmillan, President, 6/1/58–9/30/59," folder 8. Papers related to the discussions between Eisenhower, Macmillan, and their advisors between 9–11 June 1958 may also be found in *FRUS*, *VII*, 811–18.
52. Memorandum of Conversation, "Procedure for Future Meetings," 9 June 1958, El, PP (AWF-IS), Box 24, "Macmillan, President, 6/1/58–9/30/59," folder 7.
53. Memorandum of Conversation, "Exchange of Views on Limitation of Nuclear Testing," 9 June 1958, 2–3, EL, PP (AWF-IS), Box 24, "Macmillan, President, 6/1/58–9/30/59," folder 7. See also Memorandum of Conversation, "US–UK Agreement on Nuclear Weapons," 9 June 1958, EL, PP (AWF-IS), Box 24, "Macmillan, President, 6/1/58/–9/30/59, folder 7.
54. Memorandum of Conversation, "Relations with Nasser," 9 June 1958, EL, PP (AWF-IS), Box 24, "Macmillan, President, 6/15/58–9/30/59," folder 7.
55. Ibid.
56. Ibid., 2–3.
57. Ibid., 2.
58. Ibid.
59. Ibid., 3–4.
60. Macmillan, *Riding the Storm*, 502–3.
61. Memorandum of Conversation, "Military Aid to Iraq, Lebanon, and Jordan," 9 June 1958, EL, PP (AWF-IS), Box 24, "Macmillan, President, 6/1/58–9/30/59," folder 7.
62. Ibid.
63. Memorandum of Conversation, "Situation in Lebanon," 9 June 1958, EL, PP (AWF-IS), Box 24, "Macmillan, President, 6/1/58–9/30/59," folder 7.
64. Ibid., 2.
65. Ibid.
66. Ibid.
67. DDEL, PP (AWF-IS), Box 24, "Macmillan, President, 6/1/58–9/30/59," folder 7, Department of State, Memorandum of Conversation, "Situation in Iraq," 9 June 1958, EL, PP (AWF-IS), Box 24, "Macmillan, President, 6/1/58/–9/30/59," folder 7.

68. Ibid.
69. Ibid.
70. Macmillan, *Riding the Storm*, 495.
71. Ibid.
72. Ibid.
73. Ibid., 496. Memorandum of Conversation, "Situation in Yemen," 10 June 1958; and Memorandum of Conversation, "Situation in Cyprus," 10 June 1958, EL, PP (AWF-IS), Box 24, "Macmillan, President, 6/1/58–9/30/59," folder 6.
74. Macmillan, *Riding the Storm*, 496. See also Memorandum of Conversation at the White House Dinner for Prime Minister Macmillan, 10 June 1958, EL, PP (AWF-IS), "Macmillan, President, 6/1/58–9/30/59," folder 6.
75. Memorandum of Conversation, "Anglo/American Relations with General de Gaulle's Government," 9 June 1958, EL, PP (AWF-IS), Box 24, "Macmillan, President, 6/1/58–9/30/59," folder 7.
76. Ibid., 2. In an interview, Andrew J. Goodpaster observed that Eisenhower was completely in favor of sharing nuclear information with the French, and even the Dutch, who wanted to build a nuclear-powered submarine. Congress refused to go along, however. Andrew J. Goodpaster, interview.
77. Memorandum of Conversation, "Anglo/American Relations with General de Gaulle's Government," 2.
78. Memorandum of Conversation At the White House, 11 June 1958, EL, PP (AWF-IS), Box 24, "Macmillan, President, 6/1/58–9/30/59," folder 6.
79. Macmillan, *Riding the Storm*, 494.
80. See Ashton, "Macmillan and the Middle East," in Aldous and Lee, eds, *Harold Macmillan and Britain's World Role*, 47–9, and Ashton, *Eisenhower, Macmillan, and the Problem of Nasser*, 111–12.
81. Macmillan, *Riding the Storm*, 510.
82. Ambrose, *Eisenhower, II*, 469–70. See also Robert A. Divine, *Eisenhower and the Cold War* (New York: Oxford University Press, 1981), 98–100.
83. Ashton, *Eisenhower, Macmillan, and the Problem of Nasser*, 109–11.
84. Ambrose, *Eisenhower, II*, 469–70.
85. Ewald, *Eisenhower the President*, 251.
86. Macmillan, *Riding the Storm*, 510–11; Horne, *Macmillan, II*, 94–5.
87. Report Of Telephone Call Between The President And Prime Minister Macmillan, 14 July 1958, 5:43 p.m., 1–2, EL, PP (AWF-IS), Box 24, "Macmillan, President, 6/1/58–9/30/59," folder 5.
88. Ibid., 3.
89. Macmillan to Eisenhower, 14 July 1958, 1–2, EL, PP (AWF-IS), Box 24, "Macmillan, President, 6/1/58–9/30/59," folder 1.
90. Macmillan to Eisenhower, 14 July 1958, EL, PP (AWF-IS), Box 24, "Macmillan, President, 6/1/58–9/30/59," folder 1.
91. Ibid.
92. Macmillan, *Riding the Storm*, 512; Ambrose, *Eisenhower, II*, 471; Horne, *Macmillan, II*, 93–4. In his account of the Lebanon crisis, Horne contrasted the American intervention in Lebanon, in 1958, at the request of a ruler of a country under threat, with the British–French intervention at Suez, in 1956, when there was intervention without any request for assistance.
93. Ambrose, *Eisenhower, II*, 472; Watson, *Into the Missile Age*, 211–19.
94. Watson, *Into the Missile Age*, 213.

95. Murphy, *Diplomat Among Warriors*, 398–9.
96. Ibid.
97. Ibid., 400.
98. Ibid., 408.
99. Macmillan, *Riding the Storm*, 520–2; Horne, *Macmillan, II*, 96–7; Ambrose, *Eisenhower, II*, 472–3.
100. Macmillan to Eisenhower, 17 July 1958, 1–2, EL, PP (AWF-IS), Box 24, "Macmillan, President, 6/1/58–9/30/59," folder 2. See also Ashton, "Macmillan and the Middle East," in Aldous and Lee, eds, *Harold Macmillan and Britain's World Role*, 52–3.
101. Eisenhower to Macmillan, 18 July 1958, EL, PP (AWF-IS), Box 24, "Macmillan, President, 6/1/58–9/39/59," folder 5; Eisenhower to Macmillan, 18 July 1958, in Galambos and van Ee, eds, *The Papers of Dwight David Eisenhower, XIX*, 993–5.
102. Macmillan to Eisenhower, 22 July 1958, 1–2, EL, PP (AWF-IS), Box 24, "Macmillan, President, 6/1/58–9/30/59," folder 2.
103. Ibid.
104. Eisenhower to Macmillan, 23 July 1958, in Galambos and van Ee, eds, *Papers of Dwight David Eisenhower, XIX*, cable, 1013–14.
105. Horne, *Macmillan, II*, 97.
106. Nathan F. Twining Oral History, John Foster Dulles Oral History Project, Princeton University Library, Philip A. Crowl, interviewer, 16 March 1965, 13.
107. Ambrose, *Eisenhower*, 472; Divine, *Eisenhower and the Cold War*, 102–4.
108. Watson, *Into the Missile Age*, 217.
109. Eisenhower to Macmillan, 3 November 1958, EL, PP (AWF-IS), Box 24, "Macmillan, President, 10/58–3/20/59," folder 6.
110. Macmillan to Eisenhower, 7 November 1958, EL, PP (AWF-IS), Box 24, "Macmillan, President, 10/1/58–3/20/59," folder 1. See also Macmillan, *Riding the Storm*, 533–4.
111. Memorandum of Conversation, "Middle East," Camp David, 22 March 1959, 2 p.m., 3–4, EL, PP (AWF-IS), Box 24, "Macmillan Visit, March 20–22, 1959," folder 2.
112. Philip de Zulueta, interview.
113. Ambrose, *Eisenhower, II*, 486.
114. Ibid., 478–88.
115. Macmillan to Eisenhower, 7 November 1958, 1–2, EL, PP (AWF-IS), Box 24, "Macmillan, President, 10/1/58–3/20/59," folder 1.
116. Eisenhower to Macmillan, 11 November 1958, EL, PP, (AWF-IS), Box 24, "Macmillan, President, 10/1/58–3/20/59," folder 6.
117. Ibid.
118. Ibid.
119. Harold Macmillan, interview with Robert McKenzie, 14–15.

3   1959: Moscow, Washington, London, Paris

1. Kissinger, *Diplomacy*, 568–71; see also William Burr, "U.S. Policy and the Berlin Crisis: an Overview," 27 March 1992, 1–3, written for the

Digital National Security Archives, found on the Internet at http://nsarchive.chadwyck.com/bcessayx.htm.
2. See Richard M. Nixon, *Six Crises* (Garden City, NY: Doubleday, 1962; Pyramid Books edition, 1968), 253–314; Richard M. Nixon, *RN: the Memoirs of Richard Nixon, Vol. I* (New York: Warner, 1978), 250–64; Stephen E. Ambrose, *Nixon, vol. I: the Education of a Politician 1913–1962* (New York: Simon & Schuster, 1989), 520–34.
3. Kissinger, *Diplomacy*, 569–71.
4. Sergei Khrushchev, *Nikita Khruschchev and the Creation of a Superpower* (State College, PA: Pennsylvania State University Press, 2000), 302–10.
5. Harold Macmillan, "Typescript Diary," 5 January 1959, Macmillan Papers, c. 20/1.
6. Ibid., 7 January 1959.
7. Ibid., 18 January 1959.
8. Aldous, "'A Family Affair': the Art of Personal Diplomacy," in Aldous and Lee, eds, *Harold Macmillan and Britain's World Role*, 18–20.
9. Ibid.
10. Ibid., 18.
11. Harold Macmillan, "Typescript Diary," 31 January 1959, Macmillan Papers, c. 20/1.
12. Ibid., 4 February 1959.
13. Ibid., 5 February 1959.
14. Nigel Fisher, *Macmillan: a Biography* (London: Weidenfeld & Nicolson, 1982), 212–14.
15. Macmillan, *Riding the Storm*, 595, 597.
16. Macmillan to Eisenhower, 23 February 1959, 1–2, EL, PP (AWF-IS), Box 24, "Macmillan, 10/1/58–3/20/59," folder 2.
17. Harold Macmillan, "Typescript Diary," 4 March 1959, Macmillan Papers, c. 20/1.
18. Eisenhower to Macmillan, 24 February 1959, in Louis Galambos and Daun van Ee, eds, *The Papers of Dwight David Eisenhower vol. XIX. The Presidency: Keeping the Peace* (Baltimore: Johns Hopkins University Press, 2001), 1371–2.
19. Macmillan to Eisenhower, 25 February 1959, EL, PP (AWF-IS), Box 24, "Macmillan, 10/1/58–3/20/59," folder 2.
20. Aldous, "'A Family Affair': the Art of Personal Diplomacy," in Aldous and Lee, eds, *Harold Macmillan and Britain's World Role*, 16.
21. Ibid., 16–17.
22. Macmillan, *Riding the Storm*, 622–3.
23. Ibid., 622; Sergei Khrushchev, *Creation of a Superpower*, 308–10. Also, according to Macmillan, he received little help from the American Embassy during his trip. The Embassy's "only reply" to Khrushchev's toothache gambit was to encourage Macmillan "to ask for my Comet aeroplane and go home." Harold Macmillan, "Typescript Diaries," 4 March 1959, c. 20/1.
24. Macmillan to Eisenhower, 2 March 1959, EL, PP (AWF-IS), Box 24, "Macmillan, 10/1/58–3/20/59," folder 2.
25. Aldous, "'A Family Affair': the Art of Personal Diplomacy," in Aldous and Lee, eds, *Harold Macmillan and Britain's World Role*, 16–17.
26. Macmillan to Eisenhower, 5 March 1959, EL, PP (AWF-IS), Box 25 A, "Macmillan, 3/23/59–6/30/59," folder 2.

27. Horne, *Macmillan, II*, 127–8.
28. Hoopes, *The Devil and John Foster Dulles*, 475–6.
29. Andrew J. Goodpaster, interview.
30. Horne, *Macmillan, II*, 128–9.
31. Hoopes, *The Devil and John Foster Dulles*, 477.
32. Blake, *The Conservative Party From Peel to Thatcher*, 282–4; Evans and Taylor, *From Salisbury to Major*, 118–19.
33. Horne, *Macmillan, II*, 129–30; Macmillan, *Riding the Storm*, 636–8.
34. Eisenhower to Macmillan, 2 March 1959, EL, PP (AWF-IS), Box 24, "Macmillan, 10/1/58–3/20/59," folder 5.
35. Ibid., 2.
36. Macmillan to Eisenhower, 4 March 1957, EL, PP (AWF-IS), Box 24, "Macmillan, 10/1/58–3/20-59," folder 2.
37. Eisenhower to Macmillan, 5 March 1957, 1–2, EL, PP (AWF-IS), Box 24, "Macmillan, 10/1/58–3/20/59," folder 5. Camp David, of course, was originally the presidential retreat built for Franklin D. Roosevelt. Roosevelt referred to the retreat as "Shangri-La." Eisenhower renamed it after his grandson, David Dwight Eisenhower II, son of John and Barbara Eisenhower.
38. Staff Notes, 14 March 1959, 1–2, EL, PP (AWF-IS), Box 24, "Macmillan, 10/1/58–3/20/59," folder 4.
39. Ibid.
40. Ibid.
41. Visit of Prime Minister Macmillan to the United States, 20–24 March 1959 (agenda), EL, PP (AWF-IS), Box 24, "Macmillan Visit, March 20–22, 1959," folder 2.
42. Macmillan, *Riding the Storm*, 643.
43. Ibid., 644.
44. Memorandum of Conversation, "Prime Minister Macmillan's Visit to Moscow," Aspen Lodge, Camp David, 20 March 1959, EL, PP (AWF-IS), Box 24, "Macmillan Visit, March 20–22, 1959," folder 1. Papers about the discussions between Eisenhower, Macmillan, and their advisors on 20–23 March may also be found in *FRUS, VII*, 832–47.
45. Ibid., 2.
46. Ibid., 4. See also Memorandum of Conference With the President, 20 March 1959 (dated 23 March 1959), 2, EL, PP (AWF-IS), Box 24, "Macmillan Visit, March 20–22, 1959," folder 4. There are at least two records of this conversation, one taken by Andrew Goodpaster for the White House, and the other by Livingston Merchant, Assistant Secretary of State for European Affairs.
47. Memorandum of Conference with the President, 20 March 1959, 2.
48. Ibid.
49. Memorandum of Conversation, "Prime Minister Macmillan's Visits to Paris and Bonn," Camp David, 20 March 1959, EL, PP (AWF-IS), Box 24, "Macmillan Visit, March 20–22, 1959," folder 1.
50. Ibid., 2.
51. Memorandum of Conversation, "Berlin, Summitry and Reply to Soviet March 2 Note," Camp David, 20 March 1959, EL, PP (AWF-IS), Box 24, "Macmillan Visit, March 20–22, 1959," folder 1.

52. Ibid. Memorandum of Conference with the President, 20 March 1959, 6–7, EL, PP (AWF-IS), Box 24, "Macmillan Visit to the United States, March 20–22, 1959."
53. Ike's mention of leaving Nixon as his personal representative must not have appealed to Macmillan, since the prime minister was no admirer of the vice president. Macmillan made scant mention of Nixon in *Riding the Storm* or in *Pointing the Way* but Horne records some pointed criticisms of Nixon by Macmillan in his private conversations. See Horne, *Macmillan, II*, 131–2. See also Memorandum of Conference with the President, 20 March 1959, 6–7.
54. Memorandum of Conversation, "Berlin, Summitry," 20 March 1959, 2. See also Memorandum of Conference with the President, 20 March 1959, 6–7.
55. Memorandum of Conference with the President, 20 March 1959, 2. See also Memorandum of Conference with the President, 20 March 1959, 6–7.
56. Ibid., 20 March 1959, 7.
57. Macmillan, *Riding the Storm*, 645.
58. Harold Macmillan, "Typescript Diaries," 22 March 1959, Macmillan Papers, c. 20/1.
59. Memorandum of Conversation, "Reply to Soviet Note of March 2," Camp David, 20 March 1959, EL, PP (AWF-IS), Box 24, "Macmillan Visit, March 20–22, 1959," folder 1.
60. Ibid., 1–2.
61. Ibid., 2.
62. Ibid.
63. Ibid.
64. Ibid.
65. Ibid.
66. Memorandum of Conference with the President, 20 March 1959, 1–2.
67. Ibid., 2.
68. Ibid., Memorandum of Conversation, "Reply to Soviet Note of March 2," 2.
69. Memorandum of Conversation, "Reply to Soviet Note of March 2," 21 March 1959, Camp David, EL, PP (AWF-IS), Box 24, "Macmillan Visit, March 20–22, 1959," folder 1; Memorandum of Conference with the President, 21 March 1959 (dated 24 March 1959), Box 24, "Macmillan Visit, March 20–22, 1959," folder 4.
70. Memorandum of Conversation, "Reply to Soviet Note of March 2."
71. Ibid.
72. Ibid.
73. Ibid.
74. Memorandum of Conference with the President, 21 March 1959 (dated 24 March 1959), EL, PP (AWF-IS), "Macmillan Visit, March 20–22, 1959," folder 3.
75. Ibid.
76. Ibid., 2
77. Ibid.
78. Ibid.
79. Ibid., 4.

80. Ibid.
81. Memorandum of Conversation, "Contingency Planning for Berlin," Camp David, 24 March 1959, 1–2, EL, PP (AWF-IS), Box 24, "Macmillan Visit, March 20–22, 1959," folder 1.
82. Memorandum of Conversation "Nuclear Testing," Camp David, 21 March 1959, 1–2, EL, PP (AWF-IS), Box 24, "Macmillan Visit, March 20–22, 1959," folder 1.
83. Ibid., 2–3.
84. Ibid., 1.
85. Memorandum of Conference with the President, 22 March 1959 (dated 27 March 1959), 2, EL, PP (AWF-IS), Box 24, "Macmillan Visit, March 20–22, 1959," folder 3.
86. Ibid., 4.
87. Memorandum of Conference with the President, 23 March 1959 (dated 28 March 1959) 2, EL, PP (AWF-IS), Box 24, "Macmillan Visit, March 20–22, 1959," folder 3.
88. John S.D. Eisenhower, *Strictly Personal*, 288.
89. Memorandum of Conference with the President, 23 March 1959 (dated 28 March 1959), 2, EL, PP, (AWF-IS), Box 24, "Macmillan Visit, March 20–22, 1959," folder 3.
90. Hoopes, *The Devil and John Foster Dulles*, 478–9.
91. Eisenhower, *Waging Peace*, 402–3.
92. Macmillan to Eisenhower, 16 June 1959, EL, PP (AWF-IS), Box 25A, "Macmillan, 3/23/59–6/30/59," folder 4.
93. Ibid.
94. Eisenhower to Macmillan, 17 June 1959, EL, PP (AWF-IS), Box 25A, "Macmillan, 3/23/59–6/30/59," folder 4.
95. Macmillan to Eisenhower, 23 June 1957, 4–5, EL, PP (AWF-IS), Box 25A, "Macmillan, 3/23/59–6/30/59," folder 3.
96. Ambrose, *Eisenhower, II*, 534–5.
97. Ibid.
98. Andrew Goodpaster, interview. Goodpaster also mentioned, without identifying Robert Murphy's role in the Khrushchev invitation, that the "State Department dropped the ball on this one."
99. Ambrose, *Eisenhower, II*, 535.
100. Harold Macmillan, interview with Robert McKenzie, 11.
101. Ibid.
102. Ibid.
103. Macmillan to Eisenhower, 21 July 1959, EL, PP (AWF-IS), Box 25A, "Macmillan, 7/1/59–12/31/59," folder 1.
104. Macmillan to Eisenhower, 30 July 1959, EL, PP (AWF-IS), Box 25A, "Macmillan, 7/1/59–12/31/59," folder 1.
105. Ibid.
106. Eisenhower to Macmillan, 1 August 1959, in Louis Galambos and Daun van Ee, eds, *The Papers of Dwight David Eisenhower, vol. XX. The Presidency: Keeping the Peace* (Baltimore: Johns Hopkins University Press, 2001), 1614–15.
107. Macmillan to Eisenhower, 6 August 1958, EL, PP (AWF-IS), Box 25A, "Macmillan, 7/1/59–12/31/59," folder 1.

176 *Notes and References*

108. Eisenhower to Macmillan, 7 August 1959, in Galambos and van Ee, eds, *The Papers of Dwight David Eisenhower*, XX, 1620–1.
109. Macmillan to Eisenhower, 8 August 1959, EL, PP (AWF-IS), Box 25A (AWF-IS), "Macmillan, 7/1/59–12/31/59," folder 2.
110. Macmillan, *Riding the Storm*, 747.
111. Eisenhower, *Waging Peace*, 418–19.
112. Andrew Goodpaster, interview.
113. John Eisenhower, *Strictly Personal*, 244–5.
114. Dwight D. Eisenhower Library, Dwight D. Eisenhower, Papers as President, 1953–1961, Ann C. Whitman File, "International Meetings Series, London: Aug. 27–Sept 3, 1959," Box 3, State Department, Memorandum of Conversation, "Conversation at Chequers, August 29, 1959," 1–4. Hereafter cited as EL, PP (AWF-IMS), box, document, date.
115. Memorandum of Conversation, "Private Meeting between the President and Prime Minister Macmillan," 29 August 1959, Chequers, EL, PP (AWF-IMS), Box 3, "London: September 27–Sept. 3, 1959."
116. Ibid.; Memorandum of Conversation, "Nuclear Test Negotiations," 30 August 1959, Chequers, EL, PP (AWF-IMS), Box 3, "London: August 27–Sept. 3, 1959."
117. Harold Evans, *Downing Street Diary: the Macmillan Years, 1957–1963* (London: Hodder & Stoughton, 1981), 43.
118. Alexander Macmillan, interview.
119. Script of televised broadcast with Prime Minister, 31 August 1957, EL, PP (AWF-IS), Box 25A, "Macmillan, 7/1/59–12/31/59," folder 6.
120. Eisenhower, *Waging Peace*, 423; see also Macmillan, *Riding the Storm*, 749.
121. Andrew Goodpaster, interview.
122. Alexander Macmillan, interview.
123. Blake, *Conservative Party From Peel to Thatcher*, 267.
124. John Hay Whitney to Secretary of State, 8 September 1959, 2–3, EL, PP (AWF-IMS), Box 3, "London: August 27–Sept. 3, 1959."
125. Blake, *Conservative Party From Peel to Thatcher*, 24, 41.
126. Macmillan, *Riding the Storm*, 749.
127. Whitney to Secretary of State, 8 September 1959.
128. Ibid.
129. Eisenhower to Macmillan, 5 September 1959, EL, PP (AWF-IS), Box 25A, "Macmillan, 7/1/59–12/31/59," folder 6.
130. Macmillan, *Riding the Storm*, 749–50; Evans and Taylor, *From Salisbury to Major*, 118–19; Horne, *Macmillan*, II, 148–50.
131. Macmillan, *Riding the Storm*, 350–1; Horne, *Macmillan*, II, 148–50.
132. Macmillan, *Pointing the Way*, 13–14; Horne, *Macmillan*, II, 148–50.
133. Eisenhower to Macmillan, 9 October 1959, EL, PP (AWF-IS), Box 25A, "Macmillan, 7/1/59–12/31/59," folder 5.
134. Macmillan to Eisenhower, 10 October 1959, EL, PP (AWF-IS), Box 25A, "Macmillan, 7/1/59–12/31/59," folder 4.
135. Macmillan to Eisenhower, "Mr. Khrushchev's Character and Motives," 5 September 1959, 1–2, EL, PP (AWF-IS), Box 25A, "7/1/59–12/31/59," folder 3.
136. Ibid.
137. Ibid.

138. Eisenhower to Macmillan, 21 July 1959, 2.
139. Macmillan to Eisenhower, "Mr. Khrushchev's Character and Motives," 5 September 1959, 2.
140. Eisenhower to Macmillan, 10 September 1959, EL, PP (AWF-IS), Box 25A, "Macmillan, 7/1/59–12/31/59," folder 6.
141. Memorandum – President Eisenhower's Talks with Chairman Khrushchev at Camp David, 30 September 1959, EL, PP (AWF-IS), "Macmillan, 7/1/59–12/31/59," folder 5.
142. Ibid., 2.
143. Ibid., 4.
144. Thomas S. Gates, interview.
145. Eisenhower, *Waging Peace*, 449; John Eisenhower, *Strictly Personal*, 262–3.
146. Eisenhower, *Waging Peace*, 409; Horne, *Macmillan, II*, 217–18.
147. Dwight D. Eisenhower Library. Dwight D. Eisenhower, Papers as President, White House Office; Office of the Staff Secretary, Box 10, "International Meetings and Trips," Chronology of Heads of Government, Paris, December 18, 1959, Record of a Meeting at the Elysée, December 19, 1959, 5. Hereafter cited as DDEL, PP (WHO: OSS), box, document, date.
148. Ibid., 10–11.
149. Ibid., 11.
150. Ibid.
151. Macmillan, *Pointing the Way*, 102–3; Horne, *Macmillan, II*, 218–20.
152. Chronology of Heads of Government, Paris, 18 December 1957, Record of a Meeting at the Elysée, 19 December 1959, 9.
153. Chronology of Heads of Government, Paris, 18 December 1959; see also American Embassy to Sec State, Washington, 21 December 1959, 2, EL, PP (WHO: OSS), Box 10, "International Meetings and Trips."
154. Macmillan, *Pointing the Way*, 103.
155. Chronology of Heads of Government, Paris, 18 December 1959, see also American Embassy, Paris, to Sec State Washington, 21 December 1959, 1–2, EL, PP (WHO: OSS), Box 10, "International Meetings and Trips."
156. Ibid., 3.
157. Horne, *Macmillan, II*, 148.
158. Richard Aldous and Sabine Lee, "Staying in the Game: Harold Macmillan and Britain's World Role," in Aldous and Lee, eds, *Harold Macmillan and Britain's World Role*, 152–3.

4 1960: Washington and Paris

1. Harold Macmillan to Jack Page, 4 March 1960, Macmillan Papers, c. 328.
2. Richard Aldous and Sabine Lee, "Staying in the Game: Harold Macmillan and Britain's World Role," in Aldous and Lee, eds, *Harold Macmillan and Britain's World Role*, 152–3.
3. Ambrose, *Eisenhower, II*, 564–5.
4. TELEPHONE CALLS, 21 March 1960, 1–2, EL, PP (AWF-IS), Box 25B, "Macmillan, Harold, 1/60–8/4/60," folder 1.
5. Ibid.

Notes and References

6. Ibid.
7. TELEPHONE CALL – 3/23/60, EL, PP (AWF-IS), Box 25B, "Macmillan, Harold, 1/1/60–8/4/60," folder 7.
8. Ibid.
9. Memorandum of Conversation, "Nuclear Test Negotiations," 28 March 1960, Camp David, 2–3, EL, PP, (AWF-IS), Box 25B, "Macmillan Visit to Washington, 3/26–30/60."
10. Ibid.
11. Ibid., 3.
12. Ibid.
13. Ibid.
14. Ambrose, *Eisenhower, II*, 566–7.
15. Richard Aldous, "'A Family Affair': the Art of Personal Diplomacy," in Aldous and Lee, eds, *Harold Macmillan and Britain's World Role*, 20.
16. Macmillan, *Pointing the Way*, 191.
17. Ibid., 192.
18. Ibid., 191; Horne, *Macmillan, I*, 221.
19. Macmillan to Eisenhower, 31 March 1960, EL, PP (AWF-IS), Box 25B, "Macmillan, Harold, 1/14/60–8/4/60," folder 1.
20. Ambrose, *Eisenhower, II*, 567.
21. John Prados, *The Soviet Estimate* (New York: The Dial Press, 1982), 88.
22. Ibid.
23. Michael R. Beschloss, *Mayday: Eisenhower, Khrushchev, and the U-2 Affair* (New York: Harper & Row, 1986), 91–3.
24. Ibid., 93.
25. Ibid., 5.
26. Richard Bissell, *Reflections of a Cold Warrior* (New Haven: Yale University Press, 1995), 111–12.
27. Ibid.
28. Stephen E. Ambrose, *Ike's Spies: Eisenhower and the Intelligence Establishment* (Garden City, NY: Doubleday, 1981), 267.
29. Ibid.; Beschloss, *Mayday*, 81–94; Bissell, *Reflections of a Cold Warrior*, 115–16.
30. Macmillan to Eisenhower, 22 March 1957, EL, PP (AWF-IS), Box 22, "Harold Macmillan," folder 2.
31. Ibid., 2.
32. Eisenhower to Macmillan, 23 March 1957, EL, PP (AWF-IS), Box 22, "Harold Macmillan," folder 6.
33. Beschloss, *Mayday*, 103–4; Bissell, *Reflections of a Cold Warrior*, 116–17.
34. Ambrose, *Ike's Spies*, 273–7.
35. Ibid., 277.
36. Bissell, *Reflections of a Cold Warrior*, 112–13.
37. David Wise and Thomas Ross, *The U-2 Affair* (New York: Random House, 1962), 154.
38. Bissell, *Reflections of a Cold Warrior*, 122–3.
39. Ambrose, *Eisenhower, II*, 567.
40. Ambrose, *Ike's Spies*, 283; Ambrose, *Eisenhower, II*, 569; Beschloss, *Mayday*, 241–2; Khrushchev, *Creation of a Superpower*, 365–7.
41. Ambrose, *Ike's Spies*, 283.
42. Khrushchev, *Creation of a Superpower*, 367–9.

43. Ibid., 368. See also Francis Gary Powers, with Curt Gentry, *Operation Overflight* (New York: Holt, Rinehart, Winston, 1970), 79–80, and Bissell, *Reflections of a Cold Warrior*, 125–6.
44. Powers with Gentry, *Operation Overflight*, 78.
45. Ibid., 89.
46. Ibid., 90. Ironically, the first U-2 flight over the Soviet Union occurred on 4 July 1956, Independence Day in the United States. The last flight occurred on 1 May 1960, the date of the Soviet Union's national holiday.
47. Bissell, *Reflections of a Cold Warrior*, 127.
48. Ibid., 129.
49. C. Douglas Dillon, interview.
50. Ibid.
51. Khrushchev, *Creation of a Superpower*, 374.
52. Ibid., 374–5.
53. Ibid., 376–7.
54. Ambrose, *Ike's Spies*, 281–2.
55. Ibid., 283.
56. Beschloss, *Mayday*, 38–9.
57. Ibid.
58. Thomas S. Gates, interviews with Bruce Geelhoed, 7 May, 14 May 1982.
59. E. Bruce Geelhoed, "Dwight D. Eisenhower, the Spy Plane, and the Summit: a Quarter Century Retrospective," *Presidential Studies Quarterly*, vol. XVII, no. 1 (Winter 1987), 99.
60. Khrushchev, *Creation of a Superpower*, 381.
61. Geelhoed, "Spy Plane and the Summit," *Presidential Studies Quarterly*, 98.
62. Ibid., 98–9; Ambrose, *Eisenhower, II*, 572.
63. Ibid., 99.
64. Khrushchev, *Creation of a Superpower*, 382.
65. Ibid. See also Beschloss, *Mayday*, 55–7. Beschloss records that Thompson was at the reception and overheard Malik's remark, not that he was notified about the conversation by Ambassador Sulman.
66. Geelhoed, "Spy Plane and the Summit," *Presidential Studies Quarterly*, 99.
67. Ambrose, *Eisenhower, II*, 574.
68. Ibid., 574–5; Watson, *Into the Missile Age*, 721.
69. Horne, *Macmillan, II*, 226; Macmillan, *Pointing the Way*, 196.
70. Horne, *Macmillan, II*, 226.
71. Ibid. See also Murphy, *Diplomat Among Warriors*, 441.
72. Beschloss, *Mayday*, 256–7.
73. Macmillan, *Pointing the Way*, 200–1.
74. Khrushchev, *Creation of a Superpower*, 380.
75. Beschloss, *Mayday*, 264–5.
76. Eisenhower, *Waging Peace*, 553.
77. Horne, *Macmillan, II*, 226–77.
78. Khrushchev, *Creation of a Superpower*, 388.
79. State Department, cable, American Embassy, Paris to Washington, 14 May 1960, EL, PP (WHO: OSS), Box 11, "International Meetings and Trips, Summit, etc.," folder 2.
80. Ibid., 8–9.
81. Macmillan, *Pointing the Way*, 202–3; Horne, *Macmillan, II*, 227.

180 *Notes and References*

82. Statement By the President, 15 May 1960, EL, PP (WHO: OSS), Box 11, "International Meetings and Trips, U-2," folder 4.
83. State Department, cable, "Tripartite Heads of Government Meeting, Elysée Palace in Paris," 1–2, EL, PP (WHO: OSS), Box 11, "International Trips and Meetings, U-2," folder 4.
84. Ibid., 9.
85. Macmillan, *Pointing the Way*, 204; Horne, *Macmillan, II*, 227; Thomas S. Gates, interview, 7 May 1982.
86. Watson, *Into the Missile Age*, 722–3; Geelhoed, "The Spy Plane and the Summit," *Presidential Studies Quarterly*, 101.
87. Macmillan, *Pointing the Way*, 204–5.
88. John Eisenhower, *Strictly Personal*, 273–4.
89. State Department, Cable, American Embassy, Paris to Sec State, Washington, 16 May 1960, EL, PP (WHO: OSS), Box 11, "International Trips and Meetings, U-2," folder 2.
90. Macmillan, *Pointing the Way*, 205; Horne, *Macmillan, II*, 228.
91. Statement by N.S. Khrushchev, Chairman of the USSR Council of Ministers to President de Gaulle of France, Prime Minister Macmillan of Great Britain, and President Eisenhower to the USA, 16 May 1960, 1,5, EL, PP (WHO: OSS), Box 11, "International Trips and Meetings," U-2, folder 4.
92. Ibid., 16.
93. Thomas S. Gates, interview, 14 May 1982.
94. Harold Macmillan, interview with Robert McKenzie, 14–15.
95. Official transcript, Meeting of Heads of Government, Paris, 16 May 1960, 9, EL, PP (WHO: OSS), Box 11, "International Trips and Meetings, U-2 [May 16–21]," folder 1.
96. Ibid., 11.
97. Ibid., 14.
98. Thomas S. Gates, interviews. See also John Eisenhower, *Strictly Personal*, 274–5.
99. Macmillan, *Pointing the Way*, 208.
100. Aldous, "'A Family Affair': the Art of Personal Diplomacy," in Aldous and Lee, eds, *Harold Macmillan and Britain's World Role*, 24–5; Macmillan, *Pointing the Way*, 208; John Eisenhower, *Strictly Personal*, 274.
101. Memorandum of Conversation, "Invitation to Khrushchev for first Summit Meeting," 17 May 1960, Elysée Palace, Paris, EL, PP (WHO: OSS), Box 11, "International Trips and Meetings, U-2 [May 16–21]," folder 3.
102. Macmillan, *Pointing the Way*, 208.
103. John Eisenhower, *Strictly Personal*, 276.
104. Beschloss, *Mayday*, 293–4.
105. Aldous, "'A Family Affair': the Art of Personal Diplomacy," in Aldous and Lee, eds, *Harold Macmillan and Britain's World Role*, 24–5.
106. Memorandum of Conversation, "Invitation to Khrushchev For First Summit Meeting," 17 May 1960, 10 a.m., Elysée Palace, 3, EL, PP (WHO: OSS), Box 11, "International Trips and Meetings, U-2, II [May 16–21]," folder 3.
107. Wise and Ross, *The U-2 Affair*, 161.
108. Ibid., 164.
109. Ibid.; Beschloss, *Mayday*, 294–5.
110. Ibid.

111. Meeting of Chiefs of State and Heads of Government, Memorandum of Conversation, "The Problem of Convening the Summit," 17 May 1960, 1–2, EL, PP (WHO: OSS), Box 11, "International Trips and Meetings, U-2, II [May 16–21]," folder 4.
112. Ibid.
113. Ibid., 1–2.
114. Ibid., 2.
115. Ibid., 3.
116. Ibid.
117. Ibid., 4.
118. Ibid., 5.
119. Ibid.
120. Ibid., 7–8.
121. Ibid., 9.
122. Beschloss, *Mayday*, 295–6.
123. "Invitation to Khrushchev for First Summit Meeting, May 17," 12, EL, PP (AWF-IS), Box 11, "International Trips and Meetings, U-2, II [May 16–21]," folder 4.
124. Stephen E. Ambrose titled his chapter on this topic in *Ike's Spies* as "Francis Gary Powers and the Summit that Never Was," 279–92. In *Pointing the Way*, Macmillan refers to the Conference as "The Summit That Failed," 178–216.
125. "Invitation to Khrushchev for First Summit Meeting," 17 May 1960, 12.
126. Horne, *Macmillan, II*, 230.
127. Harold Macmillan, interview with Robert McKenzie, 14–15.
128. Beschloss, *Mayday*, 304.
129. Ibid., 326.
130. Don Cook, "Summit Casualty – Macmillan," *New York Herald Tribune*, 23 May 1960; Drew Middleton, "West's Future Aims: Macmillan's Summit Role," *New York Times*, 24 May 1960.
131. Cook, "Summit Casualty – Macmillan," *New York Herald Tribune*, 23 May 1960, 1, 11.
132. Middleton, "West's Future Aims: Macmillan's Summit Role," *New York Times*, 24 May 1960, 1.
133. Ibid.
134. Ibid.
135. Eisenhower to Macmillan, 18 May 1960, in Galambos and van Ee, eds, *The Papers of Dwight David Eisenhower, XX*, 1539.
136. Macmillan to Eisenhower, 20 May 1960, EL, PP (AWF-IS), Box 25B, "Macmillan, Harold, 1/1/60–8/4/60," folder 1.
137. Ibid. Macmillan's suspicions that Khrushchev had decided to "torpedo" the summit before he arrived were accurate. See Khrushchev, *Creation of a Superpower*, 387–8.
138. Macmillan to Eisenhower, 20 May 1960, see also *FRUS, VII*, 866.
139. Eisenhower to Macmillan, 24 May 1960, EL, PP (AWF-IS), Box 25B, "Macmillan, Harold, 1/1/60–8/4/60," folder 7. See also *FRUS, VII*, 867.
140. Ibid., 2.
141. Ibid.
142. Sergei Khrushchev, *Creation of a Superpower*, 390.

143. John Eisenhower, *Strictly Personal*, 263–4.
144. Geelhoed, "The Spy Plane and the Summit," *Presidential Studies Quarterly*, 100.
145. John Eisenhower, *Strictly Personal*, 263.
146. Macmillan, *Pointing the Way*, 202; Horne, *Macmillan, II*, 231–3.
147. Dr. A. McGehee Harvey, "A 1969 Conversation with Khrushchev: the Beginning of His Fall from Power," excerpted from "Playing for High Stakes," *Life*, vol. 69, no. 25 (18 December 1960), 48b; Geelhoed, "The Spy Plane and the Summit," *Presidential Studies Quarterly*, 104.
148. Sergei Khrushchev, *Creation of a Superpower*, 383.
149. Meeting of Chiefs of State and Heads of Government, Paris, May 1960, Lewellyn Thompson, Memorandum for the Record, May 16, 1960, EL, PP (WHO: OSS), Box 11, "International Trips and Meetings, U-2, II [May 16–21]."
150. Sergei Khrushchev, *Creation of a Superpower*, 387.
151. Thomas S. Gates, interview with Bruce Geelhoed, 7 May 1982. The authors do not know whether Gates or Malinovsky was first selected.
152. Murphy, *Diplomat Among Warriors*, 440–1.
153. Sergei Khrushchev, *Creation of a Superpower*, 295, 346; see also Gordon Chang, "Eisenhower and Mao's China," in Bischof and Ambrose, eds, *Eisenhower*, 191–205.
154. Meeting of Chiefs of State and Heads of Government, Paris, May 1960, Memorandum of Conversation, "Report to NATO, Berlin, Disarmament," 18 May 1960, 2, EL, PP (WHO: OSS), Box 11, "International Trips and meetings, U-2, II [May 16–21]," folder 6.
155. Ibid., 4–5.
156. Sergei Khrushchev, *Creation of a Superpower*, 390–1.
157. Ambrose, *Nixon, I*, 519, 524–5; Beschloss, *Mayday*, 191–2.
158. Dr. A. McGehee Harvey, "A 1969 Conversation with Khrushchev," *Life*, 69, 48b.
159. Memorandum of Conversation, "Summit Meeting," 18 May 1960, American Embassy, Paris, EL, PP (WHO: OSS), Box 11, "International Trips and Meetings, U-2, II [May 16–21]."
160. Ibid.
161. Nikita S. Khrushchev, *Khrushchev Remembers* (Boston: Little, Brown, 1970), 450.
162. Nixon, *Six Crises*, 335.

Epilogue

1. Memorandum of Conversation, Meeting of Chiefs of State and Heads of Government, "Memorandum of Conversation," 18 May 1960, 3, EL, PP (WHO: OSS), Box 11, "International Trips and Meetings, U-2 [May 16–21]."
2. Ambrose, *Eisenhower, II*, 584–5.
3. Watson, *Into the Missile Age*, 725.
4. Ambrose, *Eisenhower, II*, 495; see also *FBM Facts: Polaris, Poseidon, Trident* (Washington, DC: Strategic Systems Project Office, Department of the Navy, 1978), 22–8.

5. Memorandum of Conference with the President, 27 September 1960, New York (recorded 28 September 1960), EL, PP (AWF-IS), Box 25B, "Macmillan, Harold, 8/1/60–1/20/61," folder 5. See also Watson, *Into the Missile Age*, 560–70.
6. Memorandum of Conference with the President, 27 September 1960.
7. Horne, *Macmillan, II*, 233.
8. Ambrose, *Eisenhower, II*, 585–6; Watson, *Into the Missile Age*, 725; Macmillan, *Pointing the Way*, 237–8.
9. Macmillan to Khrushchev, 19 July 1960, EL, PP (AWF-IS), Box 25B, "Macmillan, Harold, 1/1/60–8/4/60, folder 3. Macmillan thought so highly of this letter, and of his speech in the House of Commons, that he included the full text of the letter to Khrushchev in *Pointing the Way*, 238–41.
10. Macmillan to Khrushchev, 19 July 1960, 3–4.
11. Ibid., 4.
12. Macmillan to Khrushchev, 18 July 1960, EL, PP (AWF-IS), Box 25B, "Macmillan, Harold, 1/1/60–8/4/60," folder 3.
13. Eisenhower to Macmillan, 23 July 1960, EL, PP (AWF-IS), Box 25B, "Harold Macmillan, 1/1/60–8/8/4/60," folder 4.
14. Beschloss, *Mayday*, 343–5, 347–8.
15. Macmillan to Eisenhower, 2 July 1960, 1–2, EL, PP (AWF-IS), Box 25B, "Macmillan, Harold, 1/1/60–8/4/60," folder 2.
16. Eisenhower to Macmillan, 11 July 1960, 1–2, EL, PP (AWF-IS), Box 25B, "Macmillan, Harold, 1/1/60–8/4/60," folder 5.
17. Ibid., 1–6.
18. Ibid., 11.
19. Ibid.
20. Ibid., 11–12.
21. Macmillan to Eisenhower, 22 July 1960, EL, PP (AWF-IS), Box 25B, "Macmillan, Harold, 1/1/60–8/4/60," folder 3.
22. Ibid.
23. Ibid.
24. Ibid.
25. Macmillan to Eisenhower, 25 July 1960, 1–2, EL, PP (AWF-IS), Box 25B, "Macmillan, Harold, 1/160–8/4/60," folder 3.
26. Ibid., 2.
27. Ibid., 4–5.
28. Ibid., 3.
29. Ibid., 6.
30. Ibid.
31. Ibid.
32. Ibid., 6–7.
33. Ibid., 8.
34. Eisenhower to Macmillan, 8 August 1960, 1–2, EL, PP (AWF-IS), Box 25B, "Macmillan, Harold, 8/4/60–1/20/61."
35. Ibid.
36. Ibid.
37. Ibid., 3.
38. Ibid., 4–5.
39. Ibid., 5–6.
40. Watson, *Into the Missile Age*, 374–9.

41. Ibid., 375.
42. Ibid., 377.
43. Ibid., 379.
44. Ibid.
45. Horne, *Macmillan, II*, 275–6.
46. Watson, *Into the Missile Age*, 562–3. See also Ronald Landa, "The Origins of the Skybolt Controversy in the Eisenhower Administration," in Miller, ed., *Seeing Off the Bear*, 117–19.
47. Watson, *Into the Missile Age*, 563.
48. Horne, *Macmillan, II*, 275–6. See also Baylis, *Anglo-American Defense Relations, 1939–1980*, 65–9; Landa, "The Origins of the Skybolt Controversy," in Miller, *Seeing Off the Bear*, 120–1.
49. Macmillan, *Pointing the Way*, 253–4; Horne, *Macmillan, II*, 276; Watson, *Into the Missile Age*, 564. Part of the problem between the British and the Americans involved the Pentagon's skepticism about the potential viability of the Skybolt project. In early 1960, Thomas Gates even warned Watkinson not to cancel the Blue Streak project before the Administration could give more concrete assurances to the British on the progress of Skybolt. Thomas S. Gates, interview, 7 May 1982.
50. Landa, "The Origins of the Skybolt Controversy," in Miller, ed., *Seeing Off The Bear*, 121–2. See also Watson, *Into the Missile Age*, 565–6.
51. Watson, *Into the Missile Age*, 566.
52. Macmillan to Eisenhower, 24 June 1960, EL, PP (AWF-IS), Box 25B, "Macmillan, Harold, 1/1/60–8/4/60," folder 2.
53. Ibid., 2.
54. Ibid., 3.
55. Ibid., 3–4.
56. Memorandum for the President, "Reply to Prime Minister Macmillan's Letter of June 24, 1960 on Polaris Submarine Facilities and Related Matters," 30 June 1960, EL, PP (AWF-IS), Box 25B, "Macmillan, Harold, 1/1/60–8/4/60," folder 6.
57. Ibid.
58. Ibid., 2.
59. Ibid.
60. Eisenhower to Macmillan, 30 June 1960, EL, PP (AWF-IS), Box 25B, "Macmillan, Harold, 1/1/60–8/4/60," folder 6.
61. Ibid., 2.
62. Ibid.
63. Memorandum of Conference with the President, 17 September 1960 (dated 28 September 1960), 2, EL, PP (AWF-IS), Box 25B, "Macmillan, Harold, 1/1/60–8/4/60," folder 5. See also Watson, *Into the Missile Age*, 567.
64. Watson, *Into the Missile Age*, 569. During the Kennedy Administration, the United States canceled its sale of Skybolt to Great Britain, causing considerable concern in the Macmillan government. But Macmillan used the action to press for the acquisition of Polaris submarines for Britain on favorable economic terms. The addition of Polaris to the British deterrent was an important feature of British military policy in the post-Eisenhower period. See Horne, *Macmillan, II*, 442, and *FBM Facts*, 5.

65. Macmillan to Eisenhower, 25 October 1960, EL, PP (AWF-IS), Box 25B, "Macmillan, Harold, 8/1/60–1/20/61," folder 2.
66. Eisenhower to Macmillan, 31 October 1960, EL, PP (AWF-IS), Box 25B, "Macmillan, Harold, 8/1/60–1/20/61," folder 4.
67. Watson, *Into the Missile Age*, 570.
68. Macmillan, *Pointing the Way*, 256.
69. Harold Macmillan to Arthur Skeffington, MP, 1 November 1960, Macmillan Papers, c. 330.
70. Harold Macmillan to Judith Hart, MP, 13 November 1960, ibid.
71. Sergei Khrushchev, *Creation of a Superpower*, 409.
72. Ambrose, *Eisenhower, II*, 589–90.
73. Horne, *Macmillan, II*, 278.
74. Memorandum of Conference with the President, 27 September 1960 (dated 28 September 1960), 6, EL, PP (AWF-IS), Box 25B, "Macmillan, Harold, 8/1/60–1/20/61," folder 5.
75. Macmillan, *Pointing the Way*, 275–9.
76. Ibid., 279; Horne, *Macmillan, II*, 278–9.
77. Memorandum of Conference with the President, 2 October 1960 (dated 6 October 1960), 2–4, EL, PP (AWF-IS), Box 25B, "Macmillan, Harold, 8/1/60–1/20/61," folder 5.
78. Macmillan, *Pointing the Way*, 279–80.
79. Macmillan to Eisenhower, 7 October 1960, 2, EL, PP (AWF-IS), Box 25B, "Macmillan, Harold, 8/1/60–1/20/61," folder 2.
80. Eisenhower to Macmillan, 14 October 1960, 2, EL, PP (AWF-IS), Box 25B, "Macmillan, Harold, 8/1/60–1/20/61," folder 1.
81. Macmillan to Eisenhower, 10 November 1960, 1–2, EL, PP (AWF-IS), Box 25B, "Macmillan, Harold, 8/1/60–1/20/61," folder 1. See also Macmillan, *Pointing the Way*, 284; and Eisenhower, *Waging Peace*, 602.
82. Horne, *Macmillan, II*, 29.
83. Aldous and Lee, "Harold Macmillan and Britain's World Role," in Aldous and Lee, eds, *Harold Macmillan and Britain's World Role*, 155.
84. Baylis, *Anglo-American Defense Relations, 1939–1980*, 66.
85. Ambrose, *Eisenhower, II*, 225–6.
86. Eisenhower Diary entry, 1 January 1957, in Galambos and van Ee, eds, *The Papers of Dwight David Eisenhower, vol. XVII. The Presidency: the Middle Way* (Baltimore: Johns Hopkins University Press, 1996), 2471.
87. Dickson, *Sputnik*, 120, 151–4.
88. Ewald, *Eisenhower the President*, 236; see also Ambrose, *Eisenhower, II*, 595; Ambrose, *Ike's Spies*, 278; Ambrose, *Nixon, I*, 539–40.
89. Eisenhower to Henry Robinson Luce, 6 July 1960, in Galambos and van Ee, eds, *The Papers of Dwight David Eisenhower*, XX, 1991–2.
90. Peter Lyon, *Eisenhower: Portrait of the Hero* (Boston: Little, Brown, 1974), 854. See also Ambrose, "EPILOGUE: Eisenhower's Legacy," in Bischof and Ambrose, eds, *Eisenhower*, 251.
91. Macmillan, *Pointing the Way*, 282; Horne, *Macmillan, II*, 279.
92. Eisenhower, *Waging Peace*, 657.
93. Ibid., 120.

Bibliography

Manuscript collections

Bodleian Library, Oxford University, Oxford, United Kingdom
  Conservative Party Central Office Papers
  Harold Macmillan Papers
Dwight D. Eisenhower Library, Abilene, Kansas, USA
  Ann C. Whitman File, International Series
  Ann C. Whitman File, Administration Series
  Ann C. Whitman File, International Meetings Series
  White House Office, Office of the Staff Secretary, International Trips and Meetings Series.

Published sources

Aldous, Richard, and Sabine Lee, eds. *Harold Macmillan and Britain's World Role*. London: Macmillan, 1995.
Aldrich, Winthrop W. "The Suez Crisis: a Footnote to History," *Foreign Affairs*, vol. 45, no. 3 (April 1967), 541–52.
Ambrose, Stephen E. *Eisenhower: Vol. I. Soldier, General of the Army, President-Elect, 1890–1952*. New York: Simon & Schuster, 1983.
Ambrose, Stephen E. *Eisenhower: Vol. II. The President, 1953–1961*. New York: Simon & Schuster, 1984.
Ambrose, Stephen E. *Ike's Spies: Eisenhower and the Espionage Establishment*. Garden City, NY: Doubleday, 1981.
Ambrose, Stephen E. *The Supreme Commander: the War Years of General Dwight D. Eisenhower*. Garden City: Doubleday, 1970.
Ambrose, Stephen E. *Nixon. Vol. I: The Education of a Politician, 1913–1962*. New York: Simon & Schuster, 1984.
Ashton, Nigel J. *Eisenhower, Macmillan, and the Problem of Nasser*. Basingstoke: Macmillan Press – now Palgrave Macmillan, 1996.
Bartlett, Christopher. *A History of Postwar Britain*. London: Longman, 1977.
Bartlett, Christopher. *The Long Retreat: British Defence Policy, 1945–1970*. London: Macmillan, 1972.
Baylis, John. *Anglo-American Defense Relations, 1939–1980*. New York: St Martin's Press, 1981.
Beschloss, Michael. *Mayday: Eisenhower, Khrushchev, and the U-2 Affair*. New York: Harper & Row, 1986.
Beschloss, Michael. *Eisenhower: a Centenary History*. New York: Edward Burlingame, 1990.
Bischof, Gunter, and Ambrose, Stephen, eds. *Eisenhower: a Centenary Assessment*. Baton Rouge, LA: Louisiana State University Press, 1992.

Bissell, Richard M., Jr. *Reflections of a Cold Warrior*. New Haven, CT: Yale University Press, 1995.
Blake, Robert. *The Conservative Party From Peel to Thatcher*. London: Fontana Press, 1985.
Bowie, Robert R. and Richard H. Immerman. *Waging Peace: How Eisenhower Shaped An Enduring Cold War Strategy*. New York: Oxford University Press, 1998.
Boyle, Peter G., ed. *The Churchill–Eisenhower Correspondence, 1953–1955*. Chapel Hill: University of North Carolina Press, 1990.
Brands, H.W., Jr. *Cold Warriors: Eisenhower's Generation and American Foreign Policy*. New York: Columbia University Press, 1988.
Brands, H.W., Jr. *Into the Labyrinth: the United States and the Middle East, 1945–1993*. New York: McGraw-Hill, 1994.
Bundy, McGeorge. *Danger and Survival: Choices About the Bomb in the First Fifty Years*. New York: Random House, 1988.
Burns, James MacGregor. *Roosevelt. Vol. II: the Soldier of Freedom, 1940–1945*. New York: Harcourt, Brace, Jovanovich, 1970.
Burr, William. "The Berlin Crisis: an Overview," *Digital National Security Archives*, Chadwyck, 27 May 1992.
Butler, Richard Austen, Baron Butler of Saffron Walden. *The Art of the Possible*. London: Hamish Hamilton, 1971.
Churchill, Winston S. *The Hinge of Fate*. Boston: Houghton-Mifflin, 1950.
Collier, Peter and Horowitz, David. *The Rockefelless*. New York: Holt, Rinehart, and Winston, 1976.
Cook, Blanche Wiesen, *The Declassified Eisenhower*. Garden City, NY: Doubleday, 1981.
Davenport-Hines, Richard. *The Macmillans*. London: Heinemann, 1992.
Dickson, Paul. *Sputnik: the Shock of the Century*. New York: Walker Books, 2001.
Divine, Robert A. *Blowing on the Wind*. New York: Oxford University Press, 1978.
Divine, Robert A. *Eisenhower and the Cold War*. New York: Oxford University Press, 1981.
Eisenhower, Dwight D. *Crusade in Europe*. Garden City, NY: Doubleday, 1948.
Eden, Anthony. *Full Circle*. Boston: Houghton-Mifflin, 1960.
Eisenhower, Dwight D. *Waging Peace: White House Years, 1956–1961*. Garden City: Doubleday, 1965.
Eisenhower, John S.D. *Strictly Personal*. Garden City, NY: Doubleday, 1974.
Evans, Brandon and Andrew Taylor. *From Salisbury to Major: Continuity and Change in Conservative Politics*. Manchester: University of Manchester Press, 1996.
Evans, Harold. *Downing Street Diary: the Macmillan Years, 1957–1963*. London: Hodder & Stoughton, 1981.
Ewald, William Bragg. *Eisenhower the President: Crucial Years, 1951–1960*. Englewood Cliffs, NJ: Prentice-Hall, 1981.
Ferrell, Robert, ed. *The Eisenhower Diaries*. New York: Norton, 1981.
Fisher, Nigel. *Harold Macmillan: a Biography*. London: Weidenfeld & Nicolson, 1982.
Freiburger, Steven A. *Dawn Over Suez*. Chicago: Ivan R. Dees, 1982.
Galambos, Louis and Daun van Ee, eds. *The Papers of Dwight David Eisenhower. The Presidency: The Middle Way*, vol. XVI. Baltimore: The Johns Hopkins University Press, 1996.

Galambos, Louis and Daun van Ee, eds. *The Papers of Dwight David Eisenhower. Vol. XVII. The Presidency: the Middle Way.* Baltimore: The Johns Hopkins University Press, 1996.

Galambos, Louis and Daun van Ee, eds. *The Papers of Dwight David Eisenhower. Vol. XVIII. The Presidency: Keeping the Peace.* Baltimore: The John Hopkins University Press, 2001.

Galambos, Louis and Daun van Ee, eds. *The Papers of Dwight David Eisenhower. Vol. XX. The Presidency: Keeping the Peace.* Baltimore: The Johns Hopkins University Press.

Galambos, Louis and Daun van Ee, eds. *The Papers of Dwight David Eisenhower. Vol. XX. The Presidency: Keeping the Peace.* Baltimore: The Johns Hopkins University Press, 2001.

Geelhoed, E. Bruce. *Charles E. Wilson and Controversy at the Pentagon, 1953 to 1957.* Detroit: Wayne State University Press, 1979.

Geelhoed, E. Bruce. "Dwight D. Eisenhower: the Spy Plane and the Summit. A Quarter-Century Retrospective," *Presidential Studies Quarterly*, XVII, No. 1, Winter 1987, 95–106.

Gelb, Norman. *Ike and Monty: Generals at War.* New York: William Morrow and Company, 1994.

Gilbert, Martin. *Churchill: a Life.* New York: Henry Holt and Company, 1991.

Hathaway, Robert M. *Great Britain and the United States: Special Relations Since World War II.* Boston: Twayne, 1990.

Hoopes, Townsend. *The Devil and John Foster Dulles.* Boston: Little, Brown, 1974.

Horne, Alistair. *Harold Macmillan. Vol. I, 1894–1956.* London: Macmillan, 1988.

Horne, Alistair. *Harold Macmillan, Vol. II, 1957–1986.* London: Macmillan, 1989.

Humes, James C. *Eisenhower and Churchill: the Partnership That Saved the World.* New York: Forum, 2001.

James, Robert Rhodes. *Anthony Eden.* New York: McGraw-Hill, 1987.

Jordan, Robert S., ed. *Generals in International Politics: the Supreme Allied Commander, Europe.* Lexington, KY: University Press of Kentucky, 1987.

Kalb, Madeline G. *The Congo Cables: the Cold War in Africa From Eisenhower to Kennedy.* New York: Macmillan, 1982.

Kennedy, David M. *Freedom From Fear.* New York: Oxford University Press, 1999.

Khrushchev, Nikita. *Khrushchev Remembers.* Boston: Little, Brown, 1970.

Khrushchev, Sergei N. *Nikita Khrushchev and the Creation of a Superpower.* University Park: Pennsylvania State University Press, 2000.

Kimball, Warren C. *Roosevelt, Churchill, and World War II.* New York: Morrow, 1997.

Kingseed, Cole C. *Eisenhower and the Suez Crisis of 1956.* Baton Rouge, LA: Louisiana State University Press, 1995.

Kissinger, Henry. *Diplomacy.* New York: Simon & Schuster, 1994.

Landa, Ronald D., Miller, James E., Patterson, David S., and Sampson, Charles S., eds. *Foreign Relations of the United States, Vol. VII, 1958–1960*, Part One, "Western Security and Integration, Canada." Washington: Government Printing Office, 1993.

Leighton, Richard M. *Strategy, Money, and the New Look, 1953–1956. Vol. III: History of the Office of the Secretary of Defense.* Washington, DC: Historical Office of the Secretary of Defense, 2001.

Little, Richard and Steve Smith. *Belief Systems and International Relations*. Oxford: Basil Blackwell, 1988.
Lyon, Peter. *Eisenhower: Portrait of the Hero*. Boston: Little, Brown, 1974.
Macmillan, Harold. *War Diaries: Politics and War in the Mediterranean, January, 1943–May, 1945*. New York: St Martin's Press, 1984.
Macmillan, Harold. *The Blast of War, 1939–1945*. London: Macmillan, 1967.
Macmillan, Harold. *Tides of Fortune, 1945–1955*. London: Macmillan, 1969.
Macmillan, Harold. *Riding the Storm, 1956 to 1959*. London: Macmillan, 1971.
Macmillan, Harold. *Pointing the Way, 1959 to 1961*. London: Macmillan, 1972.
Miller, Roger G., ed. *Seeing Off the Bear: Anglo-American Airpower Cooperation During the Cold War*. Washington, DC: Air Force History and Museums Program, United States Air Force, 1995.
Murray, Donette. *Kennedy, Macmillan, and Nuclear Weapons*. Basingstoke: Macmillan Press – now Palgrave Macmillan, 2000.
Neal, Steve. *Harry and Ike: The Partnership That Remade the Postwar World*. New York: Scribner, 2001.
Neff, Donald, *Warriors at Suez*. New York: The Linden Press/Simon & Schuster, 1981.
Nixon, Richard M. *Six Crises*. Garden City, NY: Doubleday, 1962.
Nixon, Richard M. *RN: the Memoirs of Richard Nixon, Vol. I*. New York: Warner, 1978.
Ovendale, Ritchie. *Anglo-American Relations in the Twentieth Century*. New York: St Martin's Press, 1998.
Pach, Chester J., Jr. and Elmo Richardson. *The Presidency of Dwight D. Eisenhower*. Lawrence, KS: University Press of Kansas, 1991.
Perret, Geoffrey. *Eisenhower*. New York: Random House, 1999.
Pierre, Andrew. *Nuclear Politics: the British Experience With An Independent Nuclear Force*. New York: Oxford University Press, 1972.
Pinkley, Virgil with James F. Scheer. *Eisenhower Declassified*. Old Tappan, NJ: Fleming H. Revell Company, 1979.
Prados, John. *The Soviet Estimate: U.S. Intelligence Analysis and Russian Military Strength*. New York: The Dial Press, 1982.
Renwick, Sir Robin. *Fighting With Allies*. New York: Times Books, 1996.
United States Department of the Navy. *FBM Facts: Polaris, Poseidon, Trident*. Washington, DC: Strategic Systems Project Office, 1978.
Watson, Robert J. *Into the Missile Age, 1956–1960. Vol. IV, History of the Office of the Secretary of Defense*. Washington, DC: Historical Office of the Secretary of Defense, 1997.
White, Theodore H. *In Search of History*. New York: Harper & Row, 1978.
Zuckerman, Solly. *Monkeys, Men, and Missiles*. New York: W.W. Norton, 1988.

Interviews

By Bruce Geelhoed
   Robert B. Anderson
   Arleigh A. Burke
   Philip de Zulueta
   C. Douglas Dillon

James H. Douglas
John S.D. Eisenhower
Thomas S. Gates
Noel F. Gayler
Andrew J. Goodpaster
John N. Irwin II
Alexander Macmillan, Earl of Stockton

By Columbia University Oral History Project
Winthrop Aldrich

By John Foster Dulles Oral History Collection, Princeton University
Arleigh A. Burke
Livingston T. Merchant
Nathan F. Twining

By Dwight D. Eisenhower Library
Lauris Norstad

Index

Abel, Rudolf, 137
Adenauer, Konrad, 62, 63, 69, 70, 73, 83, 93, 94, 95, 96, 106
Aldous, Richard, 29, 95, 119–20, 152
Aldrich, Nelson, 7
Aldrich, Winthrop, xxvii, 6, 7, 8, 9, 10, 11
Alexander, Charles C., 31
Ambrose, Stephen, 102
Anderson, Robert B., xxvii, xxx, 22, 35, 47, 50
AQUATONE, 103, 104
As-Said, Nuri, 44, 45, 46, 49
Ashton, Nigel, 12, 50
Atomic Energy Commission (AEC), xxvii, 15

Baghdad Pact, 16
Baldwin, Stanley, xi, xii
Baylis, John, 152
Bermuda Conference (March 1957), xxv; Eisenhower and Macmillan reach agreement on meeting in Bermuda, 13; Macmillan's hostility to Nasser expressed at, 15–16; British–American agreement on exchange of medium-range ballistic missiles, 16–18; controversy over leaked reports of British–American agreements, 17–19; and AQUATONE, 103–4
Bevan, Aneurin, 33, 88
Bishop, Freddie, 15, 23, 42
Bissell, Richard, 103, 105, 107, 108
Blake, Robert, 33
Bligh, Tim, 84
Blue Streak (missile), 143, 144
Bohlen, Charles (Chip), 118
Brook, Norman, xxix, 15, 23, 42
Bulganin, Nikolai, 4
Bundy, McGeorge, 29
Burke, Arleigh A., 142, 145

Butler, Richard Austen (Rab), 6, 8, 9, 10, 11

Caccia, Harold, xxix, 6, 14, 23, 40, 42, 48, 65, 77, 79
Camp David, 76, 79, 92, 97, 99, 100, 101, 127, 144, 146, 147, 155
Casablanca Conference (1943), xxii
Castro, Fidel, 132, 137, 138, 139, 140, 141, 149
Central Intelligence Agency (CIA), 105, 106, 110, 111
Chamberlain, Neville, 76
Chamoun, Camille, 45, 50, 54
Chehab, Faud, 45, 54
Churchill, Randolph, 152
Churchill, Sir Winston, xii, xiii, xv, xix, xx, xxii, xxiv, xxvi, 7, 10, 12, 29, 59, 65, 153, 155
Collins, Norman, 85
Conner, General Fox, xxi
Cook, Don, 124, 125
Crossman, Richard, xxiii

Darlan, François, xxi
Dean, Sir Patrick, xxviii, 15, 44
de Gaulle, Charles, 48, 62, 63, 69, 70, 73, 79, 83, 84, 89, 91, 93, 94, 96, 98, 102, 106, 113, 114, 115, 116, 117, 118, 119, 120, 121, 122, 123, 125, 129, 129–30, 132, 146, 152, 155
de Murville, Maurice Couve, 80, 129
de Zulueta, Philip, xxviii, 11, 42, 58, 150, 163 n. 17
Dillon, C. Douglas, xxviii, 81, 107–8, 110, 116
Douglas, James H., 116
Dulles, Allen, 103, 106, 109, 130
Dulles, Janet, 71, 101
Dulles, John Foster, xxv, xxvi, xxvii, xxviii, 3, 4, 5, 6, 7, 8, 11, 12, 14, 15, 16, 17, 18, 23, 24, 32, 33, 38,

192 *Index*

Dulles, John Foster – *continued*
40, 42, 43, 44, 45, 47, 48, 50, 51, 55, 64, 65, 71, 72, 81, 83, 95, 109, 130, 134, 156, 166–7 n. 122

Eden, Anthony, role in Suez crisis, 4–10, 15, 20, 103–4
Eisenhower, Arthur, xiii
Eisenhower, Doud Dwight (Icky), xiv
Eisenhower, David (father of Dwight D. Eisenhower), xiii
Eisenhower, Ida Stover (mother of Dwight D. Eisenhower), xiii
Eisenhower, Dwight D., diplomatic partnership with Harold Macmillan, xi–xii; early life and boyhood, xii–xiv; military career between World War I and World War II, xiv–xvi; presidential election of 1952, xv; first meeting with Macmillan in 1943, xx–xxii; agrees to correspondence with Macmillan, xxv–xxvi; program of defense cooperation with Macmillan, xxix–xxxi; presidential election of 1956, 1–5; meets with Macmillan during Suez crisis, 5; applies economic pressure on British during the Suez crisis, 6–10; writes to Macmillan after Bermuda Conference, 1957, 20; meets with Macmillan in Washington, October 1957, 22–5; suffers slight stroke, November 1957, 26–7; attends North Atlantic Council meeting, Paris, December 1957, 27–8; initial views on disarmament, 32; resists pressure for increased defense spending, 34–5; reaction to calls for summit meeting, 38–9, 40–1; meets Macmillan in Washington, June 1958, 41–9; responds to crisis in Lebanon, 49–8; frustrations over Republican defeat in 1958 mid-term election, 58–9; Berlin crisis, 61–3; reaction to Macmillan's visit to the Soviet Union, 1959, 65–6; talks with Macmillan at Camp David, 1959, 70–80; reaction to Khrushchev's visit to the US, 82; visit to England, August–September 1959, 83–9; congratulates Macmillan on victory in General Election, 1959, 89; hosts visit by Nikita Khrushchev, September 1959, 92; attends Western Summit in Paris, December 1959, 93–5; proposes moratorium on nuclear testing, 1960, 98–9; talks with Macmillan at Camp David, 1960, 100–2; reaction to loss of U-2 piloted by Francis Gary Powers, 109–11; holds press conference on the U-2 incident, May 11 1960, 113; meets with Macmillan and de Gaulle before opening summit conference, May 1960, 115–16; visits Marnes-la-Coquette with Macmillan during Paris summit, 119–20; reaction to failure of the Paris summit, 123–4; attempts to bolster Macmillan's spirits after the Paris summit, 125–6; and RB-47 incident, July 1960, 133–6; discusses problem of Cuba with Macmillan, 137–41; discussions regarding Skybolt and Polaris missile programs with Macmillan, 142–9; address to the United Nations, September 1960, 149–50; meets with Macmillan at United Nations, September 1960, 150–1; writes to Macmillan before 1960 presidential election, 151; impact of diplomatic partnership with Macmillan, 153–4, 155–6; as "The Man Who Beat Hitler," 159 n. 18
Eisenhower, Earl, xiii
Eisenhower, Edgar, xiii
Eisenhower, John Sheldon Doud, xiv, xxviii, 22, 77, 84, 116, 119
Eisenhower, Mamie (wife of Dwight D. Eisenhower), xiv, xv, 26, 123
Eisenhower, Milton S., xiii, 41, 46
Eisenhower, Roy, xiii
Elizabeth II, Queen, 9–10, 12, 21, 84, 89, 143
Elliot, William, 41

Evans, Harold, 85
Ewald, William B., 1–2, 50

Farouk, King of Egypt, 7
Federal Republic of Germany (West Germany), 63–4, 73, 76, 77
Foot, M.R.D., 3, 165 n. 79
Four-Power Summit Conference (Paris, May 1960), 97–8, 114–31
Freiberger, Steven, 8

Gaitskell, Hugh, 88
Gates, Thomas S., xxvii, xxviii, xxix, xxx–xxxi, 2, 92, 109, 110, 111, 115, 116, 117, 128, 143, 144, 145, 184 n. 49
German Democratic Republic (East Germany), 61–5, 66, 72, 73, 76, 77
Goodpaster, Andrew J., xiii, xxvii, 10, 17, 24, 26, 51, 68, 75, 76, 77, 79, 81, 84, 87, 91, 104, 110, 150, 163 n. 13, 170 n. 76
Gray, Gordon, 110
Grey, Sir Edward, 35, 75
Griffith, James, 88
Gromyko, Andrei, 80, 120
Gruenther, Alfred M., 47

Hathaway, Robert M., xxxi
Hagerty, James C., 51, 85, 118
Hammarskjöld, Dag, 149
Hart, Judith, 149
Hayter, William, 23
Hazlett, Swede, 26, 153
Herter, Christian, xxvi, xxvii, 23, 71, 74, 77, 79, 80, 81, 88, 99, 101, 105, 114, 115, 116, 118, 122, 125, 134, 146, 147, 150
Hill, John Bayliss (Jack), xvii
Hitler, Adolf, xii, xv, 5
Holloway, James, 54
Home, Lord, 134, 150
Hoopes, Townsend, 68
Hoover, Herbert, Jr., 4, 8
Horne, Alistair, 8, 25, 29, 149–50, 152, 170 n. 92
Houghton, Amory, 27, 94
Hoyer-Miller, Frederick, xxviii
Humbert, Russell J., 42

Humphrey, George M., xxvii, 5, 6, 8, 9
Hussein, King of Jordan, 54, 55

IRBMs, 12, 13, 17, 20, 28, 29, 34, 38, 48, 133, 142, 153
Irwin, John N. II, 77, 78, 115

Jackson, Charles D., 47
James, Robert Rhodes, xxiii, 6, 9
Johnson, Lyndon B., 1, 2, 154

Kassem, Abdul Karim, 49, 55
Kennedy, David, xv
Kennedy, John F., 130, 151
Khrushchev, Nikita S., 31, 80, 93, 94, 95, 97; and Berlin crisis, 61–3; during Macmillan's visit to the Soviet Union, 1959, 65–8; Macmillan's impressions of, 68, 72; prospective visit to the United States, 81–2; visits the United States, September 1959, 92; protests U-2 overflights of the Soviet Union, 105–6; reaction to U-2 flight by Francis Gary Powers on 1 May 1963, 108–9; speech to Supreme Soviet, 5 May 1960, regarding the Powers flight, 110; speech to Supreme Soviet, 7 May 1960, regarding the Powers flight, 111; changes tactics for summit conference because of U-2 incident, 113–14; attacks Eisenhower at Paris summit for the U-2 flights, May 1960, 116–18; visits battlefield of the Marne with Marshall Malinovsky during Paris summit, 120–1; leaves Paris after collapse of the summit conference, May 1960, 123; possible explanations for refusing to negotiate at Paris summit, 126–30; attends the United Nations meetings, September 1960, 133; and RB-47 incident, 136–7; attends meeting of United Nations, September 1960, 149–50; "shoe-pounding" interruption of Macmillan's speech to the United Nations, 150

Index

Khrushchev, Sergei, 107, 108, 110, 112, 113, 127, 128
Killian, James, 78
Kilmuir, Lord David, 10
Kingseed, Cole, 8
Kissinger, Henry, xi–xii, 12
Kistiakowsky, George, 100
Koudriatsev, Yvan, 130
Kozlov, Frol, 67, 81
Kuznetsov, Vasili, 67

Landa, Ronald, 144
Lee, Sabine, 95, 152
Leighton, Richard M., 161 n. 63
Lloyd, Selwyn, xxviii, 14, 15, 19, 23, 24, 55, 66, 67, 70, 72, 77, 78, 79, 80, 101, 125, 134, 137
Lodge, Henry Cabot, xxviii, 50, 54
Luce, Henry R., 154
Lumumba, Patrice, 150

MacArthur, General Douglas, xiv, xv
Mack, Hal, xxi, 160 n. 39
Macmillan, Alexander, xv, 3, 15, 43, 85–6, 87, 158 n. 7, 160 n. 34
Macmillan, Dorothy Cavendish (wife of Harold Macmillan), xix, 42
Macmillan, Harold, diplomatic partnership with Eisenhower, xi, xii; early life and boyhood, xvi–xviii; experience in World War I, xviii–xix; political career during World War II, xix–xx; first meeting with Eisenhower in 1943, xx–xxii; experience during World War II, xxiii; cabinet posts in the Churchill and Eden governments, xxiii–xxiv; agrees to correspondence with Eisenhower, xxv–xxvi; pattern of defense cooperation with Eisenhower, xxix–xxxi; meets with Eisenhower during Suez crisis, 5–6; becomes prime minister after Eden's resignation, 10–11; releases White Paper on defense, April 1957, 14; meets with Eisenhower in Washington, October 1957, 22–5; writes to Eisenhower after president's stroke, 1957, 26; attends North Atlantic Council meeting, Paris, December 1957, 27–8; initial views on control of nuclear weapons, 32–4; early proposal for a summit conference, 36–40; meets Eisenhower in Washington, June 1958, 41–9; commencement speeches: De Pauw University, 42–3; Johns Hopkins University, 46; role in Lebanon crisis, 50–8; attempts to console Eisenhower after Republican defeats in 1958 mid-term elections, 58–9; and Berlin crisis, 1958–1959, 61–5; visit to the Soviet Union, 1959, 64, 65–9; visits to France and West Germany, 1959, 69–70; talks with Eisenhower at Camp David, 1959, 70–80; Eisenhower's visit to Britain, 1959, 83–9; victory in British General Election, October 1959, 89; advises Eisenhower on Khrushchev's personality, 90–1; attends Western Summit in Paris, December 1959, 93–5; nuclear testing issue, 1960, 98–9; talks with Eisenhower at Camp David, 1960, 100–2; reaction to loss of American U-2 plane, May 1960, 111–12; meets with Eisenhower and de Gaulle before opening meeting of summit conference, May 1960, 115–16; visits Marnes-la-Coquette with Eisenhower during Paris summit, 119–20; reaction to failure of the Paris summit, 123–4, 134; assumes role of advisor to Eisenhower in late 1960, 132–3; and RB-47 incident, July 1960, 133–6; discusses problem of Cuba with Eisenhower, 137–41; discussions regarding Skybolt and Polaris missile programs with Eisenhower, 142–9; address at the United Nations, September 1960, 150; meets with Eisenhower at United Nations, 150–1; writes to Eisenhower after 1960 presidential

Macmillan, Harold – *continued*
election, 151; impact of diplomatic partnership with Eisenhower, 152–3, 155–6; final assessment of Eisenhower as leader, 156; establishment of intelligence cooperation with the United States, 165 n. 79
Macmillan, Helen Belles (Hill), (mother of Harold Macmillan), xvi, xvii, xviii, 10, 159 n.25
Macmillan, Maurice (father of Harold Macmillan), xvi, xvii
Mahon, George, 1
Malik, Yakov, 111
Malinovsky, Rodion, 115, 120, 121, 127, 128, 146
Marshall, General George C., xv
Maxwell, William D., 42
McCone, John, xxvii, 78, 100
McElroy, Neil H., xxvii, xxviii, 47
McKenzie, Robert, xxii, 82
McMahon Act, 25, 43
Merchant, Livingston, 23, 76
Middleton, Drew, 17–18, 19, 124–5
Mikoyan, Anastas, 67
Mollet, Guy, 6
Montgomery, Viscount Bernard Law, 14
Morrison, Herbert, 95
Murphy, Robert, experience with Eisenhower and Macmillan in World War II, xx; role in Lebanon crisis, 54–5; offer to Frol Kozlov for Khrushchev to visit the United States, 81–2

Nasser, Gamal Abdul, 2, 3, 5, 11, 16, 20, 21, 44, 46, 49, 57, 138
National Security Council (NSC), xxvii
Neff, Donald, 8
Nixon, Richard M., 26, 50, 62, 74, 82, 97, 101, 130, 131, 137, 151, 154, 155, 166–7 n. 122
Norstad, General Lauris, 14, 28, 34, 35, 78
North Atlantic Treaty Organization (NATO), x, xi, xvi, xxix, xxx, 14, 16, 17, 23, 25, 26, 27, 28, 29, 31, 34, 39, 48, 61, 64, 69, 76, 84, 86, 88, 102, 119, 129, 133, 146, 153, 155

Page, Jack, 97
Persons, Wilton B. ("Jerry"), 50
Pignard, René, 120
Plowden, Edward, 24
Polaris (missile), 133, 142, 143, 144, 145, 146, 147, 148, 149, 153
Powell, Richard, 24
Powers, Francis Gary, 98, 106, 107, 108, 109, 110, 121, 127, 137
Pulliam, Eugene, 42

Quarles, Donald, 12, 13, 15, 17, 24, 50, 51, 77, 78

Raborn, William (Red), 143
Rayburn, Sam, 1, 2
Reilly, Sir Patrick, 64, 68
Rockefeller, John D., Jr., 7
Rockefeller, Nelson A., 154
Roosevelt, Franklin D., xii, xiii, xiv, xv, xxiii, 155
Rountree, William, 45, 46
Rumbold, Sir Anthony, 76

Salisbury, Lord Robert, 8, 9, 10, 11
Sandys, Duncan, xxviii, 12, 13
Shinwell, Emanuel, 39
Skeffington, Arthur, 149
Skybolt (missile), 144, 145, 148, 184 n. 64
Smith, Gerard, 23
Spaak, Paul Henri, 25
"Special Relationship", x, 26, 152
Sputnik, 21, 22, 23, 29, 35, 153, 154
Stassen, Harold, 32
Stevenson, Adlai E., xvi, 1
Strauss, Lewis, xxvii, 15, 17, 24, 33, 43, 78
Suez crisis, 1956–1957, 2–10; Macmillan's role in, 5–10
Sulman, Rolf, 111
Supreme Allied Commander, Europe (SACEUR), xvi
Symington, Stuart, 21, 154

Taft, Robert A., xvi
Thatcher, Margaret, 11
Thompson, Llewellyn (Tommy), 111, 112, 128, 137
Truman, Harry S., xvi, xxx
Twining, Nathan F., 50, 51, 57, 77, 110, 116

U-2, 103, 104, 105, 106, 107, 108, 109, 110, 111, 112, 113, 114, 124, 126, 131, 132

Van Ufford, Quarles, 130

Warsaw Pact, 32
Washington Conference (October 1957), impact of Sputnik upon, 21; revision of McMahon Act proposed, 24–5; British–American cooperation on nuclear policy discussed, 24; adoption of Declaration of Common Purpose, 24
Watkinson, Harold, xxviii, 144, 145, 184 n. 49
Watson, Robert J., xi, 148, 158 n. 3
Wells, Herman B, 42
Western Summit (Paris 1959), 93–5
White, Lincoln, 111
Whitman, Ann C., 2, 26, 91
Whitney, John Hay (Jock), xxvii, 19, 23, 25, 77, 79, 88
Wilson, Charles E., xxvii, xxx, 12, 13
Wilson, Harold, 6
World War I, xiv, xviii
World War II, xi, xii, xiii, xv, xvi, xviii, xxiii, xxiv, xxix, 14, 75, 76, 153, 155

Zedong, Mao, 128
Zorin, Valerin, 32